Dust &
Rainbows

KIKA AMANYA

A TRUE STORY

Extreme Overflow Publishing
Grayson, GA
USA

Extreme Overflow
PUBLISHING
Grayson, GA
USA

Extreme Overflow Publishing
A Brand of Extreme Overflow Enterprises, Inc
P.O. Box 1184
Grayson, GA 30017
www.extremeoverflow.com
Send feedback to info@extreme-overflow-enterprises.com

Printed in the United States of America

Editing by Extreme Overflow Publishing Editors
Cover Design by Extreme Overflow Publishing

Library of Congress Catalogin-Publication
Data is available for this title. ISBN: 978-0-9989351-4-0

Table of Contents

Table of Contents
(Cont'd)

Table of Contents
(Cont'd)

Oh, God of Dust and Rainbows,
Help us to see
That without dust the rainbow
Would not be.

-Langston Hughes

Prologue

I lay on my left side. Just like every nurse and doctor admonished when they were at my bedside. Drab gray walls next to the only small window in the room stared back at me. All the machines I was hooked up to are making it so uncomfortable, but at this moment, I was oblivious to the discomfort. Discomfort and pain were among the few consistencies I could count on during this experience. "At least it was a better view than before," I thought, comforting myself. Laying on my back and looking at the ceiling, made the tears that sprung up, roll down my temples collecting themselves in tiny pools inside my ears. Laying on my right side, I faced the door of the room which only opened to people in scrubs, who were commissioned to see about my well being. No one else. Looking at the door reminded me how alone I was at my darkest hour.

They said we could both die, and I am here alone. I guess it was a good thing that my left side was the mandate. I stared out of the window. I had a view of the parking lot and trees outside. My condition is so dire in the moment, I can not move to change the channel on the TV. So I watched out of the corner of my eye but mostly listened to A Christmas Story on TBS for the third time in 24 hours. Eyes wide open for over 24 hours. There was no sleeping on the uncomfortable hospital bed in the ICU that night. I was told two days before, I was to deliver my baby a whole two months early.

It was a Wednesday. I came to the emergency room reluctantly that Monday on the advice of my mother. As a nurse, she recognized early symptoms of complications with my delicate condition and told me I should get checked out.

Prologue (Cont'd)

I arrived at the ER on a cold, dreary Monday morning rather exasperated, but feeling fine in general. Within thirty seconds of my blood pressure being taken, I was being told that I was being admitted and would probably have my baby that day. It all happened so fast that I didn't have time to feel anything . . .

Chapter One

Black. Gold. Green...

*"I have come to believe over and over again that
what is most important to me must be spoken,
made verbal and shared, even at the risk of having it
bruised or misunderstood."*

— *Audre Lorde*

I was born on a small island about the size of Connecticut. Jamaica sits in the Caribbean Sea, floating in a nook created by Central and South America. It is flanked by its closest island neighbors, Cuba to the North, and Haiti to the West. A lot of Jamaicans are very proud of their heritage, and most are not afraid to express it. They put flags on their license plates, pictures in their homes, and hold on for dear life to their customs and culture. Even after they've learned to get by here in America, speaking American slang, many keep the familiar rhythm and melody of "Patois". That was their first form of expression tucked neatly away at the back of the tongue, waiting for moments of release in anger, excitement, comfort, or sheer joy. They hold on to Jamaica, even if they don't return soon or often. Most of the people who hold onto their "Jamaican-ness" in more traditional ways, would probably discount my love for my culture and my homeland because I choose less ostentatious displays. I have two important and deliberate ways in which I honor the land that bore me. First, I cook Jamaican food regularly. I am always brought back by familiar smells and tastes. I love perfecting recipes that my mother and aunts taught me. The very same ones they learned from their mother. It makes me feel like the next link in the chain. All these women who came before me for generations, they left this for me. And secondly, to carry my love forward, I have endeavored to learn as much about Jamaica's history and culture that I can. These have always been the ways I have kept Jamaica close to my heart.

This tiny corner of the earth is where I made my entrance into this world on November 16, 1982. I was a baby born into a society that was still a baby itself, having been independent for a mere couple of decades. What can be a lifetime to an individual; can be a very short time with respect to a developing nation. By the early 1980s, Jamaica was 500 years deep in European colonization that took on different forms at different times, but was still ever present. By the time I made it there, the island had been nominally independent for 22 years, and the Mother Country had left her indelible mark. Her mark can still be seen on all things great and small in Jamaica. From the public sphere's architecture that line the streets of Kingston, and the parliamentary style politics, to the very personal, like our names and our language. Often, especially in America, we think history started with Europe and its influence on the world. It's as if we didn't exist until the Europeans came in contact with us, but Jamaica existed for many many thousands of years before Columbus set his sights on it. The 4,000-mile piece of land that makes up Jamaica is actually the top of an underwater mountain range. Back during the prehistoric era, there was a piece of land that was attached to Central America and connected to Venezuela. Due to changes in the earth's crust over many years, the landmass broke off during prehistoric times and sank into the ocean. As ocean levels fluctuated over a large span of time, the highest peaks on that sunken mountain's range formed the beautiful arc of islands that dot the Atlantic Ocean and make up the Caribbean. I looked at the map once, and had this crazy daydream, as I often do, that a mythical giant could use these islands as a stepping stone, and walk from Venezuela to Florida. I know that most people say that their home is a beautiful place, and I don't doubt that there are countless beautiful corners of the world, but this place has a beauty beyond words. Columbus himself called it the most beautiful place he had ever seen.

We know a little about what went on, and who lived there in the days before written records. History says, for as far back as 20,000 years ago, the island was inhabited by native tribes. The fact that there were thousands of people inhabiting the island became a minor inconvenience to the Europeans, who claim to have "discovered" it in 1493.[1] When the Spanish colonizers found the Natives impossible to enslave, they had to go with plan B; genocide of the Natives. It took no time at all. Afterwards, between the 1500s and the 1800s, the Spanish, then the British, transported Africans forcibly by the millions to live out their own personal hell in paradise. At some point in time, there were people on one of those ships who were strong enough to survive the voyage from Africa that killed a great many. These strong people survived brutality unspeakably and lived through enough to generate new life in the midst of the pain. Generation after generation, these people watched as many as millions understandably succumb to the suffering that slavery brought, but the strongest of these people survived. It was those with a will of steel, so strong that they could not be broken. They survived, kept going, and kept making a new life. In 1982, they made me. I come from

---

1   Sherlock, Philip. *The Story of the Jamaican People.* 1997

strength. I was born out of fierce determination. That is my stock.

A lot of the information I know about Jamaica came slowly over many years. When I was in school, every time there was an opportunityto choose a topic for a report or a project, I would almost always choose something or someone related to Jamaica. Except for this one time, I did a report on Nelson Mandela, which sparked a lifelong obsession with the man, his story, and his message. Even that was sparked by an interest in my mother country; I remembered hearing a reggae song as a child that chanted the lyrics "Free Mandela". I first came to The United States in 1990, the same year he ended his time as a political prisoner. I remember hearing his name a lot. I remember the pride glowing from people's faces when they mentioned his name. I just had to find out who he was and what he needed to be freed from.

All roads lead back to Jamaica for me, always. It is still my favorite place to be. Every time my feet are resting on that soil, I feel the weight of my history. I feel at home, although the majority of my life has been spent far away from there. The island has a spirit like no other place. However Jamaicans are perceived by the world, I find us to be a strong, resilient people; a people with a passion that runs so deep through our veins that creativity seems to burst out and seep through our pores. The formation of their very language speaks of their creative brilliance. Patois was created during the era of slavery. It is technically a dialect of English with heavy, West African influence, along with some borrowed words from Spanish, Portuguese, and Irish dialects. It is also further peppered with some Old English words that aren't in use anymore in Standard English. It wasn't until I was an adult that I appreciated how beautiful and ingenious the creation of this dialect was. It was the language of all the important, life-changing moments of my childhood and adolescence. It was the language of my life. The language I speak in my thoughts, long after its color has faded from my spoken word. I was fascinated to see a direct link to Africa. A large portion of our culture and language derives directly from our African ancestors who survived the Middle Passage. From the *ackee* we eat, that is only native to West Africa, but now grows abundantly in the Caribbean, to the use of certain words like *nyam* (to eat) and *unu* (all of you), they are just two of a plethora of words we use that are untouched gems from our history deriving of West African languages. Some of the customs, children's stories and parables survived the voyage across the Atlantic alongside the people.

The landscape, the mountains take my breath away every single time. Sometimes I wish they could talk. I wish they could tell us stories of the Natives and their lives. I would love to sit and hear these gigantic trees that pepper the valleys you overlook when driving around the mountains, tell tales of the people that have passed through. I would love to see what they have seen.

It seems that the soil of the land has been wrought with strife for as long as there has been written history; a land with blood-soaked soil. The concept of written history arrived in the region in time to tell us details about the bloody, genocidal killing of tens of thousands of Native men, women, and children in a short time span. That era was followed by the cruelty of the Atlantic Slave Trade, which lasted a few hundred years and soaked the land with the blood, sweat, and tears of Africans far from home. The slave ships fed the sharks in the Atlantic with the bodies of those too sick, too weak, too heartbroken, or too defiant to make it to the New World. It has been written about many times over.

There were schools of sharks that would follow the slave ships because they were guaranteed a meal. The used, abused, murdered and disregarded Black souls and bodies were the supplement of the day. When the tides turned hundreds of years later, the Africans revolted viciously and shed more blood in the name of freedom. The end of slavery forced Britain to think of a new way of maintaining control because they could no longer use literal chains. Then we entered Colonialism. During the colonial era, the British brought indentured servants and laborers from its other colonies in East and South Asia, which diversified the population over time, and further complicated the class system based on race and skin color. That era following slavery was where we saw less of the physical exploitation by the colonizer and things leaned more toward social and economic exploitation. Colonialism did its best to carry on the social hierarchy that existed during slavery. That is to say, the non-Black people were at the top of the social totem pole. Within the Black population, how you were treated had a lot to do with what shade of brown you were.

Jamaica was declared an independent nation on August 6, 1962. Poverty has been a plague to the nation and other similar nations around the world. Of course, there are some who manage to escape the plague of being poor, but most of the huddled masses, including my family, had no social ladder to climb. The causes of the poverty in Jamaica are weaved together with the effects of poverty, creating a miserable cycle that still grips the place today. Violence, a stagnant economy, and inflation are just a few of the push factors that prompt people to try and make it elsewhere. After independence in 1962, in addition to the everyday violence, there arose a tradition of gang violence attached to elections and politics. Housing schemes were built by the government with the nominal intention of easing the suffering of the people. These government housing schemes became breeding grounds for people's pain. And often, people who are in emotional and psychological pain and have no relief, turn around and inflict that pain on the next man. Many neighborhoods, especially in Kingston, were sometimes terrorized by street gangs who were merely extensions of the two major political parties. Although violence was rampant, there existed obvious and unbridled electricity running through the people collectively. This time right after independence is remarkable to read about. The influence of American and European music on the radio lit a fire amongst the Jamaican musicians. They created their own unique genres of music and eventually, that music was brought to the world's stage, most notably through Jamaica's most famous son, Bob Marley. His rise also brought to light a religion created on that soil that was thoroughly Afro-centric. Rastafarians were there for many decades before this, but the time after independence saw a surge. Rastafarians celebrated a spiritual connection to their roots. They rejected the religion of their oppressor and reveled in their African-ness. While beauty contests and positions of prestige were always won by those of the lighter hue, the Establishment was still promoting the old racial caste system and the grassroots was gaining steam. The Civil Rights Movement and the subsequent Black Power movements in America did not go unnoticed in Jamaica, serving as an inspiration to many. I have read accounts from that time that say that Afros could be seen along with clenched fists in the air. Declarations of Pride in being Black could be heard shouted into the winds in Kingston. The nation struggled economically to stand to its feet, wounded by its past, trying to prop itself up on an experiment in Socialism. The ancient Roman philosopher, King Marcus Aurelius, wrote that Poverty is the mother of crime. Jamaica was then, and still is, fertile ground.

Poverty was then and still is, breeding crime abundantly. It was into this world that my mother and father were born and raised.

I can't pretend to know everything about their upbringing or what it was like to live in that world. I have quite a few memories, but I did not spend most of my formative years there. I try to always keep that in mind when I think about the decisions they made and the paths they chose. They grew up in a completely different world than I did. If I take the little bit of life in Jamaica, to which I can personally testify, and add it to the bits and pieces my rabid curiosity has led me to find out about over the years, it can never equal living it the way that they did.

I have tried over the course of many years to ask them both about certain aspects of their lives, and they told me what they could. I have also picked up bits and pieces of them from other people. My mom was born two years before independence, to the day. My father was born a few years before her. They both lived in the Duhaney Park section of Kingston, directly across the street from each other on Dickens Avenue. Duhaney Park was the site of one of the government housing schemes that sprung up after independence. Although neither family lived there in the building, it had a looming presence on the street. I have long been fascinated with who built the Duhaney Park neighborhood and named all the streets. They are all named after famous writers. It is one of the many examples of the lingering influence of the Europeans who once ruled. It is such a contrast to see people of all different shades of black and brown walking down Shakespeare Avenue or Chaucer or Swift Avenues. I love the variety of writers used for the street names. They go from famous figures in classic literature: Bronte, Dickens, Shelley; to classic poets like Longfellow, Keats, and Emerson. There is also homage paid to some black writers like

Selvon, a Trinidadian writer who has a street named after him, and Baldwin, one of my favorite writers from the Black Renaissance of the 1920s. These narrow cracked streets were lined with rows of houses as connected in their unspoken pain as they were by their literal walls. These streets' namesakes are some of those who have helped us put the pain of the human condition into words, and that in itself, I find poetic. Whoever was responsible for this part of the development earns at least that much of my respect for being a lover of literature. Those are some of my favorite people.

As my parents came of age in 1970s Kingston, it was a time of transition for everyone. I have never heard a story detailing how my parents actually met, but as people like to say, they go way back, as far back as grade school. Although they may have grown up in close proximity to one another, and they both spent the majority of their life without a father. The similarities between them basically ended there. From early on they led very different lives.

My father was the only child born to a single mother. I have never heard anyone mention his father, not even himself. I have no idea if his father died or if he left them, but whatever happened, it was clearly too painful to speak of. His mother was Catholic, which was sort of a minority denomination in the majority Protestant Christian country. In my memories, there lives a short, petite light brown little lady who was an excellent cook. Her first name means Pure, and her middle name, very much along the same lines, means True Image. I love that. I feel like it makes one of the most common things I have heard about her ring true. She was never afraid to speak her mind. Then again, that quality is not hard to find in a Jamaican woman. Of the few memories I have of my paternal grandmother, they include her tasty food and piercing eyes. Her honey colored eyes, light skin, and hair speak of an ancestry that is not 100% African but will remain forever a mystery. By all accounts, she was feisty and hardworking. I have heard how much she loved and doted on me, her only grandchild, at the time. Every time I think about her, my heart hurts a little because I wish I knew her better. She is one of the many people who share my blood that I know very little about. I can't imagine life was easy for her, growing up in that era, in that environment, a single mother way before it was trendy. She worked hard to provide for her son. I have heard it said that she spoiled him as a child. Having been a single mom with one son myself, I am not so quick to subscribe to that judgment. I used to hear it myself all the time. The thing is, even if it is the truth, I understand. You cannot know the emotional turmoil of being a woman trying to raise a boy into a man on your own unless you have lived it. She had it much worse than I did. I didn't remain a single mom. Even at my worst points, I have been afforded a more materially blessed life than she ever knew. I was also lucky enough to come up in a society that, while still promoting this is not an ideal way to raise a child, was at least accepting of single motherhood. I can never imagine the judgment she faced, or the suitors she kept secret or turned away, or the sacrifices she made. I honor her. She is in my blood and without her, there would be no me.

My father's first name means "One with Brown Hair" which is crazy because one of the things I both remember about him and inherited from him, is an odd color brown hair. Brown is also the meaning of his surname. My father served as a sailor in the Armed Forces of Jamaica and has always been a man of the Sea. I find that so fascinating about him. I share with him a love for painting and the ocean, although his love of the open

18

water goes much deeper than mine. He has been a professional diver for decades, and diving is a huge part of his life. He has the same light brown skin with the reddish hue that his mother had.

My mother was born in a house on the corner with a view of a government living facility across the street. She began life in Duhaney Park with both her mother and father and a large number of siblings. She was right in the middle of the brood, number four of eight children born to a strong, unconventional, sharp-tongued, chain-smoking force to be reckoned with, whose name meant Holy. She was not a person you would easily forget if you were to meet her. I wish, as with a lot of things, that I knew more about where she came from. My mother and aunts have told me stories about my grandmother's parents, their grandparents. Their grandfather was a tall fair skinned man. A distant family member conducted a thorough research project on this line of our family tree, which revealed mixed roots in Jamaica that went back hundreds of years. This story goes with so many in the African Diaspora. This particular branch of the tree began with a Scottish slave owner, who was given free land by the British Empire in the 1600s.

There is not much that I know about my great-grandfather personally. The few tidbits I have heard over the years were that he was so tall that his feet would hang off the bed, and he had to duck to get into doorways. His wife was a petite woman who was said to be at least part, if not fully Maroon, and she wore her long thick hair in two waist-length braids. The Maroons were Africans who were brought to Jamaica as slaves, but who rebelled and ran away to the mountain region and formed their own free community. Many of them mixed with the few handful of natives that were still around, though their numbers were dwindling at the time. This group of people displayed an attitude that still runs prevalent in Jamaican culture: they didn't wait for any European to grant them freedom, they took it. The British tried to lay siege on their communities a few times and tried their best to destroy the Maroon colonies. Through the struggle, a Maroon community still exists in Jamaica today. Still isolated and still living a life way closer to their African roots than most of us.[2]

How this petite Maroon girl and this giant stoic fair-skinned man met and decided to start a family will be a mystery to me forever. I love to create fanciful tales in my head to fill these gaps sometimes, but no tale could ever be better than the truth. That is a truth I will not know.

My family is not quite as sentimental as most American families, but their way is very typical of Jamaican families. Painful stories from the past are told every now and then, but not very often. The funny ones are repeated with the same vitality over and over, but the pain often gets buried. It is understandable why one would not want to think and talk often about times that were so incredibly difficult. Of the few stories, they tell from the past, the one that is most imprinted in my brain is quite literally the Mother of all family stories, for without this story, none of the others would exist.

My grandmother and her brothers were booked passage to England on a ship sometime in the early 1950s. Since the beginning of the 20th century, Jamaicans had been relocating to England and had established a sizeable immigrant community by that time. Great Britain recruited men from Jamaica (and all of its

2   Sherlock, Philip. *The Story of the Jamaican People.* 1997.

other colonies) to fight in both World Wars, and a lot of these war veterans chose to remain in England afterward. These war veterans were the roots of the Jamaican communities in England, but soon after, others were joining them. At the time they booked passage on this ship, members of my family were a part of the greatest wave of migration to Britain from Jamaica. In 1944, a hurricane devastated the island, killing many people causing economic hardship that resulted from devastating floods that followed. At that same time in Britain, they were recovering from fighting two major world wars in a relatively short span of time. There was a major labor shortage as a result of the post-war economic boom in Britain. They started making it known in their colonies around the world, that there was plenty of money to be made if they would come to Britain to fill the labor shortage. This caused a massive wave of migration, from the recent storm-ravaged Jamaica to England that continued for years. I am not sure what their personal reasons were for booking passage on that ship, but they cannot be much different than most people around the world and through time who take the huge risk of moving to another country. The opportunities had to be better than what they were faced with where they lived. I am sure that most of the people who were presented with the better opportunity took it. My grandmother and her brothers were ready to relocate to Europe to make a new life for themselves. I was told that somewhere along the way, my great-grandfather heard news that his seventeen-year-old daughter was pregnant. It is said that he marched right down to where the ship was docked and pulled my grandmother off that boat. He did not feel as though she was worthy of such a hard-fought opportunity. She remained a sort of black sheep, an outcast with her family from that point on. Through the years when my grandmother was raising children of her own, there was little contact with her family.

I never personally heard my grandmother tell that story, but I imagine that it hurt to tell, no matter how old she was. It just seems like one of those moments of your life that you would think about often and wonder "what if?" I wonder how she felt as she saw her other siblings over the years establish themselves in England and lead very different lives than she did. It had to have been difficult. As thorny as this story feels, I love this story. It is one of the first pieces of my personal puzzle. My grandmother was indeed pregnant with her first child, who is still one of my favorite people in the world. He holds this family together in so many ways, and it started when he was still in the womb. His presence was the reason she did not go to England. When that child, whose name means famed, bright and shining, was a just a few years old, she met my grandfather and went on to have seven more children with him. If her father had never pulled my grandmother off of that ship in the 1950s, she never would have met my grandfather, and my family as we know it would never exist. I would not exist without this painful turning point my grandmother experienced in her youth. I was amazed when I sat down to do a count while preparing the obituary for her funeral in 2002. She had 8 children, 23 grandchildren, and 10 great-grandchildren. That's a whole lot of people who owe their very existence to that fateful moment when my grandmother was yanked off the ship to England.

As they tell it, life in Duhaney Park was alright when my family first arrived. Things were fairly normal by all accounts. It was a newly built neighborhood, meant to be a suburb. The early part of my mother's childhood seemed to be a fairly happy time. Their Dad would be away working sometimes for days, but whenever he came back, he came bearing gifts. He loved his girls. He taught them songs (I hear he was quite the singer) and doted on his little ones. We all have our faults and apparently, his was that he was an alcoholic. That ultimately was his undoing. He died from cirrhosis of the liver when my mother was just thirteen.

That's when life changed for everyone. Before this, my grandfather did a great job providing for his large brood. They were never rich, but they were not starving either. With his death, they were now starving. My grandfather was officially married on paper to someone else, and my grandmother was in effect, the other woman. Despite this fact, the love he had for my grandmother was evident. He had so many children with her, my mother and aunts always speak of their father fondly, showing that he spent a lot of time with them. However, when he died, all that he had went to his wife and their children. My family was left without a breadwinner and with no legitimate claim to anything he left behind. My grandmother never finished school and she had 8 children. These facts made her even less qualified in an already crippled economic environment. She did the best she could every day and they all made it through. Even if there was nothing to drink but water, and nothing to eat but rice, she kept everyone going. When her children had children, some of them were teenage mothers like her. She added their offspring to the load on her back and kept trudging along. In the earlier years, the hardships of the outside world and the struggles of everyday life prompted my grandfather to encourage them to stick together no matter what, because the outside world was so cruel. I think in a twisted subconscious combination of reasons, and in a way to both honor his memory, and as a result of being deeply scarred collectively, my family still lives to this day by that code of fierce protectiveness. This code sometimes is for the better and at times for the worst, but it will never change.

There were so many changes going on at that point in time, not just in their household. The political violence that they grew up in helped shape their worldview. Even though I think some of them don't know it, it still affects them today. One of the more subtle manifestations of their trauma was something my younger cousins and I used to talk about all the time; our mother's obsession with rape. They are always warning us against rape, and often their warnings come in hypothetical rants about the worst possible scenario. That scenario always ends with you or someone being raped. You could easily hear one of my aunts warning a female relative that they may wanna cover up their skimpy clothing for fear that someone could drag them into an alley and rape them. "Never open the door for a stranger, he could be a rapist." The warnings could even just be casual ones like "oh honey, close your blinds, you never know what rapist could be watching through the window." My mom could be warning me that I should make sure my son has all his shots because if it seems like I am neglecting him, they could call the Child Protective Services on me and put my little boy in a foster home where he will be...that's right, raped. This is not an exaggeration, everything you do, or don't do, for that matter is protecting you from ultimately being raped in the end. No matter where the story began, in their eyes, you should watch the company you keep. Not just because you might end up in jail, it is the inevitable rape in jail that always gets the final emphasis on the warning. Now, don't get me wrong, rape is not a joke, it is a real thing. It is a real danger and I in no way intend to minimize the fact that the possibility is out there, and people should always be on alert in certain life situations to safeguard their self. However, most people, upon observing my family would probably agree with me; they are definitely overly paranoid about rape.

On the other hand, it is sometimes difficult for those born or raised in America to wrap our heads around the level of violence they lived with. This place not only boasts some of the highest crime rates in the world, and the time in which they lived there were some of the most violent and unregulated times ever experienced in the region. With almost half the population unemployed in the 1970s, the murder rate tripled over ten years and the rate of reported rapes increased by twenty-fold. And that is only the number of people brave enough to report their rape to a justice system that was unlikely to work in their favor. There are no statistics for the countless people who swallowed the bitter pill of life's sorrow and kept going. For my family growing up in Kingston in the 1970s and 80s, being raped was not some abstract possibility like it is for us in the western world. We were living in relative safety. For them, rape was a very real, clear and present danger in their lives. I can just see how a woman with six daughters could constantly speak of the danger that could lie in wait just yards away on the streets. I can understand how coming of age in the midst of unspeakable violence can leave you with scars you might not even realize you had. Even though these women are many years and hundreds of miles removed from that world, some of its shadows still lurk.

My mother is a very unique person, and she has been set apart from the beginning. She does not come from an especially tall family, but for some reason, she shot up to six feet. Her Hebrew first name means Bitter, and I feel that the theme has definitely run through her life, from the situation into which she was born, to the many challenges life has thrown at her. Her middle name means Healer. That speaks to her destiny, which she has become now, but in a way, what she was born to be. A healer emerged from the bitterness of her humble beginnings.

My mom seems to always have had a sense that she was not meant to live out her days in Duhaney Park. Since a young age, she was different from the rest of her siblings. She didn't feel like she belonged. Everyone else was average height, and she was the only one who was unusually tall. She was the darkest, and she says that they told her she was the ugliest growing up. They grew up in a world where the lighter your complexion, the better. People were even overlooked for jobs and denied entry into schools and organizations based on what shade of black or brown you were. Often in that world, being the darkest would automatically make you the ugliest.

Their family struggled to make it. Times were hard for them growing up, especially after their father passed away. My grandfather had a cousin whose name means God is gracious, who lived out the meaning of her name when she essentially took my mother under her wing. She spent time at her home in a middle-class area of Kingston, and she helped, not just my mom, but the family in so many ways. She helped my mom get into a private school where she was a teacher. My mother speaks of this time as being both a blessing and an extremely difficult time for her socially. Many of the other kids who went to this school had parents of means. My mother felt bad about that, understandably so. A girl with one good dress at home, around the children of diplomats and businessmen every day, has to do a number on one's self-esteem. To top it off, she was dark skinned and taller than everyone else.

The gangly teenager grew into a stunning young ebony-skinned woman, who proved herself responsible, determined and ambitious (she held a job since she was very young). She also proved herself to be a virtuous woman, an active member of Open

Bible church, who carried herself with an air that she was destined for more. The brown-haired boy from across the street wasted no time. They were married very young, and pretty soon I was on the way. They both worked, and it seemed at first that they enjoyed a relatively little more prosperity than the homes in which they were raised. The next part of the story gets a little fishy for me. I can't really say for sure what happened. I have heard such vastly different versions of what went on in their relationship and how or why things ended up the way they did. It reminds me of a typical sitcom episode. You know, every sitcom has an episode where two people are telling their own versions of a story. One person's version will have them as the innocent angel, while the other person was totally evil. When the next person tells it, *they* are totally innocent and the first person was all wrong. When it comes down to it though, the truth is always somewhere in the middle.

What I do know for sure is that by the time I was two years old, my parents were no longer together and my mom went to the Bahamas. I stayed on Dickens Avenue with my grandmother, but I am not sure for how long. One of my mom's sisters flew to the Bahamas and took me there to be with my mom. Somehow, my father came to the Bahamas and brought me back to Jamaica against my mother's wishes. She didn't see me again for five more years.

My earliest memories do not consist of the things (as I came to understand later) that a childhood should. It wasn't until I was about eight years old that I even heard of things like Santa Claus and the Tooth Fairy being discussed in real life. Birthday parties, tiaras, hugs, toys and all the things western culture associates with childhood were literally foreign to me. When I found out that I had missed out on all of this, and latched onto that American sense of entitlement, I felt a little cheated.

My earliest personal memory is not with my mother or anyone in her family. My first memory is being on a bus with a woman, getting off and walking down a paved road until we reached a dirt path, the "lane" where I lived on Brunswick Avenue in Spanish Town. I lived there with my father's girlfriend, her parents, her two brothers and one sister. I think that my father lived there too, but to this day, I cannot be sure because I barely ever saw him. I didn't see his girlfriend that much either. My main caretaker was my father's girlfriend's sister, the woman I was on the bus with. She is a woman who holds a special place in my heart and always will. Her name means Prophet, which is totally fitting for her role in my life. A prophet is a leader and a teacher. She was both of those things early on in my life when I was frankly neglected. A prophet proclaims the will of God, and that is exactly what she did for me. Without this woman, my destiny would have been different. She was my personal prophet. She was the only soft nurturing hand I held at that time in my life. Her mother was also very nice to me, but she was older, and she also had the main responsibility of maintaining the household and I rarely spent time with her. Even as a child, I was observant enough to know that I was not really wanted in that house. I picked up on conversations about me, and the cold way in which most of the members of the household dealt with me did not go unnoticed. My father's girlfriend was the coldest of all. My presence seemed to annoy her tremendously.

She had two brothers, one in his late teens or early twenties and the youngest one was still in High School. I can even remember going to his graduation. What's worse is I also remember him crawling into my bed some nights; his brother too, but much less often than he did. The youngest brother molested me systematically for the entire time I lived there. I did not know that that which was happening to me was wrong until much much later.

I have vivid memories of those incidents and few other select circumstances, mostly of a negative nature. However some significant portions of time have me drawing a total blank, and I think I blocked some things out. I remember using an outhouse and always being scared to enter the dark smelly shack. I remember not always having food, and sometimes dinner was a wild rabbit that they chased between the trees for thirty minutes. It really does taste like chicken. I remember loving the smell of the rain, and the desire to eat dirt when I was young in Jamaica. That was something that I was embarrassed about for a long time, and I never told anyone. It was my secret. In my never ending quest for information, I came across a documentary about dirt eaters one day when I was an adult. I watched as adults and children alike would unabashedly eat fistfuls of mud and dry earth. I learned that people who crave dirt are normally malnourished and lacking in certain minerals and that explained a lot for me.

A devastating hurricane hit Jamaica when I was about five years old. Hurricane Gilbert was the most destructive storm to hit Jamaica up until that time. Since then, climate change has put Jamaica through much worse. At the time though, Gilbert was a huge deal. The high winds and heavy rain left scores of people dead, billions of dollars in damage and whole entire agricultural industries wiped out. From my little corner at the time, I could not fathom the devastation that spread throughout the entire island. We hunkered down where we were. We were in the dark with only cans of sardines and crackers to eat. I recall the fear I felt, but it wasn't because I knew what was going on. It was because I could feel the fear of the adults. I remember clinging onto my father's back trudging through waist-high water in the aftermath of the storm. I remember the incredible amount of debris in the street and toppled over trees everywhere. Houses with zinc roofs were topless.

Among these dark memories are the bright spots when my own personal prophet shared her little with me. She might bring home a bag of chips or some Shirley biscuits or Ovaltine crackers because she knew I loved them. She took me to church with her, which besides school, was my only consistent outlet. I would sit in the pew of the fairly large church, either reading a book I managed to sneak in or scribbling whatever came to my head on whatever paper I could find. Church on Sundays with the Prophet was something I looked forward to with excitement. Whenever she took me other places with her (which was never often enough for my liking), she doted on me. She would hold my hand, let me lay my head on her lap and hug me. Those simple gestures stood out and meant so much to a kid who got no loving physical contact otherwise. She was my light in a dark room.

I also have some good memories of the few times my father took me to do fun stuff. We went to an amusement park once, and he took me to a restaurant a few times. I would visit Duhaney Park and stay with his mother, sometimes for days, not knowing at the time that my own flesh and blood lived across the street. I saw my first movie in the theatre with him. He took me to see the feature length Michael Jackson movie called Moonwalker and I was mesmerized. I am grateful for those days that broke up the monotony of life in Spanish Town. Those few and far between days were needed. To tell the truth, what I really needed was a protector. I needed my mother, but whenever I thought of her in those days, it was in an abstract and very detached way because I had no memory of her. I needed my father too, but he was mostly gone.

Throughout those years, no one even mentioned my mother. I didn't remember her at all and I often wondered if I even had a mother. I am guilty of telling some people later on in my life that, they told me that my mother was dead. When I really thought about it though, I can't really remember anyone saying that to me directly. A couple of times I mentioned her offhandedly and was met with blank stares by all. It was obvious my mother was not a comfortable subject. I think I just assumed my mother was dead and they didn't want to talk about her. I settled on that as an explanation in the absence of answers. I had no way of knowing anything at the time. I did something back then that I still do today when things are overwhelming; I spent a lot of time inside my own head. I would often engage in these elaborate daydreams about who my mother was and what she was like. Her presence (or lack thereof) affected me so deeply early in life.

I had a lot of time by myself in those early days. On a day to day basis, no one really communicated with me or even acknowledged me unless I was in their way. I remember many times not speaking for days at a time, and always only speaking when spoken to. I stayed to myself and I was a voracious reader. I read and understood things way past my level. I imagine the members of the household who didn't want me there thought they were hiding their disdain for me, but I was extremely perceptive. It was clear to anyone who paid even a little bit of attention to me that I was an exceptionally smart child. There was often no food in that house, but always a slew of books. I had some children's books that I liked. I would read about Anansi the Spider or Amelia Bedelia. Those were on my age level, but even at four and five years old, I loved reading the few novels I would find around the house and would get excited about reading a big book. I remember reading a High School level science textbook and tingling with excitement. Maybe if there was nothing to read, I would settle for a Nancy Drew book. It was the makings of a true nerd. Although I spent most of my time amongst the trees in the large yard, or with my nose in a book, I loved music. All my life, music has been essential to me. It has had a sustaining quality for me for as long as I have been on this earth. I would learn words to songs easily and sing them whenever I was alone. I heard a lot of different Reggae songs from that time, but I also recall that there was always a lot of American R&B and pop music around. I remember Lionel Richie, Patti LaBelle, Whitney Houston and of course Michael Jackson being some of my favorites when I lived in Jamaica. There were so many R&B ballads that I knew every word to but would not find out who the artist was until years later. Aside from books and music, the small TV (when it was working), was my window into the outside world. There was only one channel, so you just watched whatever was on the TV. I was a kid who loved Dallas, The Facts of Life, and Silver Spoons, not because I preferred them over other shows, but because that's what came on.

Most of my time in that house was spent in solitude. Once my father took me to the country area, and I stayed with some people I didn't know for about a week by myself. I also remember being in the hospital once for about two weeks. It could have been longer or shorter, but that's what it felt like in my young mind. I was hooked up to an IV the whole time. I even had to walk around with it on a stand if I wanted to get up, which I was not allowed to do that much. I cannot recall for the life of me what was wrong with me. I had asthma, I knew that, but I have no idea why I was there. I don't remember feeling especially terrible, but there had to be a reason. This is one of those times where I know I blocked out some significant, probably traumatic situation. I can't really have a feeling about it when I don't remember what happened. I do remember the stay in the hospital was actually kind of fun for me. It felt like a vacation away from the house. I made friends with a boy who was in the bed next to me. All the children were crowded into a large room about the size of a typical school gymnasium. Beds were lined up in row after row throughout the large room; with the boys and girls with all different types of issues. The boy in the bed next to me had bandages covering his entire stomach. I stared with curiosity whenever the nurses would change his bandages, and I remember thinking that every time they lifted the bandages, what I saw reminded me of Vienna Sausages. He was my little friend while I was there.

One day, when I was about seven years old, my caretaker came home from her job with two huge plastic bags. I watched wide-eyed as she dumped them out on the bed, and I saw clothes and shoes and Barbie dolls and more stuff than I ever owned. I was totally elated and when she told me that these things were from my mother. Well, even now it is so hard to find words to encompass the rush of feelings that came upon me. That was one of the big moments of my life that stand out to me. In an instant, things changed, and I would have no idea the depth of the changes to come. Before that, I didn't know anything about her. I mean, I assumed she was dead for crying out loud., but here was proof, here was my own personal prophet standing in front of me bringing the good news. She lives.

The way I understood it was, that in the five years since I was with my mother, she had made her way from the Bahamas to New York when my father refused to let her have contact with me for whatever reason. By this time, she was married to someone else and had a new life somewhere else but she never stopped trying to find me. That general story is all I knew. Logically, I know there had to be ups and downs and twist and turns in between, but most of the details have been lost to me. My experiences later in life have taught me that nothing is ever that simple, but from my end, at the time this is what I knew. The entire time I lived in Spanish Town, she had no idea where I was or what I was doing. She was unsuccessful in convincing my father to let her see me, and her attempts to circumvent him to see me some other way also proved futile. I didn't even have contact with her family whom, as I stated before, lived directly across the street from my paternal grandmother, and who I would occasionally spend time with in Duhaney Park. I was so close but so far away. I am not sure of the exact story of the way these two met, but in a stroke of absolute serendipity (I'm sure, combined with my mother's due diligence), on one of her many trips to Jamaica to find me, my mother and my caretaker met one day. Living up to the meaning of her name, she helped usher in the will of God in my life and my Prophet quite literally led me to the Motherland.

Leaving Jamaica was sudden, terrifying and exciting all at once. After discovering where I was, my mother tried to go through the court system in Jamaica to regain custody of me, but in the end, custody was awarded to my father, she was allowed two weeks visitation, and I could not leave the country. Going to the courthouse was my first genuine memory of my mother. She came up to me and hugged me tight. She had other people there with her, who all seemed happy to see me, but I didn't remember any of them. The only other face I remember from that day besides my mother's, was the face of her mother.

Well, the two week visitation was granted, and immediately following the trial, I went to Duhaney Park and spent two weeks with my mom and her family. It was a great time. Everyone was so happy to see me. It was the first time I can remember feeling tenderness and love aside from the woman who took care of me at home in Spanish Town. She was the only person to be affectionate with me, and I had never before experienced that much love from more than one person. I was sad to leave when the time came and so was my mom. She asked me if I wanted to come live with her and I eagerly said yes. When she dropped me off at home, she promised me that she would take me to live with her in America.

At the time I was going to a small private school in town. There was a man who owned a pickup truck who would take the children to school. I, along with several other children in the neighborhood would wait at the end of the lane for him to stop by and we would jump in the back of the pickup. There were other children he picked up before us already there and he would take us to school. I was told by the Prophet to wait at the end of the lane as if I was going to school and that my mother would pick me up. I waited that morning, excitement coursing through my veins. Then the appearance of a car caused my heart to start beating so hard, I felt my chest would explode. I saw the car slow down, and I thought it was time to make my exit but it wasn't who I thought it was. It was my father. There he was, looking tired and pulling up to the house. Right behind him was the pickup truck that took me to school. I wasn't sure what to do so I climbed in the back and went to school like normal.

We tried it again just a couple of days later. Once again I was told to wait at the end of the lane for my mother to drive by and pick me up. I waited, and I was even more nervous than the time before. This time, as I waited and I saw no cars slow down. Once again, I ended up climbing into the pickup truck, my book bag a little extra heavy that day because it contained a few books I didn't want to leave behind, and my favorite purple shirt that had my name on it that I had made at an amusement park earlier that year. I sat, weighed down by my book bag and my expectations and I cried. I was so disappointed; I went to school and sat in class. After a little while, someone came to get me in class saying that my mother was here to take me to a doctor's appointment. I grabbed my bag and we flounced out of the school doors and into a black car. We got a ride to the airport from a family friend and we rushed straight to the bathroom once we were inside the building. I remember her being a ball of nerves. Shaking and jittery, she cried in the bathroom stall and prayed out loud. After she composed herself, my mother changed me out of my school uniform and I put on a brand new pink sweat suit. The sweat suit had the Care Bears on it. When I complained about being hot, she let me know that when we landed in America, it would be cold so I would need it. Then we went to a payphone where my mother called the woman who took care of me. She was grateful for her help and she wanted to let her know that we made it to the airport and were on our way. When she called, she let my mom know that my father had caught wind of the fact that she signed me out of school. He was looking for us and may be on his way to the airport right now. She hung up the phone, panicked; I'm sure because the airport was not a long way. She went straight to the desk to check how long it would be until the flight took off. It would be another few hours and we could not wait that long. My mother switched the tickets that we had to fly to NY in a few hours, for some tickets that would put us on a plane to Miami that was leaving in a few minutes; anything to get off of Jamaican soil immediately. She always would jokingly attribute her actions that day to "watching too many movies" but thank God for those movies, because her quick thinking got us out that day without incident. When it was time to board the plane, she wrapped a scarf around her hair and asked a random tourist if she would hold my hand and take me on the plane. The lady pleasantly agreed and took my hand as my mom walked a few steps behind us. In those days, you would have to walk out on the tarmac and go up the stairs to enter the plane. People were also allowed to stand on a balcony outdoors and watch the planes take off. I'm not sure but I feel as though she figured if he was looking for us, he would not be looking for a child in a pink sweat suit holding the hand of a White woman. We got onto the plane and settled into our seats. This was my first time on an airplane. As we waited for the plane to take off, we sat and watched his familiar frame frantically pace the balcony back and forth through the window. Once we were in the air, she breathed a sigh of relief. My mom got up to go to the bathroom. After a few minutes I started to feel a rush of panic sitting in the airplane alone. Looking back, I think I was overwhelmed by the whole experience and was just releasing. At the time, all my seven year old self knew was that I was scared and I started to cry. The longer she took to return, the louder I cried. She came rushing back to the seat and reprimanded me very harshly for crying. I remember feeling taken aback. Our time together before that had been pleasant and I was hurt, even back then, that she couldn't see that I was scared. Scared about my first plane ride, anxious because I was leaving everything I knew (although very willingly, it was still a huge turning point for me), and literally going into the unknown. I was seven years old and I had barely been outside of the parish where I lived. That exchange would be symbolic of a running theme in my mother's and my relationship. She would rescue me from terrible situations again a few times in the years to come, always with love as her motivation. There was little attention paid to how I felt or even being rebuked if my feelings were expressed too loudly. I always felt safe, but a feeling that there was a lack of empathy for me would always mar the experience. It was like fiercely protecting me was all she could see; her only goal, to get me where I need to be, under her protection. That first time, as in the times to follow, she dragged me along with the best intentions, but I was bruised and tattered emotionally with no bandage for my invisible scars. I can't remember anything else about that flight now that I am older. I can imagine that she was just as scared as I was. It had to have been so overwhelming; scared of drawing attention to herself, and probably still shaking from having executed her daring plan. She was probably more on edge than I will ever know. She was also pregnant.

Chapter Two

Red. White. Blue...

"Although she feeds me bread of bitterness,
And sinks into my throat her tiger's tooth,
Stealing my breath of life, I will confess
I love this cultured hell that tests my youth!"

-Claude McKay

On a dark January night in 1990, my mom and I were walking out of the double glass doors of JFK international airport in New York. We were ushered out of the cold, into a warm blue Buick and large loving hands, ushering his wife and her firstborn into safety. It was my mother's new husband, the only love of her life. His name means, From the Land of Strength, and I have never met a stronger man. He is the man I would call my Dad, the one who raised me. He always has been, as his name attests, a pillar of strength for our family. Their marriage may have been fairly new, but these two had also known each other for years before. They knew each other while growing up in Jamaica. They met again in New York and were married after a dating only a short time.

The image of the New York skyline, as I drove across the biggest bridge I had ever seen, is branded into my brain. I remember every detail of my first few hours on American soil. Getting off the plane in New York was an assault to my senses. We landed very late at night and still, there were more people inside that airport than I had ever seen before in life. I smelled new scents and heard other languages and accents for the first time. It was loud, and I felt like I was either being pushed by someone else, or dragged by my mom's sturdy hand grasp. I took in so much. The airport was like a little microcosm of the city with all different kinds of people rushing everywhere. I was in awe of a girl with her hair in a soft baby pink color. I saw a fur coat for the first time, and I was thoroughly amused. Our short journey from the plane to the car had me experiencing more new things in minutes than I had ever experienced in my life at the time. Nothing could prepare me for the bite of the January air outside. It was January 11th to be exact.

When I got into the car, I remember first thinking how nice the car smelled and how soft the seats were. It was an overwhelming day, and here I was sitting in the nicest car I had ever seen at that point. When we crossed the bridge, it was honestly (and still is) one of the most beautiful things the human eye can behold. I will never forget that view or that night. I had no idea what to expect. I didn't miss Jamaica; I was excited to be there. I don't remember much about the conversation that was had in the car. All I know is that it was whispered, emotional, constant and almost frantic. I think the air of excitement and uncertainty of the future ran through all three of us on that ride across the Bridge and into the Bronx.

There is a popular sentiment among Jamaicans, especially those who have family abroad. They hear stories of success in America and they come to believe that life in America is easy for everyone and that everyone here lives in abundance. To be fair, the average person here does live in relative abundance when compared to your average Jamaican. There are vastly more opportunities to make money and advance your station in life. Those who have not experienced life in America tend to have a romanticized view of the way things work. They often have misconceptions about the price people pay to live in relative comfort. Many believe the myth of the streets being paved with gold and life being a breeze here in America. What is often not understood is that the opportunities are there, but you often have to tear down walls and fight fires to get them. Working hard in America is supposed to make you successful, and while it does not always happen, just having the opportunity for success is life changing for many people around the world. In Jamaica, often there are no opportunities for people to even fight for. If you are born into a certain station in life, even hard work will have no effect on what happens. It is a blessing to be in a world where hard work can yield success, but to come to New York, and start at the bottom, and work your way up, is not for the faint in heart. Most don't understand until they have the experience.

My rose colored view dimmed with each step as we climbed the largest staircase I had ever seen. When we turned the corner and were faced by another set of stairs just like it, I grew even more aware that I was not walking into what I thought I was at first. By the time we reached the third floor, I learned a lesson without a word being spoken. By the time we got inside the apartment, I breathlessly confessed to my mom that I thought she would have had a big fancy house with fancy furniture and servants and everyone had a good laugh. Within minutes, I was hit with the reality of life in America.

All the same, our tiny apartment on Digney Avenue provided more comfort and luxury than I had ever known in Jamaica. The first thing I remember was the large TV in the living room. When they turned on the TV that first night, the Arsenio Hall show was playing. I was fascinated by everything happening on the screen. My mom asked me if I was hungry and I replied that I was. She made me some hot dogs. After I ate one, she asked me if I wanted another. It kind of took me by surprise. When I was more mature and I thought back on this moment, I realize that "seconds" had never been a concept in my world up until then. Until that moment, I had never been in a place where there was enough food for anyone to have any more than the portion they were given. I ate another hot dog, and another. Four hot dogs later, I was throwing up. Just hours into life in my adopted homeland and another important lesson learned. Just because you can doesn't always mean you should.

The next night, as I stepped out of the building, light snowflakes were floating in the air. I could see my breath! I was in awe. So many new experiences, but I was excited all along the way. We were headed to an apartment not too far away from ours, in the Co-Op City section of the Bronx. This was also for me, a sight to behold. Co-Op City was an area that had all high rise residences. Its home to tens of thousands of people, and is the largest housing development in the world. Being among those enormous brick edifices so closely built together made me feel like an ant among giants. We took an elevator up to see my uncle and his wife. My mother's oldest brother, the one whose presence in the womb helped seal our family's collective fate, lived there with his beautiful, sweet wife whose name means Humble. She most certainly was! The term that comes to mind when I think of this woman, whom I haven't seen in decades is salt of the earth. That night, they weren't the only ones awaiting our arrival at the apartment in the sky. Two of my aunts who had also made it to America made the trip from Brooklyn to see me. It was a joyous occasion. There were hugs, a few tears, and dramatic displays, but lots and lots of laughter. There is an electric feeling when my family gets together (usually around some food of some sort), and they sit around and talk about all manner of foolishness and laugh well into the night. This is still right now, one of my favorite things to observe.

I settled into my life on Digney Avenue. I started school at P.S 87, not too far away from home. I learned much more than the standard subjects going to this school. Of course, I still held onto my love of music, and I was totally enamored by Hip Hop and that new brand of R&B that arose in the early 90s. Discovering Mary J. Blige and A Tribe Called Quest (among others) was almost illuminating. I picked up on social cues very quickly, because to not do so was to my detriment. I learned the appropriate responses, slang terms, and socially accepted behavior. I learned independence because prior to that, I had never walked such a far distance alone. I stopped at the corner store on the way home all the time and bought chips, candy, soda, whatever the change jingling in my pocket could get me. I learned that people do not always react well when confronted with something or someone different, even in the supposed melting pot that was New York. I had experiences with teachers and students alike that illustrated that great American contradiction. I learned that the children were especially cruel, and due to the ruthlessness of those children, I learned to let my accent fade into the wind.

As an adult, talking to people who grew up elsewhere, I have come to value the education I received in New York. Aside from the standard subjects, I remember ever since elementary school, it was emphasized that we were the class of 2000, the first graduating class of the 21st century. We were made to feel like we were special like we could change the world. It feels like we were taught a detailed history of New York at a young age. Maybe my love for the subject just makes these lessons stand out. I remember when I first learned that the island of Manhattan was purchased from the Natives for a trunk of trinkets worth $24. I found that so amazing and fascinating. I remember one teacher even going on to say that this should almost be a life lesson for us. This purchase set the tone for New York to be a shrewd place, where even one second of naiveté would allow someone to take advantage of you. We learned to be proud of New York's role in not just the country, but the world. Anything you want to be, this is a great place to be that. They taught us as third graders, that if you could make it in New York, you can make it anywhere. That we lived in the best city in the world, the center of the art world, the theatre world, the financial capital of the world, the place people have written songs and stories about for hundreds of years. For years, I was almost obsessed with New York history. I have learned so much from the very obscure trivia facts to the most common facts. This, along with my personal experiences over the years, fostered in me a lifelong love for the place I call my hometown.

My mother went back to school at age thirty. She struggled through nursing school. She was nudged, encouraged, and thoroughly supported by my Dad, our Strength. When I first arrived, my mother told me in a very straightforward manner, that I was to always address him as Dad. No one had to know our business because as far as all parties were concerned, we were a family. As a child, I was confused. I couldn't help but feel forced to accept him, and forced to forget my old life, which aroused confused and unfamiliar feelings within. I know now that my mother did not have negative intentions. It was her way of dealing with things. She knew how much he sacrificed so that I could be there. She knew how much he loved her, and how he was willing to accept me as a part of that love. She realized how honorable and wonderful it was that this man was opening his heart, home, and entire life to us. She wanted me to respect that sacrifice and that love from the minute I got there. Now that I have matured and I realize all the factors, I can't even put into words how grateful I am for this man. I was only seven, and I didn't understand that yet. I don't know if these things were explained to me. They possibly were. All the same, I do not think I could have wrapped my mind around that at the time. I was told to address him as Dad, which was awkward for me at first because I didn't know him that well. My interactions with adults up until that point had mostly been devastating at worst and tepid at best. To say it made me shy and uncomfortable around people would be an understatement. I was painfully unsure of myself as a result.

Today, for the friends of mine who know that I have a different biological father than my siblings, recognize my personal terminology when I refer to these two men. My biological father is always referred to as my father. My step-dad (now *that* term is awkward to use) is Dad. My father made me physically, but my Dad raised me, sacrificed for me, loved me, disciplined me, and taught me valuable life lessons about hard work and faith. I see the way he was there for me, all these years, as a testament to the fact that he loves my mom so much it filled up and overflowed onto me. He was also raised in Jamaica but he came to this country as a teenager. He is the youngest of seven children, and as some of his siblings liked to say, his mother's favorite. He comes from a handsome family of fair-skinned people whose name I now bear. They are another testament to the diversity of Jamaicans. When I was a child, I spent a lot of time with them and they also embraced me as a family.

I had lofty expectations of my life in America and what my mother would be like. Those expectations were utterly shattered. In all honesty, I was angry in those early days because I felt like I was just as much of a nuisance, an intruder in someone else's family life, as I did in Jamaica. I felt as if I was being forced to deny where I came from and who I was. I felt I was being dragged around by the adults in my life with no explanation. It felt back then like she was ashamed that she had a first marriage to even speak of. I was a living, breathing, reminder, that try as she may, couldn't erase that. When I would tell people that my last name was different than what it said on my passport, I remember feeling as a kid like I was lying, and it felt wrong. I thought about how I got in trouble for lying about other things, but I would ask myself (too afraid to ask out loud), why it was Ok to lie about me. I felt like some kind of living breathing human burden, the kind you have to sweep under the rug, smile politely and explain away; a blemish on the face that needed to be covered by make-up, or a mistake that needed an explanation. I felt as a kid like I was lying because my mom desperately did not want people to know the full story of who I was. Complicated things for a child to have to work through I think, I had lived with these feelings for a long time. For a long time, these feelings of anger, the feeling that my mom was ashamed of me, governed a lot of my actions.

I wouldn't be surprised if my mother had expectations of a different child. Children who grow up in Jamaica tend to be more precocious and adult-like than the average child in America. A lot of this has to do with the hardships they are exposed to, and the adult situations many of them are forced to deal with sometimes for their own survival. I was painfully shy, timid, introverted and baby-like. Probably not as street smart as she expected and definitely not as street smart as I'm sure she was at my age.

My little brother was born just four months after I arrived. He was given an Arabic name that means "One with Good Judgment." I am constantly amazed at how much people's names have an influence on them somehow. It was as if by giving him his name, my parents pronounced a blessing on him because he has definitely grown to be a thinking man, one who displays a wisdom more advanced than his age. When he first arrived on this earth he was a big ball of curmudgeon. He didn't smile as a baby. He had a surly look on his face at all times. He was one of the only babies I have ever seen, roll their eyes at people before they could talk. I spent a lot of time with my brother in his baby stage. I changed a lot of diapers, fetched a lot of bottles and other necessities. Those first few years of his life, my mother was in school so I babysat a lot. He also went to the Puerto Rican lady next door. She was a very sweet lady whose name was Latin for Glory. She was beautiful and had a bright shining countenance about her. I used to have to pick him up from her house after school. My life and his were very intertwined, often to my dismay. See, the truth is, I was hoping for a sister. It took me a while to resign to the fact that I had a baby brother. I got used to him eventually, and even though I would never have shown it or even admitted it back then, I came to love and admire my little brother. He has a boldness that I wish I had a fraction of. He is witty and smart and inherited the level-headed strength of our dad.

For my first few years in New York, my mother worked hard to finish nursing school in a three year program. I will never forget her time in nursing school. It was definitely hard for her. I went to visit the small school she attended a few times.

The school was located in central Harlem, an area that has been beautified and gentrified over the years, but in the early 90s, the garbage lined streets were a cesspool of drugs and violence. I remember her tales of having to step over people passed out in the doorway so she could get to class. When she became an RN, it was a great reward at the end of an arduous road.

During those years in the Bronx, my mother and I would also travel to Harlem to get our hair braided all the time. We used to go to this one place regularly, it was called Billy Jeans. We would leave uptown at the crack of dawn and ride the subway from 239th street in the Bronx all the way down to Harlem. Sometimes, when we got there, the sun wouldn't even be out yet and people would be lined up around the corner so they could get themselves in a chair. I used to love those trips. We almost always bought food from someplace that day, and I got to take in a million sights. Vendors would line the sidewalk with their wares laid out carefully on blankets or shaky folding tables. It was a sea of dark faces of every variety, with every accent I could imagine. Harlem, even in those darker days, was vibrant. I just loved going there and feeling the shock to the senses, it was thrilling as a child. To this day, I enjoy being in a busy area sometimes and just watching people. I look at their outfits, try to read their faces and imagine I know things about them. I would make up stories in my head about where they came from and where they were going. I perfected this game on the NYC subway when I was a kid. The long trips to Brooklyn to visit my aunts that lived in Flatbush, and even the shorter trips to Fordham Road, a popular shopping area, were always exciting for me. My parents were still young then, and I consider that one of the best things about my childhood. They still were young enough to not just want to sit at home. Young enough to want to socialize, go to barbecues for the fourth of July, or celebrate New

Year's Eve. In general, having fun was still on the list of priorities.

I didn't realize this at first; it took a little while for it to sink in but my Dad owned the building where we lived on the third floor. It was a small yellowish tan building, having only three floors with two apartments on each floor. It was the tallest edifice on the block. We were surrounded by multi-family houses. Despite the connotation that might arise when someone says they live in the Bronx, it was a quiet sleepy block, almost tucked away. It was located on an angular, narrow one-way street that only had residences on one side. In retrospect, it was the only street in the immediate area to break up the monotonous grind of typical city streets. It felt isolated in a small way. It was one of those places you would bypass easily, and never know it's there unless you had a reason to come that way. It had a very suburban feel to it. All the neighbors knew each other, shoveled each other's walkways when it snowed, and generally acted the way good neighbors should.

I have fond memories of sitting on the concrete stoop with a ton of Barbies and accessories, as all the little girls on the block would pool their Barbie resources and create these giant elaborate scenes to act out. These were my first friends. At eight years old, I had never played with other children nor had I had anyone desire my company. I have found that throughout my life, that has been a feeling that I have felt come too rarely. It made me bitter for a while, but in the end, it taught me over the years to value the people who value me and desire to be in my company. My closest friend lived next door with her mom, stepdad, and her little sister. She was a pretty girl with caramel skin with a name I had never heard before the day I met her. It meant Youthful, and she also had the thickest longest head of hair I had ever seen on a human being. Though our parents had been neighbors and acquaintances, our close friendship also brought them together in a close friendship of their own that would last many years.

My parents were building a life not much different than other people their age. Their desires were not much different than the average person. They wanted to prosper and see their children prosper and boy did they put in the work. Both of my parents worked so very hard to build a good and stable life. Most of my younger days were spent adjusting and doing my ever so small part (cleaning, watching and caring for my brother, helping my mom when she was in school) to help stabilize our family. I see it that way now, but I am not so sure how anyone else views my contributions to my family. Although sometimes thoughts try to creep in and tell me that I didn't bring anything positive to their lives. I know that my minuscule responsibilities as a child helped things run smoothly. Now, make no mistake, I was still a child. I still had some moments that I am sure had my parents feeling frustrated. Like when I fed my obsession with WWF (as it was known back then) professional wrestling personalities by calling this 900 number they had that would play recordings of their voices. I called the number obsessively and unknowingly ran up a hefty phone bill.

I had some issues then, too that went unnoticed and subsequently untreated. I had no way of knowing what I was going through. I could barely make sense of reality much less delve into the layers of my emotional problems. I experienced bouts of what I now recognize as depression and anxiety. I didn't know what to call it when I would think about life in Jamaica and battle the sharp knot in my gut that made me cry and shake uncontrollably. I didn't know why I was ok with being in my room for days at a time, speaking to people only when necessary. I found the outside world, even within my own house to be so cold against my sensitive nature. I lived inside my own head a lot. It was fortunate that I loved to read. It allowed the world inside my head to expand, giving me room to roam. I was quiet and I seemed ok, but I needed a certain type of nurturing that I was not getting. I had been through trauma and probably would have benefited with some counseling.

My parents were at a crucial moment in their lives where they had to work hard to build a life for their family. They took care of my basic needs and then some, but there are only so many hours in a day and only so far a human being can be stretched. With all the work it took to achieve what they wanted in life, some things were overlooked when it came to me. Growing up over the years, I resented some of the ways I felt dismissed and ignored. Not that this was done with malice, I know they just thought everything should be fine now. They didn't know about the sexual assaults or the times I would be beaten right along with the family dog, putting us both on the same level. They didn't know I carried it all on the plane with me to America.

Make no mistake my early life with my parents had a flip side. While they were working hard most of the time, there were times we enjoyed the fruits of their labor. They invested in property in Florida and I got to experience Disney World and long road trips to visit my mother's family who left Brooklyn for South Florida. We had so many fun times during those first few years in the Bronx. My little brother was born four months after my arrival from Jamaica, so I am sure it was all a whirlwind; fun times, down times, somehow, somewhere through all of it, I just existed. I felt lost in the shuffle. Not that I wasn't taken care of. I was WELL taken care of. Although I waxed melodramatic on many occasions, no one was beating me or yelling and cursing at me. I was not mistreated in those ways anymore. It was just that I was coming from a traumatic past, where I was treated that way. My earliest memories are of being abused and my body used against my will. I wasn't sure who loved me, what love really meant, and I wasn't sure where I belonged. And I wanted to feel loved in a certain way and I wanted to belong. I just needed some extra attention, but I never got any. Even now, writing this, I feel silly thinking about how petty that sounds. "I needed extra attention", but that fact remains. I don't think the people who were around me saw that need. They felt that delivering me to safety was attention enough. I am sure they felt that by not mistreating me, by feeding and clothing me, and doing enjoyable things sometimes, it should have been obvious. As an adult, I have grown and learned. I now know these things to be outward expressions of love, but my seven year old self didn't understand.

This is not meant to belittle that effort, because God only knows what would have happened to me if my mom hadn't come for me. When I arrived in this country, I was malnourished and underweight, and had worms. Here I was just two years later, at Disney World, ordering what I want at Sammy's in City Island. I am forever grateful for that rescue operation. I hate to think of where my life would be had I stayed in a place with limited opportunities and hardly anyone invested in my well being. Once my basic needs were met, my more complex needs came to the forefront. As much as I was (and am) grateful for the good parts, there were a lot of times I felt bad. I know now that I was struggling with depression and anxiety, maybe even PTSD. I felt overly criticized, so I reacted by being painfully shy and unsure of myself in every way. One could almost say I was withdrawn. I never felt as if I had a valid contribution to the lives of other people. I felt like a pet, something to clean up after, teach discipline, feed and keep out of danger. A lot of times, I felt invisible, and when I would muster up the courage to speak, I would often be dismissed. I grew up believing what they said so many times in different ways, which was, that while I was book smart, I had no common sense. I took this to heart and touted it as an element of my personality until adulthood. This sentiment lasted throughout much of my life. If someone asked a question and I was absolutely sure of the answer, but someone else had a different answer, I would always defer to the other person. I always assumed that in situations like that, I was more likely to be the person who is wrong. I have had incidents in life where I am positively sure of something beyond any shadow of a doubt, but I let someone else's opinion make me question that which I know. I entered many a bad situation in my life with a wealth of knowledge in the back of my mind, but without the courage to be surefooted.

At that time, I felt a sense that no one would care if I was around or not. Sometimes, I felt just as overlooked and as much of a nuisance as I felt in Jamaica. This caused me to make up stories to make myself special. I didn't come home from school one day, convinced in my head that it would be a while until anyone noticed. I stayed at a friend's house until nightfall and her mother was inquiring when it was I would be going home. She got a call not too long later from the school that along with my mother was searching for me. I got the first and only spanking I ever received from my mom ever that night. I didn't really think consciously about why I did it, and I think I really did believe they wouldn't care. I wanted so badly as a child to feel like I was not just tolerated, but that someone would be happy about my presence. It seemed to me that I went from being one family's burden to another family's burden. I didn't feel like I belonged there when I lived in Jamaica with my stepmother's family, and I knew because of the conversations and the way they treated me, but they took care of me (barely) out of obligation. I felt almost just as much as if I didn't belong when I got to the Bronx. My different last name and my sensitive nature (which they did not share nor were especially sympathetic to) helped reiterate that feeling for me. Here I was again being taken care of because of some perceived obligation but without much tenderness. I was in desperate need of some tenderness. As soon as I was grown, I would spend my life searching for that feeling of unconditional acceptance and belonging.

When I look back on this with adult eyes, I know my parents loved me by their actions. Starting with the major sacrifice to get me here, they would sacrifice many times over in the years to come, and I would benefit because of it. Still, at the time, I felt unloved. Now I know I was loved, I was just not nurtured in the way I needed to be. I was a soft and sensitive child who needed to heal from past hurt, but I spent my childhood with people who were not very soft or sensitive and who really had little patience for it.

Something I have come to accept in my later years is that parents are still people and people are not perfect. You want to be the perfect parent for your child and even when a parent tries their hardest, they may be shocked to realize that some things are done nonchalantly, and even things they do with good intentions had an adverse effect.

Chapter Three

The House On Baldwin Drive

Love and Death on Long Island

The next few years passed by and I grew to love a lot about living in the Bronx, but not everything. I loved my new extended family and the few friends I made. I established relationships and a routine, and I became more and more American by the minute. I was 11 and my brother was 3. We were growing up before their very eyes and we were still sharing a bedroom. My dad's parents moved into one of the second floor apartments, and I got used to going down there often to break up the monotony of always being in our apartment. My parents decided that we had outgrown the place and went looking for a house. I had so much fun house hunting. For someone who loved to observe and take in details, it fed my interest, and to this day I love a good day out house hunting. My parents had every intention of staying in the Bronx, and we looked all around town, even to some of the nearby suburbs of Westchester, Mount Vernon, and New Rochelle. Looking back those days, it was so plain to see that our collective steps as a family had been Ordered, because we ended up moving 25 miles away to Long Island, into the one and only house we looked at in the area.

The story of our move starts with two people, two angels sent to usher my parents into their spiritual destiny. My dad was an electrician. He was (and still is) a member of the Electricians Union Local #3 in New York since he still had a teen at the end of his age. In the late 80s, early 90s, there was a Jewish man who was a foreman on one of his jobs and he struck up a friendship. This man lived on Long Island, in Oyster Bay. He then met another Jamaican man like himself, but this guy had some years on my dad. He was the nicest, gentlest soul. He invited my dad and our family out to his house on Long Island, in Westbury where he lived with his wife and kids. The homes of these two friends of my dad's, we discovered, were minutes apart and we would drive out there periodically. I remember these visits out to Long Island, it always felt like the longest drive in eternity to me. I would ooh and aah over the neat tree-lined streets and split level homes. To us at the time, it was like a day trip out to the country. Whenever we went to my dad's friend's houses, we would dress well and be reminded to mind our manners in the car on the way there. My dad's Jewish friend and his wife had two sons, the youngest of which is my age. I thoroughly enjoyed my time with them as a child. They had more gadgets and toys than I could probably fit into our Bronx apartment. They still keep in touch today, and for many years they were very close friends. My dad's Jamaican friend and his wife, however, became more than just close friends. They would become an integral part of all of our lives. They would grow to mean so much to us. People often say that good friends you acquire throughout life are like family, but these people deserve a category of their own. They are much more than friends and sometimes are there for you, even when family is not.

My mom had just finished nursing school, and my dad was

doing well for himself at work, when we took that fateful trip to Long Island in 1993. It started out as these trips typically did, except this time, over dinner, my parents discussed their latest mission: to move into a house as soon as they could. The relationship between our two families grew stronger over the previous years, and they were godparents to my baby brother. They had a long list of godchildren, these two, and to me, it is a testament to their dynamic nature and the incredible way they let love work in and through them. I was always mesmerized by the immense power that they would exude each in their own way. That power never overshadowed the inherent goodness that flowed between them. They led deeply spiritual lives and were always mentors for my parents. My father's friend's wife (also a nurse), had a name was unique and hard to define, just like her. Her husband had the name of a King who is noted for his fairness and a quiet humble strength. There could be no better description for this man. Their family name is one that is also used to describe a type of Sparrow. Sparrows, very fittingly are symbols of freedom and true love.

Mrs. Sparrow told my parents that the house next door was for sale. They were not looking to move that far away, they said. I get the sense that they looked at the house initially out of a begrudging politeness. We had NEVER driven this far out to house hunt so I know this location was one my parents had not even considered. Surprisingly, they ended up loving the house and buying it immediately. I think even they were surprised by how swiftly they made their decision. A very short time after that dinner, we were moving into the house. It was love at first sight with our house on Baldwin Drive.

When I first moved to Westbury, I both loved and hated it,

and I felt both feelings rather intensely. I loved adventure and new experiences so that part was exciting. New experiences were one thing, but I regarded meeting new people with dread. The Sparrows next door were inviting us to their church constantly and my parents would visit periodically. They would send me to the church because there were a lot of children there, and they were constantly doing activities with them. On my very first day at the Westbury Divine Congregational Church of God, I had no idea that this place would go on to be a special and integral part of my life. I also did not anticipate meeting people who would become extended family. On my very first day there though, I did not want to be there.

My parents pulled into the church parking lot and I squinted at the little white house sitting on a huge plot of land. I was not expecting it to look this way, such a small church with such a long name. I got out of the car, feeling awkward and waiting to depart for the African American Museum in Hempstead, a boy several inches shorter than me walked up to me and said hello. I looked down at his round head and dark, dancing eyes and said hello in the barely audible tone that was standard for me. He asked me a few more questions after that, but for some reason, only one stood out in my mind. He said, "Can I kiss you?" I was so taken aback by that until I walked away and spent the rest of that trip trying to avoid this annoying but unforgettable little boy. It seemed like he made it his mission to follow me everywhere. This boy, whose name means *meadows in the west*, came to mean a lot to me in the times to come. Meadows are wide open grassy spaces without too many trees. They contain all kinds of other plants, flowers, and vegetation that could not grow anywhere else besides these open, sunny spaces that support life. They are the best place to be in touch with nature. Meadows are symbols of vitality and freedom, and freedom is the only law by which this person has ever governed his life. He was and always has been wide open, naturally occurring, free and unencumbered by the unnecessary.

I started to attend the church regularly with my little brother. They had an active youth ministry that met every Friday night, and I went to Sunday school every week. Sometimes, my parents would show up for church and I would have to stay after Sunday school and attend the actual service. Before this, I had never experienced either of my parents being very spiritual or religious. My dad's mother was deeply religious, and while I lived in the Bronx, I went to church with her most Sundays. My parents were occasional churchgoers then too. In those years, I never really observed anything tremendously religious from either of them. After about a year of living on Long Island, I noticed my parents slowly started showing up for church more and more. Suddenly they were hanging out less with their friends, listening to different music, and making new rules. My mother began to seek official membership in the church, and it was then that I first started to hear her detail her early life in the church. She started to speak of a time when she was very young in Kingston and she attended the Open Bible Church. She had spent years not attending church regularly, and here she was, back where she belonged she testified. My father had more of a private struggle. He didn't talk so openly about things, but he was a man of action. No more cases of beer or cuss words. His growing compassion for his fellow man and his desire to be a servant of God were visible. Looking back on it, I know that there were discussions and possible mentoring by the Sparrows next door that I was not privy to as a child. For sure, they were a huge spiritual influence for my parents.

My family became fixtures at the church before long. We fell into our lives in Westbury as if it was the way it was meant to be, and I have every reason to believe it was. After finishing school, my mom got her first nursing job at a hospital in Harlem. She worked nights in the Detox Unit, a place where people (many of them homeless or disadvantaged in some way) came to get off of drugs. She dealt with dangerous, unstable people and she always had some crazy story to tell. While she was working there, it also just so happened that my dad also started a job working nights too. With both parents working nights for a few years, I would spend a lot of time alone babysitting my brother. Sometimes a few days would pass and I wouldn't lay eyes on my parents. I just communicated with them by phone and notes. When I awoke to go to school, my mother would have just come home, maybe an hour before, and my dad, a couple of hours before her. I was always admonished not to disturb them. Anyone who ever had to work nights knows that sleep becomes a more valuable commodity in your life than ever before. So they would often be fast asleep as I got myself ready and headed to the bus stop. By the time I came home, my mom was usually already gone and my dad would sometimes be gone, sometimes rushing out as I was coming in. Living on Long Island and working in the City meant that they had to leave early to make time for the trip. My dad was an electrician and drove to work. My mother took the train all the way to Harlem, which took over an hour from Westbury. When she got off of work, it would be late, so the train schedule would start becoming more sporadic. She had to leave work at a specific time in order to make that last train home at about 3 am. Her job was a little unpredictable, so she wasn't always walking out the door the exact time she was supposed to. Sometimes she missed that train and had to wait until 5 am for the next train. I am sure it was hard, emotionally, to want to be home more but feeling as if you had no choice. I also remember that it also took a physical toll. Once, she cried real tears when after working a difficult shift, she had to sit in Penn Station for two hours before she could take the hour long ride home. It was a difficult time. They talked often of wanting to change their job situations so that someone is home with the kids more, but as life often does, it left no room for change in the immediate future.

There was a lot I didn't understand about my dad back then. My views on him were ever changing and sometimes even contradictory. My dad was proud of the work he was doing on the bridges and tunnels of New York. If we drove across a bridge or through a tunnel that he worked on, he would always point out his work. After years of work, he drove us through the Lincoln tunnel showing us how he participated in lighting the two mile path out of New York City. I was fascinated by this as a child. I would look up high and wonder what kind of courage it took to be all the way up there to do electrical work, to crouch for hours in uncomfortable spaces, or working in the subway tunnels while being aware of active trains. It made me see him like some sort of Superman. He seemed stronger than anyone I had ever met, and he always seemed to know the answer to every problem. At the same time, I approached him with caution because his straightforward way of being would often chafe against my sensitive nature. I have, over the years accepted him and I love him with a love indescribable. The same can absolutely be said of my mother. At first though, because I was thrown for a loop and thrust into a living situation without much attention paid to my emotional state, I had to learn the hard way (by myself) how to navigate my relationship with my parents and reconcile my feelings for them.

In between all the work and stress, my parents were still young enough to want to have fun, visit friends and enjoy life.

We still visited the Bronx very often because my dad's family still lived there, and they still owned the building on Digney Avenue. My dad's parents were living in the building, and at that time, my grandmother had her own space in the basement while my grandfather remained in the second floor apartment. The way I understood, it was that he was a difficult man to deal with, very grumpy and stubborn. She told me so herself. We would often have these secret talks, and she would be very open with me about how she felt. Not only did they live closer than any other family members at the time, she took me to church with her every Sunday morning. I never thought anything of these talks back then but they are now some of my most treasured memories. She told me stories from the past, which she could probably tell I loved to hear. She talked about how she felt about a variety of topics and people. Now as an adult, I realize she was venting. A lot of what she said went right over my young head, and I regret not paying more attention. I would have more insight regarding the woman she was. She loved me from day one and I truly felt special in her presence. At the time she moved to the basement, she talked to me a lot about things she regretted in life. I think that after years of dealing with him, my grandmother had reached her wit's end. She told me she felt moving to the basement was actually perfect for her because she still loved him and cared enough to want to make sure he took his medicine every day and she would cook his meals and care for him. When it was all said and done she needed her peace of mind and her own personal space, such as a progressive move for a woman who came from an era where that wouldn't be an option.

My dad's mother was a sweet God-fearing woman whose name meant *Brave Strength*. She was taller than your average woman, big boned and beautiful. She had a round face, awesome skin, and the kind of voice you expected a grandma to have; when I think of her, a feeling of warmth rushes over me. While other people in their family may have made their comments that they thought I didn't hear or unknowingly sent out vibes for negative feelings they thought they were hiding, she made no distinction. I was one of hers.

My dad's father, however, not so much but he would have his moments like when he would have had a beer or two at the fourth of July barbecue, and he felt like smiling or making jokes with the grandchildren. As a general rule, he was always a little aloof, sometimes even mean. And even though I was a kid, I had dealt with my share of people who displayed negativity toward me so I learned to sidestep it. I became an expert at keeping my head down and being just polite enough to not get in trouble but making myself scarce enough to not have to deal with him. I didn't know it then, but it was my way of protecting myself.

One day when I was in the sixth grade, on one of our many visits back to the Bronx, I went looking for my grandmother in her basement apartment but she was not there. I had just walked away from a serious Barbie doll session with my old friends who I was always excited to see now that I lived so far away. When my grandmother wasn't down there, I went to the second floor apartment to look for her because it was likely that she was checking in on my grandfather or cooking something for him. My grandfather answered the door and after a quick look around, I surmised that she was not there either, and I headed toward the door to leave. My grandfather called my name from his bedroom and I changed directions and went to him. I honestly can say, that I don't really remember much of what he said to me, but I know he was talking for at least a minute. I know because I remember watching his mouth move but I couldn't get over the look on his face. It was a look that is etched into my memory but hard to describe. It was different than I ever saw him look at me. Truth be told, he had made me feel uncomfortable at other times but something about this discomfort was almost alarming. I didn't know what was going on at the time. I just knew that every cell and fiber of my being wanted to leave, so I mumbled some excuse and turned to go and that's when he told me to wait a little bit and pat the bed next to him, motioning for me to sit. The split second I sat down, he put his arms around my shoulder and pulled me in close and put his lips on mine. He pressed so hard that it started to hurt and when I felt his tongue brush my lips I started to panic. He reached his hand up and groped my newly sprouting breasts and after a few seconds I looked at him and he smiled. He put his lips on mine again and his beard stubble scratched my face so hard, I forcefully got up and walked towards the door. He screamed after me, yelling at me not to tell anybody.

The first thing I did was tell someone. I walked right out of the building that day and I told my best friend who lived next door. Her beautiful dark eyes widened in shock. I remember as she shook her head, her long ponytail that I had always been jealous of swayed back and forth across her back. I asked her not tell anyone.

A few months later, this same friend with a name meaning Youthful, moved to another town on Long Island with her family. Our parents had become very close friends, especially our dads. It was exciting that my best friend lived closer to me, and I think my parents were also happy to have their old friends move closer. We visited with each other a lot. On one of their trips to my house, they revealed to my parents that my friend told them about the incident with my grandfather. They were going to keep the secret but they felt that it was something they needed to know. My parents thanked them for being honest and promised to deal with the situation.

My parents' way of dealing with that situation was to express anger toward me for embarrassing them. Why they said, did I feel the need to go to people outside the family with something so serious. They felt I should have come to them and only them. Now, by telling other people, they will judge us. This was a private matter. I was young back then, and not too much was discussed with me after that. I will not go as far as saying they never addressed the incident to him, but I never heard anything of the sort. It was never said, but I felt it was implied that they weren't sure if they should believe me. I don't want to accuse anyone of anything I am not sure of, but at the time, that was how I felt. No one at any time sat me down and told me, or asked me anything. No one expressed one iota of tenderness or sympathy about what had happened to me. No one comforted me or even addressed the situation to me after the day they found out about it. Except for once, when a few days later, my mom sat me down in private and laid down some new rules of conduct. I was told to change the way I interact with him, and really all men in general. I was no longer a child, so no sitting on anyone's lap. No more hello or goodbye hugs and kisses, be polite but keep your distance. That was it. So for years after that, until I was in my early 20s and he passed away, I saw the person who molested me, very often, and in close quarters like dinner at an aunt's house or something like that. I was made to hold doors and be respectful. Made to speak to him. I even sang a song at his funeral. There was never ever a time when I was in his presence that I did not think about what happened. What was surprising to me was, while I couldn't stand the sight of him, the bulk of my resentment was toward my parents, my mom especially. I hated the fact that the need for saving face and being polite and not causing conflict was more important than defending me. I was not always aware of these feelings. A lot of it went by without me even acknowledging things to myself. I felt like an embarrassment, a burden.

What I needed was for someone to tell me that what happened to me was wrong and that there wasn't anything that I did to deserve it. I wanted someone to be angry because I was molested, not angry because I told the wrong person. I can't speak for what went on in their hearts and minds regarding this incident, but I can speak for myself. All the things that were expressed openly to me, I can only hope that they were outraged in private, but no such emotions were shown to me. No one said, "I'm sorry this happened to you". I needed someone to be on my side, and I felt so betrayed by them for never addressing the issue with me. I was very angry and I stayed that way for a long time. There eventually came a time when the anger simmered to a low boil but it never left for a long time. This one incident affected my relationship with my parents for years to come. I felt like they were not as horrified as parents should have been, I felt like they didn't defend me like they should have. I was twelve when this happened. It would be many years before I could even speak about their handling of my situation because it caused me tremendous pain. I felt it was adding insult to injury when I was told to change the way I interacted with him. I felt as if it were my fault.

A lot of the feelings and actions toward my parents in my teen years were filtered through this experience. It was a turning point for me. I thought about the incident a lot. My biggest question was why this happened. As I tried to work through some answers on my own, memories of what happened to me when I lived in Spanish Town, Jamaica flooded my mind. I had almost accepted that I lived a horrible life there, and I tried to put it behind me. I had days without food, only water to drink. I lived with people who didn't want me, in an overcrowded home with indoor plumbing that barely worked. I used an outhouse often. People all around me suffered. It was a sad life. Being molested was just part and parcel of the bad place I was in, but here, in this new world, I was supposed to be safe from those things. This was supposed to be a different life. How could this have happened to me by someone else's hands? Did I do something? Was there some invisible sign I wore that told these people that it was ok to touch me? I was confused and I had a lot of questions and no one to ask.

I remained throughout my childhood, a music lover and a voracious reader. My sensitive and somewhat withdrawn nature remained the same. As I moved into Middle School, life in Westbury had become settled. School, church, and home were my regular routine. My parents were really strict and I was not allowed to do much of anything. I couldn't hang out at other people's houses, nor could they come to mine. I was barely allowed phone calls from girls, let alone boys. I spent a lot of time at home sad and angry because I didn't understand for the life of me why I couldn't do some seemingly simple things that I saw other kids do. I was a smart kid. Never did I think that it would be ok to go roaming the streets until late at night and have my parents not know where I was, but the reaction I was given was as if that was what I asked. I never asked for anything that a typical pre-teen living on Long Island wouldn't ask. I wanted to go to the mall, to stay after school. It hurt me, because I was asking to do things that I felt were appropriate, but I was made to feel bad for even asking. For example, there would be times when a group of friends would want to see a movie at the mall. We were still young, all of twelve or thirteen. All their parents would be dropping them off. A couple of parents even would wait outside or walk around the mall and meet them by the door as soon as the movie was over. One parent or two might sit with the group in Chili's or something, while they have appetizers and act silly. I longed to go on one of these excursions with my friends but I was never allowed. Not even when I offered phone numbers of parents who were going to be there. When I suggested my mom be one of the parents who waited outside or in the mall, she said she didn't have time for that. I wasn't even allowed to go to birthday parties of school friends. I would be frustrated because the excuse that she didn't know the people whose house I would be going to was always used. When I tried to implore her to get to know my friend's parents so I could eventually go to their house, it fell on deaf ears. I didn't play outside and I didn't ride bikes around the neighborhood in the summertime like all my friends. It was a huge source of frustration and pain for me. It even felt uncomfortable when my friends called the house because my parents found a problem with everyone. I remember getting a serious talking-to because one of my friends called a few times and when the phone was answered they immediately said "Can I speak to Kika?" without a proper greeting. Socializing at school became awkward for me. I had friends, even people I considered best friends at school, but when I wasn't allowed to see or talk to anyone outside of school. It was difficult to really belong. A few times I was allowed to stay after school for something that I made more serious than it actually was. I would leave early and walk up Post Avenue with my friends to Gino's Pizza and race back in time to catch the after school late bus. I would treasure those times I got to feel that rare feeling everyone felt. I hated that I felt I had to lie to get just a moment of freedom.

Thank God for the church in my life at that time. If I was going anywhere, it was with them. The church youth group would meet every Friday night for service. Sometimes, we stayed at the church and had discussions or activities there. Other times, we would go on trips to the bowling alley, roller skating, gospel concerts, plays, and all kinds of other things. We did live in New York, after all, there was always some exciting activity. It was my only chance to "hang out" or socialize with people outside of school.

The things I wanted were simple and age appropriate, but I was extremely restricted and micromanaged as a child. My hair, the clothes I wore, what I did with my time, every part of my life both big and small were heavily monitored. I was often miserable. There was no talk about the birds and the bees. The day I got my period I was basically told that now I can't go around messing with boys because I can get pregnant. That was the extent of the conversation. Children sometimes can be precocious and take lessons from their friends who might know more about life than they do. So my mom by this time had discovered a few notes to and from boys and things of that nature. Maybe she assumed that she did not have to talk to me about sex. I think she would have been surprised (if she had really tried to talk to me about it) to find out that at that point, I really didn't have any real working knowledge about sex or the changes going on in my body.

When I was thirteen, I saw a porno for the first time and that was my light bulb moment. I was like "Oh, so it goes INSIDE?" Before that, I had only ever seen PG-13 sex scenes, so I kind of knew what it looked like but I didn't know what went on under the covers. I have to laugh at myself now because I have no idea what I thought people actually did when they had sex before that. I distinctly remember that moment of enlightenment. Now, among my age appropriate books like *The Babysitter's Club* and *Are You There God, it's Me, Margaret*, I started reading adult novels with graphic descriptions of sex, and my curiosity grew. Within months of learning about sex, I mistakenly started to feel I was ready. I was actively being pressured for it and that made it easier to succumb.

At the same time that I started to learn about it, I found myself having my first go round in a relationship of sorts. It was one of those situations where the girl thinks she is in love. To the guy, it was just another conquest. He was 17, I was 13. This guy went to the church and was there every Friday night. He wanted to be around me, and he literally charmed the pants off of me. He was a Jamaican guy with light brown eyes and a nice smile. I lost my virginity to him in the least romantic way possible. I cried, a little bit because of the pain but mostly because I hated the way my first time happened. At that age, you spend so much time talking about things like your first time with friends, and for me, I did a lot of reading about it in young adult novels like *Tiger Eyes* by Judy Blume or *Fly Girl* by Omar Tyree. I think I had an idealized view of what it would be like but I enjoyed not one second of it. He picked me up at the bus stop before school and within a few minutes I was in his friends pitch dark basement. I didn't get undressed, he did not kiss me, and he was not at all gentle or understanding. The good part was it was over just as quickly as it started, and before I knew it, I was getting dropped off at school, entering the building a little more of a woman than I was the day before, or at least that's how I felt then. He stopped talking to me not too long after that. It was the first of many times my illusions about relationships, and boys/men were completely shattered. I was very depressed about it and I think my first time broke me a little.

Middle school was a difficult time. I was bullied a lot and I never really understood why. I was quiet and I never bothered anybody so it was especially perplexing when rumors would fly around about me. It was hard, but not nearly as hard as the four years of High School that would follow.

Chapter Four

Community For All Seasons

"You need a village, if only for the pleasure of leaving it. A village means that you are not alone, knowing that in the people, the trees, the earth, there is something that belongs to you, waiting for you when you are not there."

-Casare Pavese

Westbury High School was a unique place. I remember the smell vividly. The sight of the front of the building will always bring a flood of feelings, good and bad. It was a school in a majority white town and county, but the school's population was mostly minority. There is only one other high school in the same area and that one was majority white. Segregation has been against the law for decades, but somehow, there are still times when things don't always look too different in modern times. Both schools were located in Westbury, but they were like two different worlds. We would sit and listen to the sports teams would tell us about the awesome food they had inside the cafeteria, while we side-stepped the buckets in the hallway that were catching the water dripping from the leaky roof. I remember the first day of my Physics class in the tenth grade. A really good friend of mine sat next to me as we patiently waited for the teacher to distribute the dilapidated textbooks. As she opened hers, she saw a familiar name scrawled in the front cover. It was her mother's name. She had the same Physics textbook that her mother had when she took the same Physics class about twenty years before. All the books we received were old and falling apart, just like the building we were expected to learn in every day. Budget cuts were often the explanation given when anyone inquired. My school had a swimming pool that had not been in use since the late 70s. It developed a crack in it, and as the story goes; while they waited for the funds to come in to fix the crack, they used the pool as a storage area for old desks and whatnot, which made the crack worse and worse over the years. By the time we got there in the late 90s, there was no hope for a pool, it was unfixable.

Old computers and school supplies were only part of what made High School a little difficult for me. I was really very quiet and unsure of myself. Looking back, I think I may have come off aloof to some of my peers. Just about everyone who took the time to know me liked me. Those people were far outnumbered by the ones who judged me using what they heard or what they saw on the surface. A lot of false rumors were spread about me. Some rumors were loosely based on a fact, but the story got greatly exaggerated. Some rumors though were pulled out of thin air. I had a tough time dealing with life in High School. Although I was hurt by a lot of the almost-fights (and one real but very unfair fight, I got jumped by four girls on the last day of 8th grade), and the crazy rumors, I had some fun times too.

When I first arrived, I think the school and even the town of Westbury itself was learning to deal with a shifting demographics. Since the 1960s, Caribbean and American Black people started to slowly infiltrate the mostly white town. As a matter of fact, our neighbors, The Sparrows, had been the first black family to live in Sherwood Gardens, (the name of our little enclave) and they arrived in the late 60s. They witnessed the initial slow trickling in of people in those first couple of decades turn into a full fledged wave of new dark faces in the late 80s and early 90s. Westbury's connection with people of African descent may seem to be a modern one, but it actually dates back hundreds of years.

Westbury, by virtue of being a town in the Northeast, is one of the older settlements in this country. It was settled first by English Quakers who came to the area in the 1600s. They, like most early Americans, were there to establish a community in which they could practice their religion freely, which they were barred from doing in their native England. The Quakers who founded Westbury (named after their British hometown) were Christians who called themselves The Society of Friends.[3] It was they who, upon arriving via a trail that had been blazed by the Massapequa tribe that lived there before them, named that trail Jericho Turnpike. The Society of Friends owned slaves when they first arrived, as was the custom of that era. They arrived at about the same time the slave trade was just beginning, so the enslaved people in Westbury were some of the earliest to arrive from Africa. The Quakers spent the first century as loyal British subjects (as did most of the colonies' residents) who were happy to practice their faith far away from those who previously persecuted them. Political strife in the colonies was built up over the years. Then in the late 1700s, the tide started to really shift in society. Unfair treatment from the British crown plagued the colonist's lives. Laws were passed and taxes were levied from an ocean away, and the colonists were no longer standing for it. The Europeans who came to the American continent were a special group of people.

---

3   Panchyk, RIchard. *A History of Westbury Long Island.2007*.

One needed a certain fire in their spirit to brave a rough two month journey on a ship that would have a chance of being plagued with infectious disease and unknown dangers only to arrive in unchartered territory and lay a foundation from nothing. There were millions of Native Americans already living in North America when they arrived; some were friendly and some were not. Some tribes were accommodating to the new settlers, but some saw this influx of Europeans as an invasion and treated it as such, attacking settlements, ambushing and murdering. Moving across the Atlantic was not for the weak. This was a continent was settled and occupied by the toughest, bravest, most independent Europeans in that era. They had to be that way to survive in the New World. These same people (and their descendants) who fought to be free and to have a society of their own did not take the injustices imparted on them by the British Crown lightly. That same fire they had in them that fueled their settlement in the Americas in the first place was re-ignited a century later. By the 1770s, the American Revolution was brewing. Influenced by Greek philosophers and the writers of the Enlightenment, the new leaders were speaking against the Crown and circulating these notions of limited government, separation of powers and a whole host of other ideas that encompassed their dream of a new and independent Democratic Republic. During this time, there was little one could do as a member of society to avoid contact with these new concepts. There were books written and pamphlets circulated. Dramatic speeches by some of the more prominent leaders sparked discussions among every sector of society. From the fancy salons down to the slave quarters; these ideas reached those on the highest levels of society and trickled all the way down to the lowest rung through the everlasting power of word of mouth. In 1776, the leaders of the brewing revolution decided to put it in writing in one official document, resulting in the Declaration of Independence. In seeking their separation from the King, the founding fathers inked an approximately 1300 word document, which with its very first opening line declares all men equal. In the same first breath, yet without a full stop, it declared Life, Liberty and the Pursuit of Happiness to be the God-given right of every man. The Quakers in Westbury were influenced in their own way by these new sweeping ideas. Their religion dictated that they be pacifists, so they generally took a neutral stance when it came to war, but they were convicted in their principles about the institution of slavery by the same sentiment expressed in the opening line of the Declaration of Independence. They asked themselves if God created all men equal, how then can we hold our fellow man in bondage. In 1775, after over a century, but still a century ahead of the country as a whole, they gave all the African Americans who were enslaved by Quakers their freedom. 154 ex-slaves built their own community on open land in Westbury. This was against the mainstream at the time. Not that black people were ignored at the time, there were some discussions about the place that a black person occupied in the American Revolution. People of African descent were here from the very beginning of settlement. There were those who brought up the question of whether African Americans were included when they spoke of equality, but there were very few who did not follow that question with excuses for why Black people should continue to be subjugated. Some people wanted to exclude the Africans because the lucrative nature of free labor made it hard to resist slavery. Some felt that the very same Christianity that the Quakers practiced and the very same Holy Bible they read was dictating the opposite, that it was the destiny of the African to be enslaved. The excuses varied widely but the results did not.

There were other communities and people across the colonies who freed their slaves during a small window of time around the American Revolution. But once independence was won, the need for money, for goods and services, outweighed anything else with respect to slavery. While the country was swept up in independence fever, there seemed to be hope for Black people. But once the dust settled, the people in power needed to clean up the mess and build wealth as fast as possible. What better way to build wealth than to have millions of people work for you for free? The slavery laws got even more severe and the development of the de-humanizing form of chattel slavery practiced in America grew into full fruition. The United States became so dependent on, even addicted to, this free labor force that it had to fight a bloody war that killed close to a million of its own sons before it was forced to let go. But one hundred years before that bloody Civil War, and technically years before the United States even became official (the Revolutionary war ended in 1783), the Quakers realized that the African Americans they held in bondage did not deserve their condition. Later down the line, but still decades before the Civil War ended slavery nationally, they helped the free African Americans in the community build the African Methodist Episcopal Church on Grand Blvd. in Westbury and the building still stands today. The Quakers took their religious convictions even further by making many locations in Westbury and its surrounding areas (mainly Old Westbury and Jericho) stops that were a part of the Underground Railroad. The route through Long Island was not the most popular route that freedom seeking slaves from the South would take. They were most often looking for the fastest route to Canada and this stop was a bit of a detour. But the Quakers were known to have one of the safest routes to freedom. Often, the enslaved people could hide in plain sight among the free Black people that already lived in Westbury, and many did stay. But for many still, it was just a stopover until they would be hustled by wagon to the water (most likely Oyster Bay), where they would make other stops along the way en route to Canada.

I love knowing that I grew up in a place so strongly connected to African American history. Westbury's small black community dwindled over the scores of decades that followed. This was especially when the bright lights of Harlem and other more urban neighborhoods that attracted black people came calling. In the final decades of the twentieth century, however, a shift happened and that which was old was new again. In 1924, the village of Old Westbury came into existence. It was basically a way to separate the more affluent members of the area and give them their own space. The contrast between the homes and median incomes in Old Westbury and Westbury differed tremendously. All one would have to do is cross one major street and you would go from regular middle-class homes be surrounded by splendid mansions like you have never seen. I once read that Old Westbury actually has the second richest zip code in the country. It was right across the highway from where I grew up. The Black people who came to Westbury in the last half of the twentieth century were often leaving the New York City boroughs for Long Island (and other surrounding suburbs), much like my family did, in search of a better life for their children. In the modern world, however, the migration looked a little different. Many of these people were not just black, but foreigners, which created a unique experience. Of the majority Black students I went to school with, the majority of *them* had parents who were born in another country if they weren't born there themselves like me. I went to school with a lot of Jamaicans and other Caribbean people. There was a substantial Haitian population, along with some Africans. The Hispanic population steadily rose alongside the Black population. They were mostly from El Salvador, although there were other Hispanic nationalities represented there. I remember Colombians, Puerto Ricans, Cubans, and one girl who was Chilean. There were smaller groups that brought even more diversity. There were a few Filipinos, a few Indians, and a handful of White people; all of the non-black and Hispanic students made up a small fraction of the population of about 800-900 students.

Chapter Five

A Reason. A Season. A Lifetime. . .

Make new friends but keep the old. One is
silver and the other's gold . . .

-Joseph Parry

L iving in New York also provided me with exposure to other people's cultures, which I have always found fascinating. I came across so many interesting people and stories that I will never forget. In the third grade at PS 87 in the Bronx, I had a teacher who was Jewish. When it was time for the annual Christmas program, she suggested we do our portion of the show about Hanukkah instead. So for the eight days of Hanukkah that year in the early 90s, we were taught the story of the Jews and the significance of the Menorah and its candles. We made dreidels (these traditional toys that resembled a spinning top), we learned traditional songs and on the last day of Hanukkah, she brought her daughter to class and with two hot plates in the classroom they taught us to make potato latkes. They were delicious. When it came time for the program, instead of Jingle Bells, our class was the only one to sing a Hanukkah song. It must have been a sight to see 30 African American children singing a traditional Jewish song inviting the audience to come light the menorah. I still remember that song word for word and I treasure these types of experiences in my life.

I have tasted cuisine from a lot of different countries I can place a foreign accent with laser-like precision. I actually really love the fact that I grew up somewhere where they taught us to respect other people's cultures. Little tidbits were always dropped on us, like the fact that you cannot call an Asian person Oriental because that term refers to objects from that region, not people. We were discouraged from calling every Asian person Chinese and were taught the differences in Asian cultures. We were taught to respect that every Hispanic is not Mexican or Puerto Rican. There are diverse arrays of nationalities under the Hispanic umbrella, so one should never assume. You learned never to confuse cultures and the right terminology to use when you weren't sure. I had a friend in middle school, who although she was from El Salvador, she had a German first name meaning Family. Her mother used to make us traditional food all the time. She was a part of my first group of friends. When I lived in the Bronx, I barely spoke to people at school and I had a couple of good friends on my block. The group of friends that started on the first day of the sixth grade in Westbury was the first experience I had with a sense of belonging. Besides myself and my Hispanic friend, there were two others. One friend lived in my neighborhood of Sherwood Gardens and rode my bus. Her name is Welsh for Fair One, and she had a Guyanese dad and a Jamaican mom. The group was rounded out by the only American who had a Jewish name that means Sacrifice. We ate lunch together, we wrote songs, we called ourselves Power Rangers (your ranger color was whatever color you were wearing that day) and we loved to laugh a lot. I still treasure the years of friendship I experienced with these girls, especially because it felt like the first time people actively wanted to be my friend and wanted me around. Our El Salvadorian group member had to move before we finished High School. Today, she lives up to the meaning of her name, she is a wonderfully warm person who lives for her family. My first male friend had a name meaning "Light Bearer" although he did not spell it traditionally. During the time period when my parents both worked nights, I would spend hours on the phone with him, talking about any and everything. We had a lot of similarities, and not just our November birthdays. I remember relating to him because we both experienced similar situations with our biological dads and the last name confusion that came about as a result. We were both very different kids, although his eccentric nature was more obvious than mine. He was close friends with one of the only white guys we went to school with (who also happened to be one of the best people I came across in my time in Westbury. His name means From the Valley). We both loved Hip Hop music, but we also both experimented with different music. I was always music obsessed. My obsession with music started as early as I can remember in Jamaica. With him was where I developed the theory that if you only listen to one type of music (like most of the kids i grew up around did), you cannot call yourself a music lover. This Light Bearer was the first person I shared the secret joy of different types of music with. Our choices would have (and sometimes did) result in derision from our peers, but we had each other. We have logged hours upon hours of conversation. I think I fell in love with him for like a couple of months and we probably kissed once, but his friendship was so important to me. He was the first real artist that I came into contact with. He used to draw these amazing cartoons all the time, and later on in High School fell in love with photography and he has made art his life from then on. He inspires me, even today. He takes his love for art to levels I don't think I could ever have imagined. He is successful and doing the thing he loves.

Church provided me with a lot of great supportive friends over the years. We were like family, and I am still close friends with some of the cast of characters I met there. A lot of these people have fallen out of regular contact, but the bond will always be there. There are others I check in with like my friend whose name means *Bee* in Greek. She has kept me laughing for a lifetime. I have so many great memories with these people. I remember countless nights of mischief with my closest friend whose name means *Defender of Mankind*. Such a mighty name to live up to, but she still is a force to be reckoned with in her own way. She is gregarious and there are so many different people who would call her their best friend. Her friendship has been one of the few constants in my life. She has been a support to me through some of the hardest times I have encountered as an adult. No matter where life has taken me, or how far apart we have lived, she has always made it her business to see about me. I have to treasure her, if only for that. She is still to this day, one of my most loyal friends. I remember the very first time I laid eyes on another of my closest friends, someone else who would become like a sister to me. She was younger than me, full of energy and electricity, and it seemed like destiny brought us together. We often were mistaken for sisters without bothering to correct people. I had such a depth of love for this girl I don't think I felt such a connection with a friend before or since. I watched her grow up it seems, into someone dynamic. Her name means *Little Girl Arise*, and that she did. I watched this little girl dust off the ashes of a bad childhood, and ascend completely into the epitome of the American Pull-yourself-up-by-your-bootstraps type of woman. Although I am sure when many people speak of that type, they don't imagine a short rosy cheeked brown girl, armed with cute shoes and the determination of a lioness. I will always be grateful for the people I met while I was growing up in church.

I had a few other people I shared special friendships with in High School. One friend was the son of Jamaican immigrants who came to America and made a success of their lives. He felt the pressure to live up to that success in a major way. It is a predicament that I think only this specific subset of people can understand. He is like a kindred spirit of sorts. We are both misfits in our own way. I was nervously approaching the bus stop on the first day of the tenth grade when two new faces stared back at me. One belonged to someone who caused me a little grief for a while, although he was close friends with my friends. The other had the biggest brightest smile I had ever seen. My close friend, whose name means *"Brave Power,"* smiles so genuinely every time he does. It's the kind of smile that lights up his whole face, makes his eyes almost gleam and gets so infectious that you find yourself smiling too. There was a third member of their group and he lived the closest to me, but he came running for the bus as it was about to pull off, which we later discovered to be the norm. I remember my attraction to him was instant as he breathlessly boarded the bus that morning. It wasn't long before he was my boyfriend and the *Brave* One served as a best friend to us both. Even after our relationship dissolved, I remained friends with both of these gentlemen, and the Brave One and I share a special bond that continues to this day. His other half is someone we went to school with also, and he chose well. There was a lot of ignorance roaming the halls of Westbury High School when I was there and somehow he managed to snag one of the sweetest souls ever.

I came across so many good people who loved me and were good to me. I am glad for that crowd of people because there were many who felt opposite. I treasured back then, those who were positive in light of all the negativity I faced. A lot of the negativity surrounded my dating habits. Basically, a lot of girls didn't like me and it was usually because some boy did. I dealt with people spreading rumors and talking negatively about me, while often not knowing much about me at all. I remember rumors about me performing sexual acts at a party in High School, which made me laugh out loud when someone tried to confront me about it. If they knew me even on the most basic level, they would know that there was no way I was at any party. My parents were super strict and I spent all of High School having attended one dance my senior year (aside from the prom) and one formal sweet sixteen, that was it. I did not hang out. I was not in the mall on a Saturday or walking to Post Avenue with my friends in the summertime like them. People did then as others have often done to me in life. They assume that I fit a certain paradigm because of how I look or my demeanor. Most people who choose to look beneath the surface find a host of complication that my outer shell does not convey.

Music was a mainstay in my life; always, since the beginning. In a sense, music was my oldest friend. Every memory I have, from Jamaica to the present day, is interwoven with a soundtrack. When I was living in Westbury, I sang on every choir imaginable at school and at church. I took voice lessons for a few years and a little piano. I developed such a love for not just listening to music but being a participant and helping to make something sound beautiful. I was less enthusiastic about the church choir in my earlier years. I still participated and I eventually grew to love it. My enthusiasm for the church choir and really for church in general, began to grow during my senior year of High School. I guess the journey to that change started the summer before senior year when I went to sleep-away camp in Southampton.

Chapter Six

Eight Summers

*What good is the warmth of summer, without the cold of
winter to give it sweetness.*

-John Steinbeck

Summer is every kid's favorite time of year, but I was
not your average kid. My parents' strictness didn't
allow me the luxury of seeing summer as some carefree
time to be young. I stayed in the house a lot and there
was a lot of effort put into monitoring me. I felt at
the time like there was a conscious effort to limit my fun and
freedom. At least during the school year, I went somewhere and
saw my friends every day. Summer for me meant devouring
books in my room, watching my little brother and counting the
days until I got to go away to summer camp for two weeks.
To say camp was the highlight of my summer would be an
understatement. It was a bright spot in my year all together.

The electrical workers union, that my dad belongs to, has
awesome benefits for its members and their families. One of the
more unusual things they offer for its members and their children
is a summer camp that could be attended at a steep discount rate.
This sleep-away camp location was one that was embedded in
American history, and although I did not know it at the time, I
swear I felt it. There are many times I have been somewhere and

was able to feel in my bones the weight of the history permeating the walls or seeping up from beneath my feet. The Hamptons was not always the rich people's hotspot in New York that it is today. Back in the gilded age of the early 1900s, the hot spot was actually not too far from where we lived in Westbury on the North Shore of Long Island. That beach community (that includes Old Westbury) was the place that was visited by F. Scott Fitzgerald that inspired him to write The Great Gatsby. In his novel, the North Shore was set in the re-named fictional community of West Egg, where he explored the joys and the disadvantages to achieving the "American dream". This concept was embodied in 1920s Long Island. It was full of affluent people and extravagant parties that seemed almost to be celebrating a new age in America. The prosperity enjoyed by the richest people in the country seemed to increase. These nouveau riche were looking for places to spend their new disposable income. Estates popped up all along the beach towns of Long Island, as far as a two and a half hour drive away in the Hamptons. The Hamptons are a group of villages and towns on the far east end of Long Island that boasts some of the most beautiful beaches and most extravagant estates in the country. In 1918, a prominent figure in American finance, Charles Sabin and his wife Pauline commissioned the building of a large estate in Southampton, which they named Bayberry Land. Pauline Sabin was the daughter of a high ranking official in the government, who was in fact a member of the cabinet of Theodore Roosevelt. The estate served as the summer vacation home for this wealthy family for almost thirty years. There were articles written about the lavish parties they would throw for some of the most prominent people at the time. Charles Sabin died in 1933 and his wife died in 1945, at which time the family put the estate on the market. Its luxurious setting most likely made the price steep and it had a hard time selling. The International Brotherhood of Electrical Workers purchased the large estate and used it as a retreat for its members. Over the years they made a lot of changes to the property, adding new buildings and swimming pools. In the early 1970s, they created Camp Integrity for the children of its members. This camp was made so that these children who mostly live in the city could experience nature and enjoy life in the outdoors. I joined the ranks of about 18,000 children who have had that experience in 1993, and it is still one of the most treasured experiences of my life. I went to this camp every year following until I was too old to go, and even then I served as a camp counselor there one summer before finally saying farewell to the beautiful place. The camp has since moved its location and Bayberry Land has been sold and turned into a country club.

Don't be misled by the fact that this camp was located on an estate in the Hamptons because there was nothing luxurious about it. We lived in the woods with no electricity in the living quarters. We lived in these enormous half cabin half tent contraptions. They had wood stairs and a wood platform served as the floor, with wood beams going up the sides of it, holding up a canvas roof. There were heavy canvas flaps on the sides of the tent that we were only allowed to roll down if it rained; they remained wide open most of the time. It was better that way, because when the flaps were down it was like a sauna in there. The beds were pushed to the outer parts of the platform close to the beams, close to nature. It basically felt like you were sleeping outside. It would not be surprising to open your eyes in the morning and see deer a few feet away from you, with nothing barring them from just casually walking into the tent, although I never saw one do it. Over the years the worst things that entered the living space were things like frogs, chipmunks and insects. The bathrooms were in a central location, so you had to take a walk to go use the toilet or take a shower, often having to wait in line to do both. The bathroom was one of the few locations that had electricity. We were in such a heavily wooded area, that if you were always mandated to go places with at least one other person, no matter what. That was a serious test of friendship when someone was poking you in the shoulder at 2am doing the pee dance in front of your bed because they have to go to the bathroom and they couldn't go alone.

I learned to swim there. I discovered my love for art there. I sang for them and helped write skits that each group would perform on the last night of camp. I got stung by a jellyfish while canoeing in the Bay. I got a spider bite on my eye that had it swollen shut. I also learned songs that still pop in my head from time to time. I had so much fun there. I made friendships that lasted many years. The majority of those people, I only saw in the summer at Camp Integrity but it felt like we grew up together. The majority of those people were also white, which was a unique experience for me.

I was usually the only black girl or one of a few when I was there. While I am more conscious of situations like that in my current life, it did nothing back then to deter Camp from being one of the highlight experiences of my life. I learned so much about myself. I came to many an epiphany out there at edge of my little world, away from everything. This experience stood out from most of my social experiences in life. The only other time I had the experience of being one of the few minorities would be years later in a brief stint I had at a Christian college in Indiana. Although I was exposed to other cultures in New York and came across people who were different all the time, my intimate life was not very diverse. I was born among Black people in Jamaica and raised among mostly Black people in the Bronx and Westbury. All aspects of my life, family, school, church, all had me surrounded by people who looked like me. If I wasn't in an environment that was majority black, which I was most of the time, then usually that environment was heavily diverse with lots of different types of people. Camp Integrity was the first (and one of the only times) I found myself surrounded by mostly just white people.

I loved every minute of every day I spent there, and my love only increased over the years. I loved all the activities, I loved the fact that we were encouraged to be creative. When I was there, I was like a different person. I was outgoing, outspoken, and confident. Mostly because I didn't feel like anyone was judging me. The parts of me that I was too timid to let loose were on full display. Weirdly, I was more myself among these strangers than anywhere else at that time in my life. There was no one telling me that I had book smarts but no common sense; no one underestimating me or ignoring me. I was always sleepless the night before I went, and I always cried sad tears when it was time to go home.

I started at the age of 9 and went until I was 16. The final year I went, I was actually a junior counselor, so I was there for a longer time and I got paid. It was my first job, but I often don't think of it in those terms. That summer, I had just completed my junior year of High School, one of the most difficult years there, and I was excited to get away. I was no longer young enough to be a camper and I looked forward to experiencing the other side of things as a counselor at camp. What an experience it was. There were many returning counselors; some of them were counselors when I was a camper. I saw a lot of those people in a totally different light. Of course in front of the campers, they presented a more wholesome image, but I soon learned of relationships between counselors and all kinds of personal things one was not privy to as a camper. One of the people who was an authority figure in the past but was now a colleague, and one of the few fellow black people that went to camp was this guy who had a biblical name meaning Rock. To me back then he was extremely good looking. Although the real details of how he looked escapes me right now, I can remember being obsessed with the dreadlocks he had hanging down his back, about six inches past his shoulders. I had a super crush on him and I didn't do much to hide it. I found myself everywhere he was. This guy (who was about twenty-two years old at the time) found it interesting that this sixteen year old junior counselor who was once a camper who he taught to play basketball had a crush on him. He would call me out on it, but not in a mean way. I could tell he was flattered.

We used to have days off as counselors and often people would use their days off to go home for a day or two and visit. Some people who lived too far would just go into town and hang out and try to stay out of the way when they were at camp so no one asks you anything. I remember one particular weekend both me the Rock and I had our weekends off, and as we were in the van that was to drop us off at the Long Island Railroad station. We were hit with a road block. Most of Southampton was shut down because then, President Clinton and his wife Hillary were vacationing that weekend. We were not allowed to drive down that road that day, and on the ride back to camp, we bonded a little more on our shared disappointment at not getting to spend our weekend off the way we wanted. When we got back to camp, I stayed with him most of that weekend and we got much closer. Soon we were inseparable and a few weeks later, I decided to give in to his sexual advances.

I lost my virginity at the very young age of thirteen. After a few times with that first person, I was not sure if I even liked sex. I was of the opinion that it was mainly for the guys because as a teenager, I never enjoyed having sex. That just goes to show that I was not ready for it. The years from the age of 13 until 16 were spent celibate. That junior year of High School, I was in a couple of "serious" relationships and felt pressured to engage in activity that I honestly did not enjoy. I could make out all day long, but I would always dread the ultimate act. So by the time I was at camp that final summer, I was under the impression that that was what was expected of me after being in a relationship for so long. I thought of it as something that guys will wanna do with me eventually, but at that point in my life, I had never felt the desire to pursue having sex with anyone; just always giving in to pressure.

I thought we were in a real relationship. It was the first, but it wouldn't be the last time in my life I was mistaken about something like that. I naively thought our late night conversations and secret rendezvous meant more than they did. I even snuck off on another weekend off to spend two days with him at his place in Brooklyn. I found out later that he lived with his mom and sister's in that apartment that he claimed was his alone. I also found out he had been in a relationship with the same girl since they were fourteen years old and they had children together. To top it off, this girl lived right across the street from him, but was on vacation that week he brought me around. All this came out from another one of the male counselors who was his "friend," but was also making advances towards me. When I told him I was dating the Rock, he laughed out loud and proceeded to tell me these things to convince me he was a better guy. It didn't make me more interested in the other guy. It didn't even make me hate Rock. All it did was shatter me.

After camp when he didn't have much use for me anymore, he discarded me in a very cold way. Even on the last day when I was running down the hill to make sure I could say a proper goodbye to him before my parents came, I could feel the coldness radiating off of him as he barely spoke to me and didn't look me in the eye. I passed off my tears that day as sadness at my leaving but deep down, I knew the real reason I was crying. I never spoke to him again and I never went back to camp.

Being treated this way had a profound effect on me. It took me to a very low place. It caused me to think about some of the things I was doing and to evaluate my reasons for doing them. This experience was not just a lesson in relationships, but being so depressed over it opened my eyes to other factors in my life. I realized I was desperate to belong to someone, desperate for affection and desperate to feel special to someone. After camp that year, like every other year, I returned to my regular life where I felt my parents ignored and did not respect my feelings (or me in any way for that matter). I was back to being invisible, doing my regular routine of church, school, home. After this experience, I knew I saw things differently. It highlighted and solidified for me that recurring feeling of being unimportant, disregarded, overlooked. After this camp experience, I wallowed in those feelings for months.

For all those years that I had been going to church, I had gone up to the altar a few times to get "saved". The church tells you that this means giving your life over to God and living by strict Christian values. I was never fully aware of what being saved entailed before, but as I matured, I saw it as something to take seriously. One day in a church, I was listening to a sermon that had me convicted about my ways, especially the fact that I had several sexual partners already by that time. I was looking for a way out from under the weight of the feelings I had because no matter how I tried I couldn't shake the depression. I saw myself as dirty and flawed and on that day, I was convinced I needed Jesus. I went to the altar that day a few weeks before I turned seventeen, so sincere in wanting to be pure and holy. I told myself that gone were the days of feeling like I didn't belong to anyone. I now belonged to God. I was baptized not too long after, and so began the first leg of my spiritual journey in life.

Chapter Seven
The Amen Corner

Growing up is losing some illusions, in order to acquire others.

- Virginia Woolf

Spending literally the entirety of my years in the church has left me with a level of expertise on the Bible that could probably rival some of the men in fancy robes. In Jamaica, I went to church every Sunday, as I did in the Bronx with my dad's mother. Even when my parents were not going to church, they sent myself and my brother. It always seemed like no matter where life took me, I always had to be in church on a Sunday. I paid attention to some of the things I heard, but honestly, even when I wasn't fully aware, I was still absorbing so much.

My mom gave birth to a baby girl when I was sixteen and my little brother was eight. We were all eight years apart. That event also had an effect on my life. I loved my little sister so much from the minute I laid eyes on her. My mom had a difficult pregnancy, but we all anxiously anticipated her arrival. She was a big baby, and she was born tall too. Seriously one of the cutest babies I had ever seen. She was planned, and wanted and loved by all. I loved her too, but her presence served to intensify my feelings of inferiority. I hated that while I loved her tremendously, I couldn't help my negative feelings when I would see the way, not just my parents, but other family members doted on her and showered her with love. It only highlighted for me once again, that I never got that. I would try to convince myself back then, that I wasn't with them as a small toddler. Maybe if I was, they would think of me differently. I didn't talk much about feeling that way because I was ashamed. Talking about the past was not exactly encouraged, but truthfully I don't know if I really made full sense of the feelings I had at the time. I kept it inside or I took it out on myself. That's how I dealt with almost everything. These negative feelings would creep up every so often, but I always tried hard to suppress them, always acknowledging the selfish root of my issue. Ignoring those feelings was absolutely made easier by my baby sister's sweet lovable nature. She was a good baby and she made everyone smile. It often feels like we did not grow up together because of our age difference. I was a junior in High School when she was born. When I became an adult, she was still a toddler.

By that time I started to take my walk with the Lord seriously, I was deeply immersed in my church in Westbury. Both of my parents served in several different capacities, and I was forced to participate also. I never really had much of a choice. For the most part, I enjoyed my participation in the church. We would go to Bible Study on Wednesday nights, and sometimes it would drone on and on until really late. It was probably my least favorite of our church activities, but it was where I gained a lot of knowledge about the bible and the church itself. I asked a lot of questions, most of them internally (I was way too shy to really speak), and whether they knew it or not, it was where I developed a lot of my personal spiritual base, sometimes in contradiction to what they were teaching. I learned a lot directly, but there were so many indirect lessons they taught through word and deed. On Friday nights, the young people would have a youth service. That sometimes consisted of outings. Sometimes there were in-house activities that varied vastly on the fun scale, and other times we would have to sit for a lecture and have to just be grateful for the time to socialize out in the parking lot. We even took trips at the end of every year to a youth convention that was sponsored by our denomination. It was always in a different city, and it provided me with the opportunity to see new places and meet people from all over. Saturdays were usually either a choir rehearsal, or I was helping with the food pantry that my church ran for the needy people in the community, sometimes both. Of course, there was church on Sunday, and about half of those Sundays had us at two services that day.

Church was my whole entire life up until that point. No matter how much teaching I received, no matter how many songs I was forced to sing, or how much of the Bible I was forced to read, nothing made me take my spiritual life seriously up until then. My camp experience with Rock and subsequent depression was the biggest part of the catalyst into a more spiritual life. Before camp, I had a rough time that culminated with my experience that summer.

I dealt with so many emotions, all the while bumping heads with my parents on a regular basis. I felt like no one cared, and I was just looking for someone to care. I was looking for someone who I could be important to because I felt unimportant to everyone around. I'm not sure if the people around me would have sympathized with that, but it was what was in my heart. I needed to talk; I needed to feel like someone was seeking me out. Boys were the main people seeking me out at the time, so I indulged in the attention. Every time my mom became aware that I had contact with boys (mostly by catching me sneaking on the phone or skirting the rules somehow), she was always so angry and disappointed. Her disappointment was always so stinging.

With the shame from my mom's disappointment from earlier in the year being combined with the shame of my camp experience, I had reached a critical point. The desperation to feel special was somewhere along the line, transferred to a desperation to not feel ashamed of myself anymore. A large driver of my new found religious awakening was, I hoped that my mom could finally be proud of me. By being holy, I could take the shame out of her eyes. In my mind, it was her shame that made her leave me in Jamaica. She was profoundly hurt and ashamed by my father publically cheating on her and mistreating her, so she left. She left me too in the process. I was the product of this shameful union. I felt that it was her shame that made her return and get me. Shame had her tell me to lie about my last name and keep mum on the subject of my father. In turn, I always felt ashamed that I had a different name; ashamed that I looked different from my brother and sister and I stood out. I thought sometimes, maybe people could tell that I did not belong. I was anxious about it in situations where people couldn't possibly know, or in situations where it didn't matter. I walked around with my shame on me like a cloak of elvenkind. This cloak is an element in the game Dungeons and Dragons. When a player was able to obtain a cloak of elvenkind, they could put the hood of the cloak over their heads and it made them invisible. The shame I felt was draped over me and at all times. I felt it rendered me invisible. For now, shame did its bidding and pushed me to the church altar and made me want to change my life.

Chapter Eight
Candles In The Wind

Closed eyes, heart not beating, but a living love.
- Avis Corea

My dad's mother, the woman who was always warm and who accepted me as her own, passed away a few months before my High School graduation. She had a series of strokes and was in the hospital for some time. At one point, it seemed that she might recover, even being alert enough to talk to us. I can still see her laying there; her usual rosy cheeks and fair skin were ashen. With her chapped lips and mouth only slightly opening, she whispered and gently reminded me of the oranges I had left behind the last time I came to visit her. That was our last conversation. She took a turn for the worse and slipped into a coma days after that. While she was in the coma, the doctors informed our family that even if she recovered from the stroke, she was still suffering from advanced stage cancer, which would likely end her life soon also. This was news to everyone; she had not shared her cancer diagnosis with her family. The whole family was allowed to gather. Those that lived in New York were all there, gathered at her bedside as she was taken off of life support and drew her last breath. We were to also discover, she had already purchased a plot for herself and her husband. It was way upstate near Pleasantville, NY overlooking a breathtakingly beautiful scene. It was so out of the way that everyone wondered out loud why she would choose such a remote place. I think the consensus was, she knew how deeply attached to her the family was, and didn't want to be buried close so as not to be a burden of sadness. The conclusion was that she didn't want people coming there every day, visiting her grave and being sad. She made it so that visiting her grave site would require preparation and effort. We will never know her reasons, but this conclusion was not far-fetched at all. That was just like her, always thinking about the family and what was best for them. The day we buried her was the first and only time I saw my dad, our Tower of Strength break down. It was a difficult time for everyone.

My senior year of High School went by so fast. I was in advanced classes, so I technically could have taken a gym class in summer school and graduated a year early, but I chose to do my full senior year. I didn't share with my parents the option I had. I made the decision on my own. I took every chorus and choir and art class possible, and basically sailed through the whole year. I did all the rites of passage, including an uneventful prom, all the while anxiously awaiting adulthood. I thought that so much was going to change for me, and I was looking forward to it. I applied to about 10 colleges, all in New York except for Temple University in Pennsylvania. I remember first hearing about Temple when I was a kid. I read a magazine interview with Bill Cosby where he spoke about attending that school. He was one of my favorite people ever, and as a kid, I loved his TV family sometimes more than my own. He was the dad I wish I had. I wanted to go to Temple when I read about his experiences, and I spent many years dreaming of the day I would leave for College. I got accepted to every school I applied to. I was totally elated when I was offered a first year scholarship to Temple. I was excited and I didn't think anything stood in my way from that point forward. My mom was in total disagreement with me going to Philadelphia for college. Mainly she said, because I was still going to be 17 during my first semester of college. I wasn't technically grown yet. I think deep down, she was worried that I did not have the street smarts to move to Philadelphia on my own. I think she (and others) saw me as weak, naive and easily manipulated. I would often hear some variation of the statement, "you are really book smart but you don't have any common sense", told to me by one of my parents. I heard them repeat these things to my aunts or close friends. Those people would in turn have the same opinion of me. Even when these things were being said, I didn't feel like it was true, but I quietly absorbed it, too timid to defend myself. Before long, I internalized it and found myself saying it about myself.

With much arguing, followed by rivers and rivers of tears, I bitterly accepted my fate, said goodbye to long time dream of attending Temple and chose a school nearby. Instead of accepting that first year scholarship, my parents paid out of pocket for me to go somewhere local. I was to take the train back and forth to school and stay living at home. This is one of the moments in life that I used to think about and wish I could do over. I wish that I could have stood firm in the potential that only I was convinced I had, and went to Temple anyway. I often wonder how things would have turned out differently. At this time, I was deeply religious and the feeling of wanting my mom to like me and be proud of me was overriding everything.

I sailed through my first year of college at Stony Brook University with fairly good grades. The year was mostly uneventful, except one major event for my family on my mother's side. One of my maternal grandmother's eight children, one that was in the middle but given a name that means "the greatest" passed away from Ovarian Cancer. She lived in Jamaica, and had started to display some horrible symptoms. In a country where you cannot get medical attention without money, this poor woman sat at home and suffered greatly. It still breaks my heart to think about it. If she were here in America, she would likely still be alive today. I think that is the most heartbreaking part of it all. By the time our family in America came to her rescue, the doctors in Jamaica could do nothing for her. They managed to secure her an emergency visa so she could get some treatment in Miami, Florida where we had some family. It all came too late, as she succumbed to her illness only a few months after coming to the U.S. She was only in her 30s and she left behind five children. The grief that came seemed epic at the time, maybe because I had not seen them so vulnerable. They were clearly mourning and uncomfortable in their vulnerability. They had no time to heal it seems. A year later, my mother and her siblings lost their mother. This time their mourning had less bewilderment about it but the sadness seemed so definite. My maternal grandmother's passing was so heavy, it seared into their collective flesh and the brand remains. It has become a part of them; a permanent tattoo that moves with them and may fade but will never leave. I was devastated. The sadness that gripped my family is hard to put into words. Probably because they didn't put it into too many words themselves. We were so heartbroken. The grief that pulsated through the whole clan was palpable. They cried tears of indescribable sorrow, especially at the funerals. Through tears and voices muted by grief at the funerals, they told happy stories. They don't forget about them. They talked about them, but they didn't talk much about their sadness. Maybe culture is to blame, for Jamaicans can be rather stoic. I believe the experience was traumatic and the hurt is too great to speak of.

Chapter Nine

Tale Of The West

Love is never any better than the lover. Wicked people
love wickedly, violent people love violently,
weak people love weakly, stupid people love stupidly,
but the love of a free man is never safe.
                                        - Toni Morrison

I started directing the choir at my church and was heavily involved with the Youth Department, as they called it. My heart and soul were all in. I hung out with people from church, and began dating someone I met many years before, on the first day I came to church. The same boy who followed me around without really knowing me, whose name means *"Meadows in the West,"* became something more to me. We were both sincere in our spirituality, and it made for a strong spiritual connection between us. It was a love story for the ages.

When all was said and done, it dawned on me how much this was like the great story of Mt. Vesuvius. I first was mesmerized by this story when it was told to me in Latin class. I had the same Latin teacher from the 6th grade up until I left High School. She added so much to my life. I always said learning Latin has done wonders for my English. A large part of the Latin class was vocabulary and learning sentence structure and conjugations. It felt like more than half the time, she regaled us with some of the best history lessons I have ever had, even to this day. The way she taught her class, her interesting way of telling stories from the ancient world just fueled my history loving fire. In the ancient Roman era, people built towns around the base of this humpbacked mountain. The mountain itself was said to have been covered with vegetation, gardens, and vineyards. People lived for hundreds of years close to and on this mountain. Until one day, in 79 AD, molten lava and ash spewed from the top. It was a volcano the whole time and no one knew. Lava ran down the mountain faster than the people could. The catastrophic event killed an estimated 16,000 people. For hundreds of years prior, this volcano was dormant. So much time had passed that people began to settle close by, thinking it was a mountain, never suspecting the fire within. When it erupted, volcanic material rained down on the towns for hours and hours, burying them in thick layers of ash. Many, many years later, the thick layers of ash were excavated and there it was found that the towns were preserved well. There was little air and moisture that could get beneath the surface ash. Because of this, there was little to no deterioration of what was underneath. There were bodies frozen in time, suffocated by ash where they stood that day. The lost cities of Pompeii and Herculaneum were discovered, with the streets and houses perfectly preserved. This site gives us a real-life glimpse into ancient life. It taught us what kind of food they ate, how they built and decorated their houses, how they lined the streets and so many more details. It gave us concrete evidence on some things that we could only speculate about before this. To this day, anyone can visit this site and see the bodies of families and their dogs, kitchen tables with food still on them, preserved for all time.

West and I knew each other for a long time. We were always friends and we built that friendship around this mountain for years and years, all the while never suspecting the fire within. Our metaphorical volcanic eruption happened one night on a trip with other people from our church. We took a Circle Line cruise around Manhattan. The skyline from that night is etched in my brain with a needle and thread. At one point, it started to rain and everyone else out on the deck ran for cover except us. We kissed under a full moon that hung almost gently, cradled in the clouds that were visible in the dark. Earlier that morning, when I woke up, we were friends. When I was to lay my head on the pillow to go to sleep later that night I was in love. Just like that. Once the eruption took place, there was no stopping the effect it had on our lives. We couldn't outrun the passion and almost frantic fervor with which we loved each other. We were so young, with little to no responsibilities and still learning about life. We had very little corrupting influences in our relationship. Our love was on fire just like particles spewing from Mount Vesuvius. It rained down for a long time, but when the fire cooled and the passion was gone, what remained was perfectly preserved for all time. There were so many grand romantic gestures over the two years we were in a relationship; never an argument or unkind word. He always came in a room and never took his eyes off of me. He made me feel like the only girl in the whole world. One day, he sat me down in front of a piano and played a song that he wrote for me. I was surprised because I never knew he could play. When I asked him about it, he said that he learned to play just so he could write this song for me. He couldn't find a medium that expressed how he felt. A poem wasn't enough. He wrote over 40 different poems and songs for me, all of which I kept neatly preserved in a binder. He had one that contained the many overtures I had written him. He taught me to say romantic phrases in Creole, a language he hadn't mastered but understood well because of his Haitian parentage. Both our parents disapproved of our relationship, and I think the intensity of it caused many of the adults we were around in church to feel uncomfortable. Often if we were at church, they would find reasons to separate us. All these adversaries fueled the passion. We both did crazy things like walking ridiculous distances to see each other for only a few minutes. In all fairness, he did a lot more of the walking but I did my share. He would come to school with me some days and sit through my lectures just so we could take the train together and be alone, all the while with my mother scolding me about the relationship.

My mom used to tell me as a little girl that when I was sixteen, I could have a boyfriend. When the time came, she reneged saying she didn't feel I was mature enough. Wait until you are eighteen she said. So now here I was eighteen and she still told me that she felt it was inappropriate to date. This time, the reason was that I shouldn't date until I was ready to get married, especially since I had pledged to not have sex until then. "So why" she said, "does it make sense for you to date him if you are not going to get married anytime soon?" That was a point of extreme frustration for me. I just wanted my mom to understand, and not make it seem like I was such a terrible person for doing what every other human being my age wanted to do. Her pressure had the opposite effect of what she probably hoped because it caused us to double down on the determination to stay together and even to contemplate eloping. It never went beyond the contemplation stage though. This relationship was important in my life for so many reasons. The biggest reason was that it had me for the first time feeling good about who I was. He told me I was awesome and I believed him. He used to look so intensely into my eyes, I would start to see myself and I didn't mind what I saw. I admired him so much and I thought of him as brave and fearless and cool. I never saw him this way with a girl in all the years I knew him. Not before me and not for a long time after. I loved him with my whole self. I also felt like if someone so cool thought I was worth all this, there had to be some good in me. He indirectly convinced me of my worth. He loved me completely and I could never forget that.

The same way the site of the volcanic eruption in Italy taught historians things they did not know before or confirmed things that were only theories before, the love between us two taught me so much about life and about myself. It illuminated for me what love was supposed to look like. He showed me for the first time what it felt like for someone to tell me they love me and not have anything negative to say about me. I, at last, felt loved beyond a shadow of a doubt. I was not a nuisance or an obligation like I felt I was to my family He chose me. I didn't have to be something else to belong to him. Finally, there was someone who did not feel ashamed, but the opposite. He didn't ask me to be anything other than who I already was. He didn't pressure me into meaningless acts of lust just for his own pleasure, like the boys I had encountered before. He respected me, and he respected the spiritual life I was trying to live because he was living the same way. After it was all said and done, I realized that what we had was real love because it still exists, just in another form. This experience taught me that true love doesn't die, but it can change.

The fire from Mt. Vesuvius' eruption destroyed the towns of Pompeii and Herculaneum as they were known before. That same fire though created the ash that served as the preserving force. Although destroyed, in a strange way, those towns still exist and will always exist, but not in the same capacity. You can't live in those places anymore. Just like the decades following the eruption of Mt. Vesuvius, where no one came around because they figured all was lost because all that was visible was destruction, it also took me some time before I sifted through the aftermath. I realized that even though for a long time I thought everything was ruined. Beneath the ashes, there lay perfectly preserved lessons that were meant to be learned. I referred back to those metaphorical ruins in my mind for many years after. It was not just a reference point for relationships, but for life. I instinctively knew I would never have that again, but in the long run, it didn't make me sad. I was actually really grateful to have experienced it. It made me curious about what was next. What other brand new experiences did life have for me? He left me with the desire to live life as freely as he did, and if nothing else, he taught me to do exactly what I wanted to do all the time.

Needless to say, our breakup was hard for me in the moment. He broke up with me on my birthday. He gave me a birthday gift and basically told me that he felt like being with me was all consuming and it left him little room to be passionate about anything else. I agreed that our relationship was all consuming, but I didn't mind that fact. I didn't have anything else to be passionate about. He was it for me. I think that our relationship opened floodgates of expression and emotion within him that lay dormant before his experience with me. I don't think either of us realized that we were capable of this level of passion. He discovered a part of himself that he was unaware existed, and true to form, he wanted to take this newfound passion as far as he possibly could. This new level of passion he had to be channeled and there was no room for me. I took up too much. He was always doing something artistic, but his first love was acting. He has and still does live and breathe art in every way.

When it ended I was sad, devastated, and emotional but never angry. Even through my tears, I understood. We both discovered ourselves through this relationship. It's like our spiritual connection gave us an understanding that surpassed everything else. He got me and I got him, always. Our season was over, but it didn't mean that our time together was not totally written in the stars. I am convinced it was. I moved on, loving West in a different way, taking from this experience so many lessons about love and about myself. After him, I spent eight months on a purposeful sabbatical from dating, and I emerged eager and open to falling in love with someone else again.

Chapter Ten

Bildungsroman

A son is a son until he takes a wife.
A daughter is a daughter all her life.

- Irish Proverb

The summer after my freshman year of college, I worked for the same union my dad belonged to. I did some apprentice work for the electricians on various construction sites around New York City. It was a physical job and I absolutely loved it. I even considered joining the union for good and becoming an electrician. I worked under several different foremen and it was interesting to see their various reactions to a young woman on the site. Some were accepting, but most were subtly annoyed and kept me busy with trivial tasks. Either way, I enjoyed every minute of it that year. The pay was awesome, and the job was interesting.

Outside of work though, I felt stifled, like I didn't have control over a lot of things in my life. I tried to exercise as much control over whatever little I could. I cut off all my hair my first year of college and I wore it short for a while, which was a point of frustration for my mom. That was always a debate my mom and I had. She never liked for me to do too much to my hair, so as insignificant as it seemed. Changing my hair in drastic ways just because I could was my own silent, lame way of declaring my autonomy. I started to wear my hair natural right before my sophomore year of college. Although a lot of black women have natural hair these days, back then, naturalistas were much fewer in number. At the very beginning, I got a lot of questions and some stares. My mother hated it so much. It was interesting over the years to watch as natural hair became accepted and even encouraged. The curious stares turned into looks of admiration at my billows of hair because I got a head start growing my afro before it was popular. The questions like "why would you ever want your hair to be nappy?" were replaced by "what products do you use?"

My sophomore year, I convinced my mom to let me stay on campus at the local university I was attending. I was excited to live away from home, although my mom still made me come home every weekend. That was something that used to make me so angry. I still had rules. I was a year out of high school, knew what it meant to work for my own money, I was directing the choir at church and still heavily involved in the Youth Ministry. Although my church commitments would have had me home very often anyway, it was the laying down of the rules that I felt stripped me of my ability to make choices for myself. I wanted more independence and I thought it would come by that time. It seemed like the more I tried to stand on my own and make my own decisions, the more my mom felt she needed to keep whatever control she could. Every time I would make a step toward independence, some small act would be performed so I would know she was in control. Rules about what time I could come home, chores doled out to me like a child, and I felt powerless. I let this powerless feeling permeate my whole life. I was so bad at speaking up for myself; I had a hard time trusting myself. Although she has always thought the opposite, I really hated the fact that she was always disappointed in me, and I wanted always to be on her good side, though my actions often had the opposite effect.

At eighteen and nineteen, my mom still questioned me about every detail of where I was going, and who I was going with, what time I went to sleep and woke up, what I was wearing to church, and it seemed like every detail of my existence. My friends would look at me with surprise when I told them at 9:30 that I had to be home because my mom would be mad, even when she knew I was with church people before I left the house, I still never escaped the complaints about my actions. The tone and the implications she made were just the same as if I had come in drunk or something. It felt like she couldn't see that I was trying so hard to be good, and it became frustrating and hurtful. She would complain when I came in after a certain hour, that was our biggest fight in those days, regardless of who I was with and what I was doing. I think it made me especially angry because I had no intentions of doing anything she was worried about.

I was sincerely living this Christian life, and so were all the people I hung out with. My friends at home that I grew up with were all Christians, and I even found me a set of Christian friends on campus and joined the Gospel Choir when I moved there. I loved hanging out with those people I was friends with in college and my church friends from home. I don't believe there was ever a point in my life where I laughed as much. I had so many great times. I didn't want to go to the club, instead, we loved to visit other churches' youth groups, go to plays and gospel concerts. I didn't want to drink or smoke, instead, we loved to find new places to go out to eat and explore the city. I had no desire to have sex because I started to see it for the sacred act it was. My friends and I would go to the North Shore, play on the beach, sit and talk for hours. These were some of the best times of my life and still to this day, the memory of these days is marred by mother's constant disapproval of my every move. It seemed that my hopes that she would finally be proud of me were not going to come to fruition.

Regardless of what kind of life they live, no one at that age wants to be micromanaged. I was young, and I had spent all my life under their thumb and unable to express myself and do what I considered simple things. It was the turning point in life that most young people have to figure out themselves and their boundaries. I felt stifled like I was not given the space I needed to become my own person. And I hadn't realized yet that freedom can't be granted from someone else, it is something you achieve for yourself. I worked and went to school, but was still mandated to clean things I didn't mess up and babysit on demand. Not too much had changed since I was a child.

I was subject to constant criticism about my clothes, my whereabouts, and my ever expanding waistline. At the time, the asthma that I had suffered from my whole life flared up pretty badly. I was on steroid medication to treat it, which was responsible for some of my weight gain. But I cannot deny that I ate out of control during that time too. I am a foodie, and I always have been. I did not heed the warnings about overeating while I was on this medication and I soon saw myself ballooning. I hated the way I looked, but at the same time, food was my vice. This dynamic created for me a cycle of misery. My parents were very critical of my weight gain and warned me that I would not be able to find a husband if I was fat. I remember hearing that a handful of times. And each time I would point out that they are not exactly skinny and they managed to marry each other they would respond that they were older and settled, I was going to be entering the world looking like this and it would lower my chances of finding a suitable mate. This was true, but hurtful nonetheless because it was not told to me in the gentlest of ways. I remember when we went to Jamaica for my aunt's funeral. On the last day there, we squeezed in a couple of hours on the beach. I paid to get on a horse that took a leisurely stroll through shallow water. It was fun, and peaceful, a good way to end a sad trip. When we got back, a few of my friends from church came to my house to pick me up for one of our outings. They came inside to say hello to my parents. They looked at pictures from the trip, and when they got to a picture of me on the horse, my dad made a joke about how fat I looked on the horse, almost like I was gonna break its back, he said through laughter. I was embarrassed and I stormed out and went to sit in my friend's car to wait for them. When they got in the car, they apologized and told me how uncomfortable it made them, especially since I was visibly upset. When I got back home, my parents told me I was being too overly sensitive and I was wrong for storming out like that. I was incredulous when they refused to see their comments as hurtful and refused to understand my reaction. This is just one example, there are countless stories of them being careless with their words, and they would remain unaffected by how it made me feel. I am glad there were other people in my life who would tell me I was a good person, that I was smart, and who had some semblance of respect for me because if it weren't for them, negative opinions of me would have been all I heard. I constantly fought with myself over who was right about me.

The summer after my second year of college was a great one. I worked with the electricians again that summer and it was even better than the first summer I did it. I enjoyed working in New York City every day and I loved the independence of it all. I started dating someone else. His name was from the Greek meaning carrier of Christ. He is still one of the nicest guys around. Just completely awesome and sweet, and the way he felt about me added a lot of joy to my life for the time we were together. He was two years younger than me which was a big deal, back then. But time would tell that even though I had apprehensions about him being younger, he was the more mature of us two.

Chapter Eleven

That Tuesday

Because things are the way they are,
things will not stay the way they are.
                                        - Bertold Brecht

E veryone who grew up in New York who was there when 9/11 occurred has a "where were you when…" story. Some of them were mundane, like "I had just arrived at school when someone told me to the news." Some were utterly miraculous, like the lady who lived in our neighborhood Sherwood Gardens, who worked in the building who was running late, and should have been exactly where one of the planes hit, but instead was impatiently waiting in the lobby for an elevator and managed to rush right back out the door when the building shook with terror. It is a time I could never forget. A wave of mass trauma hit the city. Just like when an individual experiences trauma, the event shocks you but it is the aftermath of the trauma that changes you.

I was supposed to be in class at Stony Brook, but I chose to sleep in that clear and sunny Tuesday morning. I had just started the new semester about a week before and had to stop working as an electrician's apprentice the Friday before the fateful day. The site we were working on was a few blocks from the towers. We were renovating an office space high up in one of the skyscrapers that surrounded the area. We would look out of the window and see the World Trade Center every day. When I walked out of there that Friday, some of the guys seemed a little sad to see me leave, as was I. None of us knew that four days later life would never be the same again. I often think about how close I was to being in the immediate vicinity and what my reaction would have been. I would not have been nearly as close as the lady waiting for the elevator in the lobby, but I would have been covered in debris and running for my life, and I just cannot fathom the sheer terror. The story I heard afterward was that when the first plane hit, the guys decided it was a freak accident and kept working. The second impact made them pack up and leave. Apparently, they didn't all make it out of the area before the towers fell. There were other members of the union that worked directly in the towers too, and they lost a total of 17 men in the tragedy.

Instead of being downtown with those guys and getting ready for my 9am coffee break, fate would have it that I was in my bed on Baldwin Drive, safe. My dad woke me up, calling my name from his bedroom. I walked in and was jolted to life by what I saw on the screen. He happened to be watching a newscast that caught the first impact, and about 30 seconds after I walked into the room, we witnessed the second impact live on TV. It was horrific to watch. And to this day, I limit my exposure to footage from that day because it is one of the most heart wrenching things I have ever seen. Maybe it was the personal element and the fact that everyone I knew was impacted or knew someone who was affected in some way by the terrorist attacks. As news would flood in about D.C and Pennsylvania, we were convinced that the county was under attack. Most of us had never even heard the name Osama bin Laden before that day.

In the days and months (even some years) following, it seemed the city was gripped by a collective PTSD. When an individual suffers from Post Traumatic Stress Disorder they are likely to be on edge, tense, explosive temper, even paranoid. They deal with depression and anxiety and everything they experience after the trauma is tainted by the memory of that trauma. As a city, there was mass paranoia, so that every time something went wrong, people wondered out loud if it was a terrorist attack. Even almost two years later when there was a massive blackout in the whole eastern seaboard were something like 50 million people lost power for days. New Yorkers suspected that terrorists were responsible. People with PTSD are also prone to angry outbursts when triggered by the memory of their traumatic event. A lot of people displayed a lot of ignorance toward Muslims. A few people got lost in their anger and were violent toward American Muslims and anyone who even remotely looked Muslim. The community of Sikhs who aren't even the same as Muslims (they are a religion that started in India, but the men wear turbans, which some ignorant people saw and assumed that they were the enemy) suffered at the time too. There was no excuse to justify the violence but there was no denying that the hypersensitivity was a side effect of the collective trauma. All the same, while people spewed a lot of heated rhetoric and sometimes violent action toward Muslim (or perceived Muslim) people, there were a lot of people who condemned those actions.

The city tried to pick up the pieces and move on, as any strong individual who went through trauma would do. However, just as if it were an individual survivor, the city was forever changed by that day. In some ways, the changes were for the better, and some things just nostalgia. The new New York that sprung back to life after hatred tried to crush it was alive and as vibrant as ever, but those of us who knew her before cannot deny that she is not, and has never been the same.

I have always been a sensitive person, but the fact that the events of 9/11 would have such a profound emotional effect on me was still surprising. I found myself wanting so very badly to leave New York. Just a little while after when I was still dealing with things, I read this novel called The Secret Life of Bees. In the book, there is a special character named May. She was someone with a heightened sensitivity. Her family always tried to keep things from her, because she would go reeling into a deep depression, even over things that don't normally affect people that deeply. If she heard a news story about a missing child, and she didn't even have to know that child, but she would carry any sadness she came in contact with around with her. When I read that book, I related to that character so much because I feel that is essentially what I often do. I take on other people's sadness, I cry about news stories days later and pray for people I have never met. If I pass an accident on the street, my heart leaps, tears often spring up and I will often clutch my metaphorical pearls and say a quick prayer for that person and their family. I am a sensitive soul. If someone else cries in my presence, I will cry for sure. People were strong, the city got moving again and life went on. It went on with a mist of sadness in the air. The sadness that was radiating everywhere in New York following 9/11 was strangling me. I wanted to get away from it, and to get away from my parents' watchful and critical eye, I just needed something new.

Chapter Twelve

Thou Mother Of The Free

"Here's the thing, say Shug. The thing I believe. God is inside you and inside everybody else. You come into the world with God. But only them that search for it inside find it. And sometimes it just manifests itself even if you not looking, or don't know what you looking for. Trouble do it for most folks, I think. Sorrow, lord. Feeling like shit.

It? I ask. Yeah, It. God ain't a he or a she, but a It. But what do it look like? I ask. Don't look like anything, she says. It ain't a picture show. It ain't something you can look at apart from anything else, including yourself. I believe God is everything, say Shug. Everything that is or ever was or ever will be. And when you can feel that, and be happy to feel that, you've found it."

- Alice Walker
The Color Purple

Our religious denomination that we belonged to, The Church of God was based in Anderson, Indiana. This organization has been around for over 130 years and is still thriving today. I worshipped with a majority Black congregation and it seemed like all the congregations under the Church of God umbrella that was full of brown faces like ours had their own offshoot, a sub-denomination if you will. This sub-denomination, the National Association of the Church of God, had their own central place in West Middlesex, Pennsylvania, their own officers, and even their own separate conventions. One of them was the youth convention I went to with my church every year for about seven years in a row. It was always my favorite time of year after my birthday because Convention

120

always felt like it scratched the itch I had to be free. I would be able to socialize and meet other people from across the country. A lot of the cities I have pinned on the map to indicate I visited there were because of the National Association of the Church of God's Youth Convention. I have heard it has gotten smaller over the years, but when I went, I remember most vividly being on stage, singing in the choir and looking out at the sea of chocolate faces. I did not realize at the time that our presence there, and not with our white counterparts in the Church Of God at their convention, was because of one of America's most pervasive traditions: racism.

Our "offshoot" denomination essentially seemed like the Black division of the Church of God in Anderson to me when I was younger, and it was confirmed the first time I went to the campground in West Middlesex. I heard this story from an older church member from Chicago who detailed to us how and when the land was purchased and the major events that happened over the years. She told us how the church wasn't racist at heart. The Church of God allowed Black people to worship freely during the first few years it was formed, but essentially cast out its black members as the membership grew. This was because of pressure from influential people who felt differently joining the church. After being relegated to the balcony for a while, they were eventually given the funds to go their own way and get their own building. She explained that we still refer to the headquarters in Anderson, and we are still a part of them. What started as a banishment of sorts evolved into a tradition? For close to 100 years, black members of the Church of God had been coming to this campground. So many people who still participated had parents and grandparents who helped build the structures and pave the roads of this campground. They were proud and they held tightly to their traditions. It surprised me even then that this history was kind of hush-hush and that there was always respect for the headquarters in Anderson despite the facts.

I learned during my study of History, that after the Civil War, which freed the slaves, there was a huge spiritual movement in America. The United States was devastated in the aftermath of the war. Two percent of the entire population (almost a quarter of a million people) died during the fight the South waged to keep their slaves. Imagine how devastated we would be if one major event caused the death of two percent of the modern American population. That would mean the death of about 6 million people today. There was death everywhere in the 1860s, and there were not many people who escaped being affected in some way by the war. The American people became more spiritual after the catastrophe. Many of the newer American Christian denominations were formed during this time, including the Church of God. After the Civil War, the former slaves were free on paper, but as we know, discrimination and terrorism against them still continued. The Church was not an exception. Discrimination and intolerance followed Black people even there. Some churches, like ours, started out with the noble intent to have Black people worship alongside them, but gave in to the growing white membership who did not want to sit next to a Black person, even in the Lord's house. Most African Americans at the time left the church altogether and formed their own offshoot church under the same denomination (like the one I belonged to), or they started their own denomination altogether, like the African Methodist Episcopal church.

The Church of God always kept close ties and was considered our headquarters. They expanded to countries in Africa and the

Caribbean over the years. In 1917, they founded a University in the Indiana town where they were based; all the while we belonged to the denomination, I always heard the name of the town Anderson being tossed around, but I was always very disconnected from it. I would never have imagined all that would take place for me with respect to that place. Anderson University is a small Christian college in Indiana about an hour or so north of Indianapolis, It would play the most unexpected major role in my life.

My times at the campground in West Middlesex, Pennsylvania were always fun, and I met a lot of good people there. It was there at the campground I met one particular charming young man from Chicago who I was enamored with. He told me about another two week program in the summer that took place in Anderson where you do classes and workshops on leadership and the Bible. It was mainly for people looking into ministry. At the time, it was almost a given to me that I would be heavily involved in some aspect of ministry. I feel like it was one of the key teachings of my church and also the example I had growing up from my parents. You don't just sit on your faith and all that God has blessed you with. You should always give back, and no contribution was too small. From the person who cleaned the church right on up to the Pastor. I was taught through words and example, God honored everyone who served him sincerely and so should we.

I took two weeks off my construction job that first summer I graduated, and went on a plane by myself for the first time to Anderson Indiana to take part in this program. I loved it so much and I met so many great people, that the next summer, I did it again each time, heavily admiring the Chicago guy, sometimes from afar, sometimes not so far. We kept a connection for a long time and he told me he was attending the University come this fall. I loved the abundance of awesome people I met from different places in the country, the great time that I had, and the knowledge I gained. Though it might seem strange, I was most in love with the beautiful campus I stayed on for the two weeks. The campus of Anderson University is still one of the most beautiful landscapes I have ever laid eyes on. There is something about the sunset in Indiana that was always so moving to me. Never as moving as the first time I saw it. I was fascinated by Indiana. I had never been on that sort of terrain; flat roads where you can see so far ahead without a twist or a turn. The flat ground on either side of you just seems like the earth and the sky met without interruption. The landscaping and architecture on the grounds of the school were always so gorgeous to me. At that time I felt it was just what I needed.

Chapter Thirteen

Mid-West With The Night

"I have learned that if you must leave a place that you have lived in and loved and where all your yesteryears are buried deep, leave it any way except a slow way, leave it the fastest way you can. Never turn back and never believe that an hour you remember is a better hour because it is dead. Passed years seem safe ones, vanquished ones, while the future lives in a cloud, formidable from a distance."

- Beryl Markham

There I was, ready to leave New York. Ready, really for anything to drastically change for me. Though the term Anderson was tossed around as casually as it always was, this time, a light bulb went off. I should go to Anderson University. It was perfect. My mom was always apprehensive about me straying too far from under her thumb, but she was comforted some by the fact that it was a Christian school and that I had been there and known people. I was just ready to get away. I was sad to leave my new baby sister who was a toddler at the time and also the boyfriend that I had at the time, but everything else in me was dying to go. He was also leaving to attend college in Statesboro, Georgia. I would be missing him whether or not I went to Indiana. I transferred from Stony Brook and hurriedly took care of all the loose ends so that I could go out of state. It was a last minute decision and it became a very crucial turning point.

I announced my departure and waited anxiously for the month or so to pass until the date I was to leave. I had my plane ticket and everything booked from an early date. I went around spending time with my friends and my boyfriend, tinged with a slight sadness, but so ready for the world. My mom insisted that before I left for Indiana, I should take care of my glasses prescription, go to the dentist, go get my check up and all that just in case, being that I would not be back home for a few months. Before this time, I had been to the gynecologist just twice in my life, and it still filled me with enormous dread to think about it. I was a girl with an irregular cycle but the doctors always assured us that I was still young, and sometimes it took a few years for people to get regular. It wasn't something that I paid a lot of attention to, but that year, I was nineteen years old and went without a cycle for about eight months. I am sure that was also part of what prompted my mother to insist on a checkup before I left.

Ever the procrastinator, I made the appointment with the doctor (who had just delivered my baby sister a few years before) for about a week before I had to leave for Indiana. I don't remember too much about the exam that day, all I remember is that after it was all said and done, the doctor sat in the office and told my mom and I that I had Endometriosis. This is a reproductive condition that sometimes prevents ovulation (hence the missed periods) and causes infertility. He also said that because I hadn't had a period in so many months, the lining of my uterus was so thick that they would need to go in and surgically remove the thick membrane that was supposed to be shedding every month but wasn't. He said that while we are there, he would need to do a biopsy on my uterus to see if there are any cancerous cells. I would need to be admitted to the hospital for the relatively minor surgery. I was to be kept overnight for observation because of the anesthesia they would have had to administer. I informed the doctor that I was supposed to fly to Indiana in about a week. He repeated himself and stressed the importance of taking care of the situation right away. If we went by his schedule, I would most likely have to postpone my departure. He gave me another option. I could do the procedure in the office sooner, but he would not be able to give me anesthesia in the office because of regulations that said only an anesthesiologist can administer it in the hospital so they can observe your vitals the whole time. Since I couldn't get any anesthesia if he did it in the office, I could go home the same day. I jumped at the second option, thinking to myself, how bad can it really be? I walked out of there a little bit dazed. I remember being stunned and a little numb. There were no abundance of feelings, just mainly uncertainty. I had thought about having children in a very detached way before that day, but I was forced to accept that I had a condition that may make having children difficult.

The day of my procedure, I was a bundle of nerves. The first part of it is called a D and C. It is actually the same exact procedure used to terminate a pregnancy, only mine was to get rid of excess tissue. The machine was loud and I gripped the nurse's hand trying to soothe the moderate pain and extreme pressure I felt. When it was over, it was time for the biopsy. An approximately one inch piece of my uterus was cut off with surgical scissors with no anesthesia. I cannot begin to describe the pain which I was totally unprepared for, but it was all over after about 20 minutes in the chair. I hobbled my way onto my feet with the nurses telling me how brave I was. Even on the ride home, my mom told me that she probably would not have chosen that route. I was just glad that I could still leave when I planned on leaving.

I went home and painfully continued my packing. I was uncomfortable and in pain still when I dragged those heavy bags to the counter and boarded a plane for Indianapolis. I was met at the airport by one of the recruiters who drove me an hour away to the campus. She walked me through everything, and before long I was settled in my room. I lived in the only co-ed dormitory on campus. Every other building only housed one gender. One side of my building housed females and we were separated by a lobby. On the other side lived the males. We wouldn't even have to pass each other going up and down the stairs. I also lived in the only dorm that had suites. We didn't have to share bathrooms with a whole floor. There was a bathroom built in between each room and the neighboring room, so only those four people shared the quarters. I was on campus approximately one week before classes were to begin, with all kinds of orientation events, being a new student, I was required to attend. I walked around the beautiful campus that first day and I went to an orientation event later in the afternoon. I was a little taken aback by the sea of white faces. While I knew that I was both going to a white town and that the majority of the school would be white, I wasn't quite expecting to see so very few black people. When I visited for the two summers before that, there were a lot more brown faces on that campus, and I remember thinking to myself at orientation, "I guess this is the real student population." I felt a little silly for expecting more diversity. It took a little reflection to realize that I had never been in this type of situation before, with such little diversity. Even when I went camping as a kid, I may have been one of the few black people but there wasn't just one type of person. There were Hispanics and Asians, and almost half the staff was made up of foreigners; Irish, Australian, and British people who also came in different colors and from different walks of life, with different perspectives. Even within the white community I came in contact with at camp (and this rule might be able to be applied in general to people I came in contact with from New York), there was a level of diversity. The union members all sent their kids to camp, so there would be one girl who was a wealthy contractor's or a board member's child who had every luxury in life. Most often their other parent was also in a high earning profession, and they lived in places like Park Slopes, Brooklyn. That well off girl would share a tent with another girl who was also white, but whose dad was an electrician and their mom is a teacher and they lived in places like Coney Island, Brooklyn. Park Slope and Coney Island are only about 20 minutes away from each other. Despite their proximity, these two places were two very different worlds then. These two girls would have been raised so differently, with different influences, different styles, and a different way of speaking even. People had immigrant parents or practiced other religions. They had different experiences to share with one another, different outlooks on life. Camp was still diverse even though African Americans, in particular, were scarce. The majority may have been white but there were so many different types of people. There wasn't the homogenous carbon copy element that there was in Anderson. It wasn't so much about them being white that had me in culture shock, it was that they were white and all the same.

I remember a time a few months after I arrived in Anderson. Some of us sat around and counted the black students. I don't remember the specific number but I know it was in the 70s. Of the over 2,000 students, only seventy odd of them were black. I remember we took it further and did a count of what we considered at the time the "real" black people. There were a large number of that 70 something who clearly grew up around white people and saw us (and the world) the same way they did, which was not always in a positive way. These people were more comfortable around white people, and their behavior ranged from shunning other black people completely, to associating with other black people only casually. Then there were those who grew up in a different world, who were not so used to being the only black person. Those who came here from places like DC, New York, Chicago, and the nearby city of Indianapolis, who knew the subtle realities of black life in America, not the isolated small town bubble that some of the African Americans who went to Anderson had lived. Whether we were politically correct, or even generally correct for separating ourselves from them, I still can't say. We counted 32 "real" black people. We realized that we all associated with each other. We all knew each other and socialized, even though we could point to a few people who didn't like each other, the "real" black people were almost always getting along and doing things together, sometimes in smaller sub-groups, but always together. We all could not escape having white friends and roommates, but it was almost as if we clung to each other out of familiarity sometimes. This and other complexities of life on the campus at Anderson would teach me so much over the next year.

I went back to my room that first night after orientation and looked around at the blue-gray walls and the empty bed across from me and I started to cry. I was thinking to myself, wow, I probably won't be a mom. Throughout all that happened to me the past week, the procedure, and all the chaos of moving, it was ringing in my head over and over. Even though I was doing a lot, I couldn't concentrate on anything else. I thought about it constantly.

This was the first moment that I let myself cry about it, and cry I did. For a week, I didn't go to any more orientation events and I stayed locked in my room, reading, writing, crying, sleeping, in any order that felt right. The only person I spoke to was my boyfriend, whose name means *Christ Bearer*, who was 700 miles away at a college in Georgia. It almost felt like I was mourning. In the end, I gave myself a pep talk and told myself I was done being sad about this. After all (I heard myself lie), you never wanted kids anyway, so this doesn't matter. Repeating this phrase to myself became the band-aid I would put over the wound every time it would be opened up by a friend having a baby, a TV commercial or simply someone commenting on my future children without knowing my secret. I would shake it off and remind myself that I never thought that deeply about having children before so it didn't matter. Every time the thought snuck up on me, I would repeat my I-don't-care mantra. Thinking these new thoughts caused me to emerge from my den of misery the evening before classes began.

Chapter Fourteen

Anderson

Words are flowing out like
Endless rain into a paper cup
They slither wildly as they slip away
Across the universe.
Pools of sorrow waves of joy
Are drifting through my opened mind
Possessing and caressing me.
Images of broken light, which
Dance before me like a million eyes,
They call me on and on
Across the universe.
Thoughts meander like a
Restless wind inside a letterbox
They tumble blindly as they make their way
Across the universe.

- The Beatles

I was really hungry and hadn't eaten all day. I got myself a gyro and stood awkwardly with my tray, looking for a place to sit. Long, lean brown arms waved in the corner of my eye, and when I looked, I saw a table full of (mostly black) girls, with the one guy sitting with them waving at me to come sit with them. I sat and he introduced himself immediately. His name is very pious; it means "God has Shown Favor." When I looked into those eyes, I was immediately hooked for life. I remember sitting there while he dominated the conversation thinking that this might possibly be the most beautiful member of the male species that I have ever laid eyes on. He was tall and lean and had smooth chocolate skin. He had the entire table of women captivated as he spoke with flair and flamboyance. I don't know if it was my upbringing in New York, but his sexuality was clear to me from that first conversation. But my upbringing also had me wise enough not to assume out loud. This beautiful, well groomed young man told us how he was from Evansville, Indiana, a few hours south of where we were. He told us he modeled, and even pulled out his headshots. He wore tight jeans when baggy jeans were still the normal style for men. He lit up with delight when I told him I was from New York and he declared that he would go there one day that he planned on being famous. When he got up to go to the bathroom, I couldn't help but laugh inside when some of the girls talked about how cute he was and wondered out loud if he had a girlfriend. I thought, wow, they are really naive. He came back to the table and we talked and talked for hours after the food was eaten. There was another girl who I had a connection with at the table and her name meant Sparkling. She was jovial and very smart and outgoing. She was from the Washington D.C area, and like us, not your typical Anderson University student. The three of us laughed so much, and that night became the beginning a short lived trio. Sparkle and I fell out of touch before I even left the school, but Favor came to play such a huge role in my future, especially in the immediate years following. I met someone else that same night while the three of us new friends continued getting to know each other as we wandered around campus. This guy was sitting on a couch in the lobby of a dorm building none of us lived in. He won me over almost instantly with his wit and humor. He had a special way of making fun of you while still remaining likable. I was intrigued by his unique sense of humor. I have always been a sucker for a person who can make me laugh.

His name means *Wise Protector,* and he was probably the reason destiny brought me to Indiana. Knowing him changed everything.

He walked and talked with me that first night, and as I usually find with people I meet that end up important in my life, there was a spark from minute one. We had similar taste in music and we both loved to laugh. He was outgoing and sociable and I got the vibe that he was intrigued with me that first night because I was unlike anyone he had ever met. I didn't fit into any mold. I got that a lot when I first moved to Indiana. People weren't quite sure what to make of me. I was a Jamaican girl who didn't have an accent. I was from New York, but not rude or loud or any of the other stereotypes of New Yorkers. I had an Afro way before it was cool to have natural hair. Very often, people would take just one look at me and declare that I must not be from around here.

For the first time in my life, I was around people who would boldly make some unabashedly ignorant comments. It was a serious shock to me. Black people and white people had their own brands of ignorance, but it was all ignorance just the same. I would get really frustrated by white people who would treat me like a museum exhibit, asking if they could touch my hair or making unintentionally racist comments. I gave the majority of the people who made these comments to me the benefit of the doubt that they were not being intentional with their prejudice; sometimes, even when other black people would get upset at a comment here and there, I would encourage them to take it in stride. It was clear that a lot of these people really honestly did not know better. It wasn't right, and it wasn't always an easy thing to deal with, but I realized early on how lashing out about it was futile.

Of all the major racially tinged incidents I experienced,

the first one wasn't the worst but it jolted me the most. It was a simple thing, but it was very hurtful and eye-opening, although not the most egregious incident by far. It happened one evening when we (the black people) decided to have a water fight outside. It was an unseasonably warm fall night and we gathered all the water balloons and water guns we could find and we were having an all out battle of the sexes. It was the boys versus the girls. We were pelting each other with water balloons, ambushing and soaking each other with water guns ranging from super soakers to dollar store water guns we bought that day, all with the obligatory loud talking, laughing and shrieking that comes along with a water fight. I did see several people come outside and look out their windows, but we carried on. A group of girls and I ran inside one of the nearby female dorms to fill our water guns. We were dripping wet, running through the halls, racing to the bathroom so the guys wouldn't get the best of the few girls we had left outside holding down the fort. It was all innocent enough or so we thought. While we were leaving the bathroom, a girl stuck her head out of her door and told us we were being rude and loud and that we had better clean up the mess we were making with the water in the hall. She was clearly angry, but we ignored her. Someone mumbled a joke and the whole crowd laughed. As a testament to how low it was mumbled, I didn't even hear the joke. The girl yelled at us as we rushed out of the double doors that we "don't even live in this building."

A few minutes after we went outside, we were approached by a staff member who asked us girls to step inside the lobby. She informed us that one of the females who lived inside the dorm was in tears saying we were being wild and crazy and we purposely splashed water all over the pictures she had on her door. She told the resident director that she politely asked us to clean up the water and we cursed at her and splashed her pictures. She said we were intimidating to her and she felt scared that one or all of us would attack her so she went to get help. We explained our side of the story and the staff member seemed to listen intently. The girl came to the lobby. The same person who was angrily making demands, and arrogantly yelling when we were there before, was now talking in a soft whisper about how she thought we looked angry and she got scared. After we spoke, the RD made it clear that the dorm resident felt threatened and since we don't live in the building we were now banned from ever entering that building again. Just like that. With no third party witnesses and no proof, she took the other girl's story as fact and banned us. She warned us that we were lucky she didn't fine us for the use of foul language, which none of us did. This was the first of three incidents that happened in my first semester that opened my eyes to the way we were seen on campus. The way the white students saw us, even the friendly ones, was often as threatening. When we would just be sitting in a lobby together watching TV, people on campus were always obviously intimidated when there was a larger group of us, and often reacted extremely to minor actions.

I didn't have a roommate when I first came; they assigned me one about two weeks into the semester. I met her mother before I met her. A short heavy set middle aged brunette woman knocked on my door one Saturday morning and introduced herself with a huge smile. She told me how her daughter had some medical issues. She had to take care of before she came to school. She asked me a lot of questions about myself and she seemed to be assessing the room while I spoke nervously to this stranger. Her father walked in a few minutes later with a suitcase and she trailed behind him, a fragile looking girl with very pale skin and short curly strawberry blonde hair. Her eyes were a honey brown color and they were striking. Her small lips were almost always expanded into a smile. She graduated early from school, she told me, so she was only seventeen. We got along really well at first, I thought. We were not best friends but we ate together on occasion, and talked often and were respectful of each other. We got close enough for her to tell me that if I couldn't make it home to New York for Thanksgiving, I could come to her family farm in Ohio. She was from a small town in the Buckeye State, where she was homeschooled and rarely left her rural surroundings.

She lived an extremely sheltered life. Her grandmother, she said, spoke badly about Black people but her parents always taught her different. That was evident in the fact that they did not treat me negatively at all whenever they came (which was about every other weekend). Her town was so small she said, that it only consisted of a handful of large farms, and they have to go to the next town to go to any stores or things like that. That next largest town was still small. It was so small that she had never actually seen a black person there in real life. I was so shocked that we were at the beginning of the 21st century and there were still people like that. She said that she was glad she had a black roommate so she could experience what different people were like. I told her about some of my experiences in life too and I was glad we got along well enough to have these types of conversations. We shared things and looked out for each other. After about a month of living together, I was sitting in the Campus Security office being indirectly accused of stealing her money, I was floored.

On her birthday weekend, which was just a few weeks before mine, she went home to Ohio. She came back excitedly telling me that she had gotten a total of $600 for her birthday from various family members. The next day, I came back from class to find her tearing the room apart with tears in her eyes saying she lost her money. I helped her retrace her steps on campus, helped her search both my side and her side for the money with no luck. I felt really bad for her. The next night she went to spend the night in a friend's room and I didn't see her all of the next day, but I thought nothing of it. Campus Security called my room and asked me to come down to the office to talk. I wasn't sure what it was about and as I opened my door to leave, I ran into my RA who was just getting ready to knock on my door. She was there to retrieve some of my roommate's belongings because she had been granted her request to move to a single room. I wasn't aware of the request and it caught me off guard but I went on about my way, confused but it's still not connecting that any of this had anything to do with me. Not even thinking at that point how strange it was for the RA to come move her stuff and not her. I sat down in front of the Security Officers and they wasted no time getting to the point. One man asked me if I knew about my roommate's money being missing. He said that she filed a complaint with them about the money and mentioned me because she said I was the only one who actually knew how much money she had. They told me that if I had anything to say, I should say it now because getting caught always has worse consequences than confessing. I felt my ears getting hot and my stomach churning, angry, but feeling like I couldn't freely express it at the moment. I calmly told them that I didn't steal her money. They quickly told me that they were not accusing me, just asking questions, but it felt like they were. They told me that they would be conducting an investigation and that I could leave.

I walked out of the office fuming. I was so furious that she couldn't just come talk to me, I thought we were friends. I was angry about the accusation, and I thought she knew me better than that. I thought things that I would never say out loud, like, I really don't need her $600, that's not even an amount worth stealing. I didn't consider myself or my parents rich by any stretch of the imagination but i didn't feel like I would need to resort to stealing. If I needed that much money I had several means that were legal and ethical that I would have chosen to get that money before I would *steal.* I was just walking and letting these thoughts take over, and by the time I walked into the lobby of my dorm and saw her sitting there, I just unloaded on her. I never got close or was physically threatening, but I did have some choice words for her. I stormed off and slammed my room door. I was so angry; I was ignoring the knocks on the door from the RA who was insisting I come out and talk to her. I sat there quietly looking down at my hands crying until she gave up and left. I was sitting there for a while before looking up and realizing that my roommate's side was empty. She had moved completely out while I was at the Security Office.

Chapter Fifteen

School Spirit

The hardest thing on earth is choosing what matters.
- Sue Monk Kidd
The Secret Life of Bees

Despite all that, the first semester, my grades were pretty good. I skipped class a lot, but I did that when I was at Stony Brook too. I got drunk with the power to do what I wanted. I literally did everything that was possible that I felt like doing. I blew off class for simple things like an interesting conversation. I was smart enough to average about a B, only being in class about half the time I was supposed to be. I spent a lot of time with the Wise Protector I met that first night and with my two close friends. I saw the guy I met from Chicago, although my crush on him had fizzled. We became good friends and I spent a lot of time at his apartment also with his friends. It was nice to be somewhere new, nice to meet people who were actually interested in getting to know me. I felt more confident at that point than I ever had. I still had some issues with depression. I was still figuring out who I was, and every time I would try, I would hate what I saw. All I saw was my past, full of shame, and I let it swallow me whole some days.

I struggled with my weight, I was the heaviest I had ever been before (and since then) and it did a little number on my self esteem. My weight started to increase right before I moved there. I had a bout with asthma that had me on steroids for a short time. Weight gain is a common side effect of the drugs I was on and I did nothing to curb my eating habits or get extra exercise. So by the time I was well enough to not take them anymore, after about six months on steroids, I saw a more expanded version of myself in the mirror. It helped that moving to Indiana, no one knew the slimmer version of me, so they had no visual of a slimmer me with which to compare. I took that as a new beginning and tried to be more confident in my new body.

We saw each other at least once a day, Wise and I. The spark that lit up the first night we met turned into a prolonged flirtation. I started to hang out regularly (with groups of people) at his apartment; all the while in denial about my growing feelings. We generally hung out at the apartments of people who lived off campus because there were so many rules in the dorms. This was a Christian school after all so they tried to maintain order as much as they could. We were not allowed to have people of the opposite sex inside our rooms except during certain designated hours, which were only a few hours on the weekend. During that time, we had to have to door wide open. We were barred from public displays of affection and even foul language; with the threat of a $50 fine if you were caught violating their puritan rules. We were mandated to be present at a church service on Tuesdays and Thursdays, only being allowed to miss a handful of services (we had to sign in on time and stay the whole time to get credit for being there. If you came late or left early, it was the same as you not showing up), or face a fine at the end of the semester. There were dress codes and inquiries into your personal life by the staff. It all became very overwhelming for me very quickly.

Although we exchanged flirtations, I would chastise myself every time I thought about Wise in that way in the beginning because I was committed to my boyfriend. I logged many hours on the phone maintaining my long distance relationship with a guy who was once a dear childhood friend. I had a love for him that ran really deeply. The fact that we grew up together held a lot of weight for me. As I mentioned before, he was about two years younger than I was, so this was his first year in college, and I believe his first real relationship. It was my first serious relationship after breaking up with West and it was going well. I know he loved me with all his heart. This teddy bear of a guy was just the sweetest person, and that's what made betraying his trust one of the most horrible things I have ever done. Just to solidify how horrible my actions were, Karma paid me back and then some.

Chapter Sixteen

Birthday Blues

It's my birthday
No one here day
Very strange day
I think of you day
Go outside day
Sit in the park day
Watch the sky day
What a pathetic day
I don't like this day
it makes me feel too small…

- Blur
Birthday

My birthday came around. I was anxious about what kind of day I would have on my first birthday away from home. I have always had this thing about my birthdays. I don't know what it is, but I always end up upset or crying or something. As an adult, I always try to ensure that I have a good birthday because of how things always went when I was young. I don't remember ever celebrating a birthday when I lived in Jamaica. My first "birthday party", was when I was turning 9 and I lived in the Bronx. The reason the term birthday party has quotes around it is because I didn't really feel like it was meant for me. They tried to get me excited about it but even as a kid, I was smart enough to know the reality of the situation.

My father has a niece who has the same birthday as I do; she is just a year older than I am. When we were young, people on that side of the family often lumped us together on our birthday, and that was the first time I had experienced it. She had her party already planned and the location of the party was set to be in the basement of the apartment building my dad owns. Her parents found out we had the same birthday and very graciously invited me to share the birthday party. It was a gesture meant to be welcoming and I do believe the intentions were good.

The party was full of her friends, who I barely knew, her family from her mom's side who I barely knew, and some people from her dad's side (which is how we were connected). I had ONE friend come to the party. She spent most of the night in a chair in the corner crying because a song played that reminded her of her grandmother who recently passed away. The people were crowded into the small basement space and it was starting to feel extremely hot and overwhelming. I was feeling a little dizzy so I opened a side door and stepped outside for a second. I remember looking up at the moon; taking a deep breath and watching the smoke from my mouth disappear into the crisp autumn sky. It was a very cold night, as a matter of fact; there was still snow on the ground from an earlier snowfall, so the chill sent me back into the noisy hot space after less than a minute. When I stepped back inside, my dad was standing there looking frustrated. He yelled at me about being outside without a coat, asking condescending rhetorical questions about why I didn't know better and yelling about how I was going to get sick. People who were sitting nearby stopped talking and were staring at our little exchange, which embarrassed me to no end.

I look back now at how silly that was, getting upset over

that, but it ruined my night. It felt like I couldn't escape harsh criticism for my every move, even on my birthday. I cried a little bit because of the embarrassment and the frustration that came when he wouldn't let me explain that I was feeling a little dizzy. There was nothing I could do but helplessly accept what I felt was harsh words, without any recourse. To make matters worse, my friend left before it was time to cut the cake. That may have been a good thing, because when they opened the cake box, I saw that my name was literally added onto the cake at a different time, in a different frosting color and everything. If I had any doubts whether or not I was an afterthought, they were gone. Most birthdays thereafter were terrible. My subsequent birthday emotions all ranged from being depressed, because I barely got any recognition, to outright frustration and anger because my plans were disastrous.

I had a couple of years in there where things were ok, like when I turned 15 and my mom let me have friends over and we went to the movies. That might seem like a normal Saturday to most teens, but for me, it only happened that one time. I wanted a sweet sixteen but it wasn't surprising that my parents didn't approve. I got a book, a new coat, and had a happy birthday that year. West broke up with me on my birthday too, which was just completely devastating when it happened. That first birthday I spent in Indiana was probably the most disastrous of all. I think all the time about the fact that my actions that day set in motion a new set of events for me. I have reason to believe my entire life would be totally different had my actions that day been different.

Chapter Seventeen

Twenty

It is in your moments of decision that your

destiny is shaped...

-Tony Robbins

I woke up in my small bed inside my dorm room the morning of my birthday, feeling optimistic. I did not see this day coming. There was a football game that day, so as I was getting out of bed, I heard the cheering in the distance, and the muffled voice of the announcer and I immediately decided I would go. That's where everyone was going to be anyway. On my way to the game, I checked my mailbox and it was empty. I felt a slight tinge of disappointment because I was sure there would be something in there from my boyfriend. I knew that he was a broke college student, so I wasn't really expecting a whole lot. I also knew that he was a poet, and a romantic, so while I didn't expect anything expensive, I was expecting something sweet.

I went on to the game only slightly less happy than I was but still all smiles. I sat with Wise Protector and some of his friends. I had a good time in the stands with them, but it was very cold. He had a blanket and he shared with me. After the game, we went to hang out inside one of the dorms close by. We sat on a couch and talked. I expressed my disappointment in the fact that I didn't get a phone call or anything in the mail from my boyfriend. We talked about everything under the sun, it seemed, until the actual sun went down. I went to the Olive Garden with a bunch of people from campus and had a good time.

I went back to a friend's apartment and called my boyfriend in Georgia. I was so upset with him, but that's all I remember. I can't remember his explanation, probably because I was irrationally angry. There was no reasoning with me. I left there and went to Wise's apartment where we watched movies until really late. When everything was over, and everyone had left, I stayed there with my head in his lap, facing the TV. As we spoke, I turned on my back and he leaned down and kissed me for the first time. I was surprised by how much I liked it, and how little guilt I felt. The events of the day definitely contributed to my lack of guilt. We took things back to his bedroom that night, where I broke nearly four years of celibacy. I hadn't even had sex with my then boyfriend or the one before him. Although thoughts of guilt tried their hardest, it just couldn't permeate the sheer electricity I felt being with Wise. I stayed the night that night.

In the morning I took the coldest longest walk back to my dorm and called my boyfriend almost immediately and broke up with him. I didn't give him too much explanation, I just declared it was over and hung up. I didn't break up with him because I thought me and Wise were headed for a relationship, it was more about trying to assuage the hint of guilt that wouldn't go away without facing what I had really done. It didn't work. I broke up with him hastily because, in my mind, it was righting the wrong. I still had feelings for him and he was such a good guy who was obviously headed for a successful life, and I felt like I didn't deserve him. I truly felt like he deserved better than what I did to him. So after I hung up the phone that day, I avoided all his phone calls because I was ashamed of myself. I am sure it didn't come off that way to him, but that's what was in my heart.

I was conflicted because it felt right when I was with the Wise Protector. I should have felt guiltier about breaking my vow of celibacy but I didn't. Mostly because being together didn't feel wrong, it felt like the natural manifestation of several months of heavily flirting and a strong connection. It didn't feel wrong but thoughts of my boyfriend sauntered around the back of my mind. All the while, I knew what I was *supposed* to be feeling. I was supposed to be racked with guilt not just for breaking my vow but also for breaking someone's heart. Even when these thoughts slithered in to disturb the cloud I was walking on, I went through this mental gymnastics routine to absolve myself. I kept thinking to myself, is it possible for something to be wrong and right at the same time? It felt right to be with Wise, but it sure did feel super wrong to break the Christ Bearer's heart. I agonized over whether I was wrong or not very often. And like I said before, it often didn't take me that long to justify my actions with "you were just following your heart."

We spent time together in the next couple of weeks, Wise and I. I enjoyed it immensely, and I had come to a conclusion within myself that made me feel ok with what happened although I shouldn't have been ok with myself at that point. I spent the first part of the semester so immersed in depression and now, being around Wise made me feel like that gasp of air you get when you finally come up from under the water just when the air in your lungs was running out. I wanted to breathe; I was tired of treading water, almost drowning every day. I admitted to myself that I was wrong, but I never talked to Christ Bearer on the phone about the situation. I reasoned with myself that ignoring him was about this or that, but deep down, I knew it was just me being afraid to face the music. He even got in his car and drove all the way to Indiana from Georgia out of frustration with the way I ended things. Being the nice guy he is, he didn't speak harshly to me, he spoke from a place of hurt. I felt terrible but I knew what I wanted to do deep down. I was enjoying the moment with Wise and trying not to think about anything negative. However no amount of denial, self-inflicted punishment or self evaluation could let me escape karma. Wrong is wrong, and there is always a price to pay.

Wise and I spent so much time together at first. I spent almost every night at his apartment; night and day, actually. It was a snowy month. Snow was perpetually on the ground and it probably snowed once a week. It was perfect weather for cuddling. For a month we barely spent time with anyone else, and if we did, it was always together. We would leave for food and other necessary things but we both barely went to class or even left the apartment for that matter. We watched a lot of movies, listened to a lot of music which was a shared passion for us, and were just so absorbed with getting to know each other. He was going through a rough time when we first met also. His nephew, the first child of his older brother, the first grandchild for his parents, passed away at the age of 3, and it happened months before we met. His parents, who had been together for all of his life, were splitting up and his father fell gravely ill a short time later. He was in the hospital for a while, fighting for his life, and after making a recovery that was against the odds, had his leg amputated and was recovering and trying to make a new life for himself. His mom was also embarking on new territory; she had just purchased a home on the west side of Indianapolis. When I met her for the first time, she wasn't even fully unpacked yet.

Chapter Eighteen

Push And Pull Factors

If you build the guts to do something, anything,
then you better save enough to face the consequences.
- Criss Jami

W e shared a depth of intimacy on so many levels that I had never experienced before. The connection between us was just so different than the one I had with anyone else and I jumped in with both feet. It was exciting I am the type to always welcome a new adventure. I was in love. After spending some months in the clouds, Academic Probation brought me back down to earth with a thud. We both landed ourselves on Academic Probation and he chose to move back home to Indianapolis. I petitioned the school about their decision and won my appeal. I spent one lonely horrible semester at Anderson after he was gone. Without the shield of my relationship, I re-entered social life on campus very half heartedly. I was only halfway present. I missed Wise and I spent all of my weekdays working on finding a ride to Indianapolis to spend the weekend with him at his mother's house.

Campus life started to feel like high school all over again, with petty dramas and rumors. Some of my old friendships didn't survive the time I was holed up at Wise's apartment. My trio fell apart. My friend Sparkle and I grew apart, for reasons that still aren't really clear to me, but I took it in stride. Even my enigmatic friend who I met at the lunch table, Favor, had also left after one semester. He came out to me a few weeks after the day we met but he didn't need to. When he told me his story, it made me want to hug him close to my bosom and never let him go. We shared common experiences, like being molested at a young age, complicated relationships with our mothers who we loved beyond understanding. I felt such a deep protective and nurturing feeling toward him early on. I have always felt that it was meant to be for us to meet in Anderson when we did. Our presence in each other's lives had a tremendous effect on us both.

After one half-assed semester holding on to something I didn't really want, I didn't raise my GPA enough to stay in school. I have to admit that I didn't really try. My mind and heart were in Indianapolis. At this point, it wasn't just Wise; I had fallen in love with his whole family. They were everything my family wasn't. They loved being together, loved to joke around with each other and never really had anything seriously bad to say to or about one another. They did things like sit around the table together to play monopoly on a regular basis. They were so warm and welcoming. They shared what they had with me and treated me like I was family since the first instant we entered each other's lives. I lived for the weekends I spent in Indianapolis.

A part of me felt bad that things ended that way at Anderson University, but that only came from knowing that I disappointed my mother once again. Disappointing my mom clouded the happiness I felt leaving that place behind. I hated that she was mad, but I could not deny what I wanted for my own life. If only I knew then that it would be a dilemma I would face a few more times in the future. I know she probably would have a different opinion, but it killed me every time I disappointed her. I really hated that part of it. It was just really unfortunate that the more I grew up and developed my preferences and personality; it was often different from my mother's views. It was always hard for me, but I more often than not, I chose to be true to what I wanted. I don't know who it frustrated more that I had a different way of being than her.

My mother has always been extremely frustrated by this and often says in an exasperated tone that I never listen to her. I remember often thinking to myself, she got to live her life the way she wanted. She made decisions that were not always met with approval by her mother or the people around her, but she always did what she wanted. Her example of being so self-assured and independent, always going her own way with her head held high regardless of what anyone said, had more of an influence on me than her attempts to lay down rules and control my life's course. Her actions and her unspoken notions were a much more powerful model. I know for a fact that all this came from a place of love. She was trying to protect me from the hardship and heartache that one faces in life when they take the path less traveled. I know that she was trying in her own way to guide me into what she considered a good life. Her intention I think was always to raise a good person and a productive member of society. I also believe that her desire to do so would often override me as an individual.

I felt a lot of times growing up that she was overly concerned with how things appeared to other people. She didn't often put herself in my shoes or express much sympathy for me. Not that she may never have felt it, but her expression of it was rare. She always saw the facts, and what was on paper was always more important than my feelings. This rule of thumb applied to all things big and small. If my explanation for something ever involved the statement "I didn't feel like..." or "I feel like..." it would be repeated mockingly at best or with disdain most of the time. How I felt was almost never an important factor. My feelings were often brushed aside as I was either told that I was book smart and had no common sense or that my mother knew me better than I knew myself. I grew up not trusting myself or my feelings. Even when I was heavily involved in church and committed to being "saved", I faced just as much criticism from my parent. I was still a disappointment, and the things I felt still didn't matter. I recall the soul crushing hurt I felt when I realize they still didn't trust me even though I was sincerely trying to be "good." I felt like I could never live down anything I did in their eyes, never.

This is exemplified in an experience that I had in the early 90s. I was about eight years old and I had a TV in my room, my mom woke up in the middle of the night to see lights from the TV flickering in my room way past my bedtime. I was up watching the Arsenio Hall show when I was supposed to be asleep. The next day as a punishment, the TV was removed from my room and I never ever had a TV again. Even almost a decade later as a teenager when I begged, I was told no and the reason cited was the time they caught me watching late night TV all those years ago when I was eight. I was never forgiven for that and I was punished for that one night for the rest of the time I lived with them and never given another chance to prove that I could be trusted. The TV situation was just one example of pretty much how they handled everything with me. I never lived anything down. I was always judged based on my mistakes and was never fully able to recover from them. The more mistakes I made as life progressed, the more those mistakes were used to justify the notion that what I felt wasn't important and

I couldn't possibly know better than them what was good for me.

I learned from them not to trust myself. I don't know if this hurt so much growing up, because I organically felt things so deeply or if it hurt so much because it played into my naturally emotional nature when I felt my feelings were being ignored. Regardless of how it came to be, I got into the habit as I grew older and more resentful to go with my feelings all the time, partially because I felt for the first part of my life that my feelings were unimportant. It's like I was making up for lost time and consoling myself by always doing what I felt like doing. I spent so many years being criticized and controlled in what I felt was an extreme way, and it felt like I was finally free to be me. When I first lived in Indiana, I can't exaggerate enough how good it felt to be left alone. No one was there to criticize what I wore as I walked out the door like I had to deal with every day at home. No one giving me a hard time about every single choice I made, big and small. "Are you eating again?!" (It was making me self-conscious about my weight.) "Your hair makes you look rough," (self-conscious about my natural hair), "give me that knife; let me cut that for you. You're left-handed, you will end up stabbing yourself" (of course I was always awkward with a knife with this running through my head). "Why are you still sleeping? Why are you still awake? You've been reading all day, put down the book. Why do you want to go anywhere? You went somewhere with the church last week so you can sit this one out." I was micromanaged to the max. Every move I made garnered negative criticism. All the phrases that swirled in my head started to quiet in Indiana.

People there actually listened to me sometimes and didn't just dismiss me as a book smart fool with no common sense. No more feeling guilty for wanting what other people wanted. No one telling me that it didn't matter if I was only at the movies or outside talking to friends, that it was indecent to be out past a certain time. It didn't matter what I was doing. No one was there telling me how wearing my hair natural made me look less ladylike; none of that kind of stuff. I was so far away from home at that time and I felt like I could make any choice I wanted to for the first time ever. Not having to deal with pressure from my mom definitely made it easier for it to occur to me that I didn't have to go back to New York. I decided I would move to Indianapolis and live with Wise and his mother, much to my mother's dismay.

Chapter Nineteen

A New Kind Of Family

Call it a clan, call it a network, call it a tribe, call it a family.
Whatever you call it, whoever you are, you need one.
- Jane Howard

I moved in at the beginning of the summer and I loved my life at that point. I loved experiencing life in a new city. There was a lot to love and hate about Indianapolis. It wasn't the country town that Anderson was, but not anything close to the metropolis of New York. Wise had three older brothers and one younger sister. His oldest brother, whose name means "Wealthy" lived in Chicago and was, married to a woman everyone hated and who had the same birthday as me. His next oldest brother's name is Greek for Healer. He had three kids, one of whom lived at the house with us, and the other two lived with their mothers. His next oldest brother was just a year older than Wise and his name is Hebrew for Lion, which is interesting because he kind of resembles one. His younger sister was a precocious being who made me laugh often. Her name means Brave. I felt bonded to several different members of his family in different ways. His mother's name means Keeper of the Keys and it was quite the fitting title for this matriarch. She was a church-going woman with a sweet disposition and I felt close to her while I lived there. I felt like this family brought sunshine to my life. It's not that they were perfect or had no disagreements, but there always remained a common thread of love and connection between them.

Coming from the emotionally stifled and rigid family I had, it was like I needed to see that there were people in the world with different ways of doing things. My family was what it was and I had to accept that but it was so nice to feel included, sought out, to be hugged tightly. I felt lucky to not just witness the closeness and the love they felt and showed but I was so glad to be a part of it. I didn't know any family like them. I loved them and those early days getting to know them made me happy.

The summer went by in a flash and as the summer days came to an end, I spoke to my mom, who I had been mostly avoiding this whole time. She made a convincing appeal for me to come home to New York but I stood my ground. I was finally happy and I was afraid to mess that up. "Well at least come for a visit", she said. Apparently, everyone at church had been asking about me, and everyone missed me. They were going to visit some of my mom's family who had recently moved to a suburb in Atlanta, Georgia. She offered me a one-way ticket to Atlanta so I could spend time with them and then drive back to New York and spend a little while there. I told her it sounded nice and all but I didn't want to go because then I would have no means of coming back to Indianapolis. She assured me that when the time came that I wanted to go back, she would buy me another one-way ticket back to Indiana, so I went.

I met them in Atlanta and had a wonderful time with my family who I didn't get to see much. We drove back to New York and everyone at church seemed happy to see me and it was great seeing all my old friends. It was my first time at home that I got to hang out and do what I wanted for the most part, which was of utmost importance to me back then. I think my parents were treading lightly at first because it was a delicate situation and they really wanted me to stay. After a couple of weeks of being brushed off whenever I asked about the ticket back to Indiana, I started to get frustrated. My mom got frustrated right back. "Why do you even want to go back to that place, you need to stay here and finish school instead of living in this lady's house!" Some variation of this statement was spoken in an ever increasingly aggressive way to me. It took me longer than it should have to understand that it was her intention just to get me back to New York, not to help me leave again. I hated myself for falling for it, but my immediate reaction was to try to think of a plan that would get me where I wanted to be.

By this time, I had been there for about a month and the fall/holiday season was approaching. I started working at Kohl's department store near my house. I worked there for one month and saved all my paychecks so that I could buy a plane ticket. When I went into my parents' bedroom and told them that I planned on leaving within the next week or two for Indiana, it erupted into a huge argument. The result was me paying the extra money so that I could fly out within two days instead of two weeks. I was sad about the rift with my parents, but I gave in to the wanderlust, and I left.

Chapter Twenty

Exhale

It's empty in the valley of your heart
The sun, it rises slowly as you walk
Away from all your fears
And the faults you've left behind…
Cause I need freedom now
I need to know how
To live my life as it's meant to be…
- Mumford and Sons
The Cave

Back where my heart wanted to be, I felt like I could be me again. I got a job with my boyfriend and his brother at a warehouse in nearby Avon, Indiana and I worked there for a few months. Things were not as prosperous as they could have been at that point. I spent money stupidly. I quit my job because I was immature and still living in my "I am always going to do what I feel like doing" stage so when it got stressful I stopped going. I was clearly not in the right state of mind. I was also slipping back into a depression for several different reasons. I had gained some weight and it felt at the time like I had no control over how I was feeling. Some days I would wake up on an almost manic high where I would be happy and optimistic, in love, glowing and just radiating with joy. I would thoroughly enjoy being around Wise and his family and soaking up all the cozy aspects of it all. Sometimes it could last for a day or two. And some days I would be so low and so depressed that I couldn't see my way out of bed. I would just eat and sleep and cry over a variety of issues. I was a mess.

It was on one of those low days that sunlight in my window forced me down the stairs, and as I sunk myself into a chair in the dining room, the Keeper of the Keys introduced me to a skinny girl with the longest ponytail I had seen since my friend in the Bronx. She was pregnant. She stood before me with her glasses fogged and her blue coat still on. She was the mother of one of the Keeper's grandchildren and she was named after a Roman goddess who was the protector of marriage and the home. Her name literally means Young, and it fits her well. She has always been young at heart, and as long as I have known her, she has looked much younger than her years. I remember the first day I met her clear as day. What was also clear was that the Keeper wanted us to be friends, probably because she was tired of seeing me depressed and moping around the house.

About a week after we met, I went to Young's apartment which was about 10 minutes from where I lived. She lived there with her new boyfriend, the father of her new baby. She had her three-year-old daughter and another one on the way and wasn't feeling all that great physically or emotionally. She gave birth not long after we met, and we started to hang out all the time. We became really close really fast despite a few years of an age difference between us. She was my closest friend and only confidant in that city for a long time.

Things started to fare a little better for me. Around this time, I started to communicate with my biological father again after many years. I had sent him a letter and a picture when I graduated High School and I received one back, but that was all the communication I had with him since I left Jamaica fourteen years before this. Over the internet, my father and I found each other and started to communicate again, which made my heart glad.

I got a job at a department store and I had registered for college in Indiana and was ready to continue my education. After about eight months of living with Wise's family, I was able to get an apartment right near the campus of IUPUI where I was to attend. Indiana University and Purdue University of Indianapolis were large schools located in downtown Indianapolis in the heart of the city. The schools were integrated into the landscape of the metropolis, the borders between the school and downtown were not always apparent. When driving through downtown, one drove through the campus. I loved that aspect of it. I loved living downtown, being able to take the bus and walk places, and soaking up the feeling of being in an urban area. I have always loved the city and told myself as a kid that I would grow up to have an apartment in Manhattan. That was until I grew up and realized living in a studio apartment in Manhattan required a small fortune.

I enjoyed not only living downtown but living alone. It was strange and interesting in a lot of ways but I loved it. I made other friends, while remaining best friends with Young who were, I think, going through something that I could never have understood back then. Her son was the nephew that Wise mourned for when we first met, and her daughter was born a year later. Following the death of her son and the birth of her daughter, she went through some rough times, having to do what she could to support herself and her child, while trying to deal with a tragedy that often breaks the strongest of people. The fact that she lived, loved and carried on was amazing, but I don't think I had the emotional maturity back then to even fathom what she might have been feeling. She was no longer in the relationship with Wise's brother, the father of her first two kids. She lived with someone new with whom she had her new baby. He was a good guy who was happy to stay home and allow us to go have a good time. We partied a lot, both of us nursing our emotions and looking for an escape.

I joined a theatre group and it was great. We traveled to nearby cities like Chicago and Louisville, to visit other campuses and perform. Wise would come spend the night with me at my apartment sometimes but neither one of us had a car at that point and it limited how much we were able to see each other. For the first time since the beginning of our relationship, we were in the same city at the same time and we were not seeing each other every single day. I started to really feel a little bit more like an adult. I was finally living my own life. I was not only far away from my parents geographically, but I kept my communication with them at a minimum. I hated to talk to my mom, she would always manage to say something about how she hated what I was doing, and she would try to tell me that I was ruining my life. I was always reduced back to the same little girl when we talked; the one who never had any valid feelings or thoughts. Blinded by my hurt feelings, I couldn't take in anything she was really saying. I just endured it. Every conversation took time to recover from.

On the other side of things, I had more and more communication with my biological father who by then had moved to St. Lucia. I was having a more active social life and delighting in my relationship. I was learning a lot about life and I enjoyed most of it. After just a couple of months of living alone, I got back into contact with another person, but this time he was from my more recent past. After a few months of living in my small one bedroom home, I spoke to my friend who I met that first day in Anderson, whose name means Favor. We had such a strong connection from the moment we met and we had stayed in touch sporadically in the year since he left college after just a semester. It just wasn't the place for him, but he certainly didn't belong where he was at that time either. He was back in his hometown of Evansville Indiana. He was born and raised in this small town that was about three hours away from Indianapolis. It was actually closer to Louisville, Kentucky than it was to where I was living. He was miserable there, he said. He had issues with his mother (who he was living with) that ran deep and it was hard for him to be there when he didn't want to be. He also told me about ending a relationship with a guy there who he deemed crazy. He was stalking him even though he told him in no uncertain terms that they were over. He felt depressed and at a dead end, which isn't hard in a tiny town like Evansville where there is one factory where everyone works, everyone knows each other and nothing exciting ever happens. How, he asked, is he supposed to get anywhere in life being stuck there? He sounded like he was on the verge of tears when his voice cracked as he expressed to me how much he wanted to get out of the hell hole that was Evansville. I blurted out without hesitation, "come live with me in Indianapolis!" And he, without hesitation, exhaled out a "yes let's do it." It was the beginning of an era.

Chapter Twenty One

Wanton Favor

Never fear quarrels, but seek hazardous adventures.
-Alexandre Dumas
The Three Musketeers

A week after our conversation, Favor arrived in Indianapolis via the pickup truck of a friend of his who he also met when we were in Anderson. Favor had a special relationship with this guy. He was a conservative Christian who had been engaged to a girl since he was 18, and was for all intents and purposes a straight man. He became close with Favor and they shared a borderline flirtatious energy between them. There was a clear mutual interest. It was always so interesting to watch and I think the dance was something Favor enjoyed but it may have been a little more torturous for the guy. He drove hours to pick Favor up and drove hours to bring him to my place. We were so happy and excited to see one another.

We lived together in the one bedroom through the rest of that winter and into the summer. When I began school earlier that year, I took out a student loan and I paid my entire lease off at once so I wouldn't have to worry about rent. I had quit my job when I moved out of the Keeper's house to downtown because I was still carless had no way of getting there every day. Although we both loved that place, eventually my lease was up; I was searching, not just for a job but for an apartment with cheaper rent. When I lived in the apartment with Favor all of those months, we looked for jobs, and I briefly worked as a waitress for a few weeks, but without a car, even downtown, our prospects were dismal. But I did end up finding a place that rented to me without a job because I was registered in school. The new place was right around the corner from campus and they offered specials for students. When we moved in, there was no deposit and the first month's rent was free. After that, we agreed would split the $600 rent every month. This place was such an awesome find. They were two tall buildings that overlooked the skyline of downtown Indianapolis. The rent we paid every month included all utilities, basic cable, and a landline phone. All these amenities were so unheard of, and we felt so good moving into our new two bedroom apartment. I should have done the smart thing and saw the one month of free rent as a way to get a head start on things but instead, I kept thinking it meant I had more time. I have to admit that I could have been a little more aggressive on the job front but I was really enjoying my life. I realize with age and maturity how crazy it was for me to live that way, but back then I was reveling in doing what I wanted when I wanted. I treasured this experience of being able to be myself, or at least that's what I thought I was doing. I now know that I didn't know myself at all, I was still searching. What I did know was that I would enjoy life more if I had money to spend and that was often the dilemma; aside from that pesky little money problem though, we had an awesome time.

When I introduced Favor to my friend Young, they also had an instantaneous spark. The three of us spent more time together than I spent with my boyfriend. We partied a lot. We were out somewhere more nights a week than we stayed home.

I was doing all the taboo things that I wanted to do and I loved it. Even if we had a little money, we would save it and count out some change so we could buy a 99 cent chicken sandwich at McDonald's and that would be our meal for the day. We were ok with that as long as there was money to have fun later. I smoked weed and drank regularly. We had a hole in the wall gay club called the Ten that we would frequent. The DJ was always great, the drinks were cheap and we brought the party with us. A lot of times there were other people but our core trio remained constant.

Looking back on it, all three of us were running from ourselves and our lives at that point. And we enabled each other in the same irresponsible behavior that would annoy the other two when the repercussions were nigh. We got kicked out of clubs, got ridiculously drunk and then drove home at least twice a week, saved our last dimes to go out at night, lived by the day, sometimes by the hour. I woke up every day excited for a new adventure. Favor and I had money sometimes but we were often broke. We absolutely were not spending our money wisely. And there were times we paid dearly for our financial irresponsibility but that never seemed to deter us from living the way we did. We didn't need too much of an excuse to do something. Even with all the going out, some of our best times were when we would just hang out at her apartment with the other people Young introduced me to. She was also from a small town in Indiana (there are hundreds of small towns there) and she had family in town, and her gregarious personality ensured that there was no shortage of old friends and new acquaintances of hers to meet and sometimes party with. The times when we were just hanging out, drinking, playing spades or having crazy conversations were some of my favorite memories.

Wise and I were still going strong. We barely argued, especially now since we went stretches of time without seeing each other. I was enjoying being with my friends and I believe he felt the same way. I wasn't just depressed and moping around his mother's house anymore and depending on him to be my only company and entertainment. It had put a little stress on the relationship so we were both just fine with a little room to breathe. A few months after Favor arrived from Evansville, he was lamenting to the same friend who drove him to Indianapolis how hard it was that we did not have a car, and he informed us that his brother was selling his old car. He went on about how even though it was an older model car, the car had barely been driven and was in such great condition. He even volunteered to talk to him about us making a payment arrangement with him because we couldn't afford to pay it all.

Favor's friend worked it out for us and within a week of the initial conversation, we were in a small town almost two hours away picking up a black 1995 Chevrolet Beretta. From the second I laid eyes on the car, I was in disbelief, and not in a good way. The image I had in my mind of a car that was in good condition started to deteriorate. It was clear from moment one that he gravely exaggerated the condition of the car. We opened the door and the whole inside of the car was stripped down. There was no upholstery anywhere; the only material was on the seats, none on the doors, none on the ceiling, just exposed metal. On the dashboard, in the place where there was usually a radio, a clock, and/or heat and AC knobs and gages, there was nothing but empty space and exposed wires. We showed up that day with $500 and shook hands with the man and promised to make payments that would total $2,500 when it was all over with. By the time we were halfway home, we knew that this man would never see another dime for this car. As a matter of fact, we concluded, we may have overpaid him. Within minutes of getting on the highway in the middle of the thunderous pouring rain, the passenger's side windshield wiper gave out and I don't recall that it ever worked again the whole time we had the car. A little while later on our journey home, we turned on the headlights, but they switched off and were also not working properly the entire time we had the car. We went to get new bulbs; thinking (or rather hoping) that it would fix the headlight situation. The guy at the store helped us replace the bulbs in the parking lot and we quickly found out the problem was much deeper than that. We could barely afford the bulbs we just bought much less any other work that needed to be done.

The guy felt sorry for us and after getting us to swear that we wouldn't tell anyone, showed us how to strip some wires and twist them around onto the nodes of the battery which turned on the headlights. The problem was, they would stay on forever and drain the battery so we had to open the hood and manipulate these wires every time we needed the headlights on. When we got to our destination, we would open the hood and remove the wires to save the battery. Sometimes we would hit a bump or maybe not secure the wires well enough and the lights would just go out and we would have to pull over so we can get under the hood to connect wires. Our bumper promptly fell off in the street a week after we got it and was shoved into the back seat. This car was a disaster, a "death trap", to quote one person who looked at it for us. A few days of driving it and it was making this loud grinding noise that we found out were the brakes that needed fixing. We still drove around with bad brakes for a while because we didn't have the money to fix it. Finally, we just got the parts and read a do it yourself book and asked questions at places like

AutoZone or friends who knew about cars and we did the brakes ourselves on one brutally hot summer day in front of Wise's mom's house. I like to say we but the truth is, Favor did most of the manual labor. It was a rough day for both of us because we kind of both had the same level of daintiness approaching the situation.

I haven't mentioned yet that this was all being done with no insurance on the car, the registration still in the guy's name, plates expired and neither one of us had a valid driver's license. His was suspended and I had a permit from New York, I never took the test to get my license. We were asking for something to go wrong while driving this car, but we always skated by unscathed. How, is a total mystery and a miracle. We got into a fender bender with this lady once and when she got out of her car, she looked at our scared faces and said right away "y'all don't have no insurance, do you?" We shook our heads and she cursed as she climbed back in her truck and drove away without saying another word. We thanked our lucky stars. We got pulled over on several occasions and when officers questioned us, we would always make up the story on the spot and somehow always ended up driving away with no problems.

On one of our many drunken nights leaving the Ten, we sat peacefully at a red light at an empty intersection waiting for it to change so we can make the less than 10 minute drive back to our apartment. I recall the headlights approaching behind us and it felt like at the same instant that I realized that the car behind us was not slowing down, it ran right into the back of us, thrusting our car into the intersection. We looked at each other and Favor put the car in drive and we just drove away. We shared a laugh mainly because it was better than being sad or admitting that even though my neck kinda hurt, if we got the situation addressed, it would land us in trouble in some way.

Favor and I started working for this "modeling agency", they had us recruiting people for their company. At the end of the day, they made money off of telling regular people that they could be models or actors and convincing them to pay hundreds of dollars for some headshots. They knew the majority of them will not find a modeling job in that city. We would recruit people, tell them to come to a meeting which was basically just a sales pitch for the headshots. After landing those jobs, we were able to come up with some of the rent by the time we had to pay, but I still had to call my mom and ask her for money to make up the balance. We quit the agency not long after that and we both got jobs at a warehouse where a lot of people we knew worked, including Young.

We were getting to the place now where we realized that in order to survive we had to be more responsible and hold down a job so we zeroed in on one. We heard about it from Young's new boy toy. Her previous relationship had fizzled and she had moved on with a new guy. The pay at the warehouse was better and more consistent. I noticed right away how when I went inside the warehouse, my asthma would flare up ever so slightly and my breathing would become just a little more labored. I wasn't sure what it was that affected my asthma like that, but it made me very miserable at this job and I hated going there. It didn't make it easier that I worked the day shift and Young and Favor both worked nights. It made me feel so separated from them. I saw them getting closer and felt increasingly on the outside. Still, I felt like we were our own little family and that we depended on each other and would help each other out no matter what.

I have to admit my feelings were hurt and I was a little taken aback when Favor decided it was too much for him to drop me off and pick me up because we were on opposite schedules. I knew within myself, I was willing to cut into my sleep and make the sacrifice so when he complained. Although I was miffed, I accepted it and I started to spend the night at a friend's house who also worked the same shift so I could make it to work. I hated it but I couldn't escape feeling like Favor and Young were leaving me out. Whenever the feeling would creep up, I would just convince myself that it was because they were working together and he was sleeping at her house often so they were spending more and more time together, but, I would tell myself, it wasn't about me. I tried to be ok with it but I just couldn't shake the feeling. I felt an awkward vibe every time I was around them.

One particular day, my asthma was worse than ever so I told the supervisor how I was feeling and she suggested I go home because she didn't want anything to happen to me while I was working because they would be liable. I called Favor at Young's apartment and he was very annoyed because he had only been asleep for a few hours and he had to be at work later that same day. I felt terrible about it, I really did, but I couldn't stay at work. I don't think they really believed that anything was wrong with me. I think they thought I was making another excuse to quit a job and continue my cycle. I can't say that they weren't justified in feeling a little distrust in my motives. After all, that was my M.O. to work a job for a little while and when I didn't feel like going anymore, I just stopped going. I think had they thought about it a little deeper than that, they may have saved themselves from frustration because I never needed a good excuse to quit. In fact, my excuse was often "I hated that job."

I was a little insulted also that they would feel I needed to fake an asthma scare to get out of work. If I wanted to just quit, I would have. Anyway, that day I sat outside my job for over an hour waiting for someone to come get me. I squinted and looked up when a set of car tires came to a stop in front of me. It was Young's new boyfriend. He was at the apartment when I called and he told me that after I hung up, they were expressing their annoyance with me and no one really made a move to get in the car and come. He told me he volunteered to pick me up. I drove back to the apartment so hurt I didn't speak much. When I got inside Young's apartment, the air was chilly and it wasn't just the AC. They both barely spoke to me and were acting a little strange. I picked up Young's phone and called my mother and when she got on the phone, I said, "Hi mom" and she immediately heard the wheezing and asked me about my asthma. With her prompting, I went to the hospital where they gave me a shot and a nebulizer treatment, wrote me a prescription for a steroid inhaler and sent me home. I had a letter from the doctor stating I probably shouldn't go back to the warehouse for a few days, that way I could really determine if that's where the asthma flare up was happening or if it was just a general flare up. My job said that I had two days to bring the note to them or I would have to lose my job. I stayed at Wise's mom's house with him for a few days, and I tried so hard to get Favor to pick me up and take me to give them the doctors note but he was annoyed with having to do that too. I probably could have asked someone else but I think I was trying to prove to myself that I was important to him because I wasn't feeling it at that point. I think I wanted him to be as accountable to me as I felt I had been to him. I didn't get the note to them in time and ended up losing my job. I can truthfully say that I was more heartbroken over what I felt was a turn in our relationship than I was about losing my job.

A few weeks later, as rent day came near again, one of our friends inquired how we would pay the rent and I responded very confidently that Favor would pay the rent this month. I figured he was making enough money, and whether or not I was right to do it, I assumed that he would cover it until I found another job. A little while after, Young told me that Favor was very offended by my comment, he felt it was presumptuous of me to assume that he would pay the whole thing when the original agreement was that we would split the rent. He didn't pay it. He insisted he didn't have it but in my heart, I knew he did have it, it just would have left him totally broke to pay all of the rent. I was very hurt by this. I was never in the business of keeping score before that, but I felt the way he treated me in this scenario was cold and that I deserved more as a friend.

When he moved in with me in the first apartment, he didn't pay rent at all because I took out the student loan to pay my lease off. And we were only in the current apartment because of my full-time student status, which also gave us the free rent for a month special. And even the one month where we finally came up with some money, we were still a couple of hundred dollars short and I had to call my mom and ask for money to supplement us. I felt like up until that point, we were just making it however we could, and we did a lot for each other. And truth be told, he really hadn't come out of his pocket for too much where rent was concerned so I honestly thought he would have had different feelings about this. I was wrong.

Our rent went unpaid that month, and I spent a few more tension filled weeks thereafter that until we approached our second month of unpaid rent. He took the Beretta without really consulting me and drove back to his hometown. I found out much later that he got pulled over in a small town on the way and went to jail for a night for driving on a suspended license and the car was impounded. It cost more to get out of impound than we paid for the car. So just like that, the death trap of a car succumbed to a fate unknown and our fun life and wild times had crashed and burned. About five days away from eviction, I called my mom, and she came to my rescue. True to her style of doing things, this rescuing didn't happen on anyone else's terms but hers.

Chapter Twenty Two

Cry On The Shoulder Of The Road

Freeing yourself was one thing, claiming ownership of that freed self was another.

- Toni Morrison, Beloved

My family was coincidentally planning to drive to Atlanta to visit my mom's side of the family. The plan was to spend a few days in Georgia and drive to Orlando so that my sister who was just about three or four years old can have her Disney World experience. It was one of our unspoken rites of passage in our clan. I went when I was about eight or nine when it was exciting for me, and my brother was just a baby. We returned when I was about fifteen and my brother was about seven so that he could enjoy his Disney experience. I had fun that time too, although it was made slightly less fun by my brooding teenage life. This time, I was in my early twenties, my brother was the brooding teen and my sister was in her wonder years.

When I originally called my mom for help, I asked her for the money to pay one month's rent. I was confident with that boost I would be able to get things working for myself again. I had a couple of job prospects and our apartment was right next to a bus stop. Taking the bus in Indianapolis was a challenge. The schedule was scant and the busses only ran in a limited area, but it was somewhat of a solution for me. My mother argued that I needed to give it up and just come home so I can get back on my feet. I really wanted to stay and try to pick up the pieces and make it work but I literally had nothing. After the gentle back and forth (I couldn't be too aggressive, I needed her help after all), I resigned myself once again to my mother's powers of persuasion. It was really out of desperation, I had nowhere else to turn. I would have to leave town in two days. I was incredibly sad about it. I cried myself to sleep on the floor of the living room in the empty apartment that Favor and I had been too busy partying to furnish. I have this vivid snapshot in my head of the light from the skyline of downtown Indianapolis, my head cradled in my arms, the tears rolling like a river down my nose.

When they got there, my parents rented a small trailer to pull behind their SUV. After my dad saw the apartment, I had a private conversation with him about my plan to turn things around. I remember him approaching my mom with the idea of just maybe giving me the rent money for the month like I had originally asked. My mom insisted that the only way she would help me is if I came home to New York. In the end, just like when I wanted to go Temple University on scholarship, she ended up spending triple the money to have it her way. They planned to haul my stuff all the way to Georgia, to Florida, and finally back to New York. It didn't take too long to pack, all I had in there was my clothes, a couple of boxes with a few personal items and a bed. This was a rough time for me. My mom charged onto the scene ready to take care of business. She talked to the leasing office and even worked with a family member in Georgia who was faxing papers and doing all they could to get me out of the lease without any consequences. I am still so grateful for that to this day. My mom sacrificed and did a lot that day so that I would not have that eviction on my credit. That day was so emotionally charged for me because mixed with my gratefulness for her help, there was a bedrock of resentment for how she treated me during the process.

It began when Wise's mom the Keeper of the Keys showed up at my apartment in the middle of the day. All the faxed documents we needed to take care of the business with the lease was coming through the doctor's office where she worked. She helped us out tremendously by receiving the papers and driving them to me on her lunch break. For the couple of years that Wise and I had been dating, our moms had spoken on the phone a few times but had never met face to face. When she called to say she was on the way, she expressed that she was looking forward to meeting my mom but was sad she couldn't stay because she was on her lunch break. I told my mom what she said and it was met with stony silence.

When she was outside the building, I naturally expected her to come meet the woman I lived with for more than half of the time I was in Indiana. When I asked her if she was coming down to meet his mom, I remember her cold response, clear as day. She said "I don't want to meet anybody". I felt my heart drop into my stomach and my ears were hot with anger and embarrassment as I plastered on a fake smile and made something up when the Keeper looked at me with curious eyes and asked why I walked out alone. I was really angry with her about that. I tried to explain to her that I really loved that lady and that she took care of me on certain levels, and she all but ignored me. Her only concern was taking care of the things we had to get straight before we left in the morning.

The day progressed and I realized that Wise was not going to be able to get a ride to come to my apartment and see me before I left. I hadn't seen him for a couple of days before. I started frantically trying to think of solutions because it made me so anxious to consider leaving to go back to New York without saying goodbye in person. The time between when I made the decision to return to New York and when my family arrived was only a couple of days. I spent a significant amount of time on the phone trying to find a ride to his house with no success, and as a last ditch effort, I begged and pleaded with my mom to either allow me to drive or someone to drive me the ten minutes away to see him, return the Keeper's house key and say goodbye to his other family members. I was met with closed eyes, pursed lips and her head shaking back and forth as if she were saying no and smelled something foul at the same time. My heart was breaking with each negative statement, and even my tears were callously dismissed. There was no valid reason given to me, just no. This was one of the most frustrating moments of my life.

To my relief, Wise found a way to me at the last minute. I had so many feelings swirling around me that day. Saying goodbye had my stomach all twisted up in knots, partially because I would miss my boyfriend, and partially because of the frustration with the manner in which I was leaving and frankly, I was harboring a deep red hot burning coal of anger in the pit of my belly for how my mom was acting that day. I was hoping, as I had so many times before that she could see my heart.

Even though I was absolutely grateful for my family's help, what kept coming to mind was the many times in the past that I would talk to my mom with the best intentions in my heart and was treated with suspicion, and reminded of whatever mistakes I had made before. I felt unable to live anything down or to be forgiven. Like when I got caught watching TV after I was supposed to be in bed one night when I was about nine years old. The TV was removed from my room the next day and I never got a TV in my room again. I lied about staying after school for tutoring once in the 7th grade. I just wanted to hang out with my friends. When I got caught, I had a hard time getting permission to stay after school all the way up to the 12th grade. I couldn't make up for anything. It felt like every mistake was filed and stored and used as a reference. And here I was, adding to the list.

When I was about 18, one day she left early from work and turned down a street she didn't normally have to drive down, only to see me getting off the train, where I was not supposed to be. She was understandably angry with me. Then over ten years later, when I was an adult after she saw me drive past her on her way to work in the wee hours of the morning, she called me to say she saw me and that she knew in her spirit that I had just come from the club, partying my life away and nothing was farther from the truth. Even when I was telling her that it wasn't true, she believed her spirit, not me, even though when she saw me I had just returned from spending an uneventful night at a friend's house. I think it just made her uneasy to see me driving at that time of the morning and she assumed I was out at some wild party. Very often she is right about her premonitions but there are times when she is not. When she is not right, there is nothing I could ever think of to say that would convince her otherwise. My words have never held too much weight.

I have seen my mom exhibit the Christian charity that is supposed to be characteristic for followers of the faith. Often people profess to be Christians and forget the part about Christ loving, accepting and sacrificing for people. Unlike a lot of Christians, that is one thing she has never forgotten. Throughout her nursing career, she has mostly worked with people who were not on the upper crust of society. She worked first with detoxing drug addicts, and for many years has been a community health nurse. She chose to not make the top pay so that she could talk to teen moms and all different kinds of young people she saw headed in a bad way. I believe the Spirit has placed many people in her path to which she has been a sage mentor. She has countless stories of patients who cried on her shoulder and she showed compassion and understanding to them in a non-judgmental way.

I have seen her exhibit this quality in ministry, with even some of my close friends telling me how talking to my mom made them feel so much better and how she gave great advice and they felt comfortable. I didn't have too much personal experience with this side of her. She judged me harshly and often when I was younger and I felt she was less sympathetic to me, even when she showed compassion to other people going through the same thing. Through my years of deep contemplation about our relationship, combined with years of life experience I came to realize and understand that she wasn't all that strange after all. As a matter of fact, I had a mother on the better end of the spectrum mistakes and all. The day eventually did come when I accepted that my mom was a human being first and foremost. I have accepted her for who she is, and by doing so, I lifted a heavy weight off of my life. I wish that day would have come sooner. I wish that I had the maturity and insight earlier in life; I wonder how things would have been different. I also came to learn that people feel differently about their family than strangers, and tend to have higher expectations of them. I am guilty of it too. I have never expected perfection from anyone out there in the world, I have always been pretty accepting of human faults. It just occurred to me how unfair it was for me to expect her to be perfect and to do everything right just because she is my mom. She did get a lot right. It's just natural for the wrong to stand out, especially when you are hurting. Laying there on my last night in my apartment with my family camped out in the living room, I was hurting tremendously.

That night before I left town, I was angry about her actions toward me and the people I cared about. I went to sleep with anger in my gut. Morning came and we left Indianapolis and drove south. The trip was miserable for me. I was still absorbing everything that happened.

Chapter Twenty Three

The Crash

*It has not been in the pursuit of pleasure that I have
periled life and reputation and reason. It has been the
desperate attempt to escape from torturing memories,
from a sense of insupportable loneliness and a
dread of some strange impending doom.*

-Edgar Allan Poe

I was basically coming off of a year long party binge and like most binges, things ended in a horrible way. I was upset that I had to leave my boyfriend behind. I was so in love with him at the time and I was absolutely sure that I never wanted to be in a relationship with anyone else. We had been together for a few years and I didn't want to just throw everything away. I thought things were perfect, but later on in life, I would realize that the first crack in the relationship appeared when he subtly suggested we part ways for good when I go back to New York. I quickly bulldozed over that whole notion and insisted that we try, insisted I would be back, all the while ignoring the doubt in his eyes. After persuasion from me, we agreed to do the long distance thing and to see how it worked. We both realized we were still young and agreed that if we were interested in anyone else, we wouldn't put any harsh restrictions on going out with other people. If things took a sexual turn or anything remotely more serious than hanging out, we would be honest with each other.

I was absolutely determined to see things through in New

York and return to Indianapolis to be with him when I was more financially stable. For the nine hour drive to Georgia, I was mostly silent, looking out the window thinking about him, and a host of other things. My brother and sister fought in the typical way that kids do on road trips. My family made it easy to miss the carefree life I had lived for the past couple of years. My sensitive nature was back to being bruised by their harsh judgments immediately, which made me even sadder about being carted away with them. I was really also still angry, and still holding it in, not daring to tell my mother that I felt she had acted in an extremely insensitive way toward me. I remember before I left the apartment, when I was trying to plead with her to either let me drive to his house or maybe her and my dad could drop me off, I asked her to please try and understand how I was feeling. I said, "What if it were you and dad, and you had to leave suddenly, you would at least want to see him face to face to say goodbye wouldn't you?" Her answer was that I could not compare my relationship with Wise to her marriage to my dad. It really hurt me that she felt it was ok to gloss over my feelings as if they didn't matter. It was nothing new, it was just that I had been in this place where everyone I had around me treated me the exact opposite way for the past couple of years. The old feelings I had about myself faded up until that point. Being on that trip was a harsh thrust back into insignificance. The sting of their words, the feelings that followed, all had memories attached to it, the pain was woefully familiar.

We spent a few days with our family in Georgia and continued on to Florida. All the while, I was distant, full of angst and just over the whole trip altogether. In the midst of my brother and sister fighting, I was also nursing the hurt I felt about where my roommate Favor and I had left off as friends. I thought about him a lot and I would be lying if I said I wasn't angry with him. I was also thinking about the details of what I would need to do to get back to Indiana as fast as I could. I was aware that this wouldn't be a quick process but I was already anxious to get it underway. Frustrations inside the truck reached a boiling point as we pulled up to our destination, and my mom said something really harsh out of her own frustration.

Often when we as human beings go through something hurtful, we tend to block things out subconsciously. I want so badly to remember the exact words she said but I can't. What I do remember is the way it crushed me. I remember the feeling like the general idea was that having me ruined her life, that she would have had a better life if it weren't for me. As I said, her exact words escape me, but not her sentiment. This is how I took what she said, but I always like to give people the benefit of the doubt so I will say that it is possible that this is not what she meant to say. I wasn't making up in my mind the way it came off because my silence moved her to make the first apology she had ever made to me.

The next morning after she apologized, I was still feeling a myriad of emotions when she came into the room I was sharing with my little sister to get her ready. She expressed her frustration with me about not getting over the situation and declared to me that if I decided to keep being upset then that was really my problem, and left the room with my sister. Needless to say, I had a miserable time at Disney that week and was anxious to get back to New York.

Chapter Twenty Four

A Heart Without Words

Some changes happen deep down inside of you. And the truth is, only you know about them. Maybe that's the way it's supposed to be.

- Judy Blume
Tiger Eyes

It was great seeing my old friends, both from church and from high school. Some of my old high school friends also still lived at home. When I came back from Indiana, would often hang out; reminisce about high school and our old shenanigans. Sometimes we made new memories with brand new shenanigans. I really loved my church friends too, and it was easy to pick up where we left off with most of them. I was not quite the same person as I was before I went to Indiana though. Thrust back into life in the church I was basically raised in, I was forced to confront my spirituality. Some of my church friends were disappointed and felt like I had strayed too far. Truth be told, according to their standards I was living like a total heathen. I faced a little judgment from a few people, but I didn't really care. I felt the weight of the things I had been through and that was the first time in my life that I started to explore what religion and spirituality really meant to me. I had smoked weed, drank, had sex with my boyfriend, and partied a lot for the past year and a half. The guilt didn't take too long to subside because for some reason I was sure that these trivial things and that God would love me anyway. In the midst of that, I never stopped going to church. I went every Sunday just about with Wise's mother, and as far as I was concerned, I maintained an open line of communication with God.

I had been going to church since my earliest memories in Jamaica. My caretaker would take me to church with her every week. When I moved to the Bronx, my father's mother took me every week with her. By the time we moved to Long Island, my parents were heavily involved in church, so I never escaped going to church every Sunday at any stage of my life. Even with all my extracurricular activities, it never felt right to me to not be in church on a Sunday morning. Someone cannot possibly go to church their whole life and not come away with some indelible imprints on their life. However, the more I learned about some of the principles I held so dearly, the more disillusioned with the actual church I became over the years. I started to learn more about the different denominations and the pettiness that separated them. The different seemingly mundane rituals and rules that some people would declare could send you straight to hell depending on whether or not you were doing them. I started to despise knowing that people who are studying to become preachers are schooled in the art of emotional manipulation, or that Christianity was used to justify the enslavement of my ancestors.

I know in my heart that I have had spiritual experiences in life, so I have never denied the existence of God, but I was increasingly upset about the way the church packaged the Message. I felt it was convoluted with things that didn't really matter, and it grew more and more unattractive to me. I started around this time to develop my own beliefs. I believed what felt right to me. I still loved the church; I don't think I could ever replace the sense of community and belonging. Through the years I can say, I have had genuine spiritual experiences through my involvement with church and have learned so much. The most important lesson I learned was to discern what's meant for me and leave the rest.

I have always been a silent praying type of person; ever since I was a little girl. I have always talked to God in a very candid manner in my head. Back then, I wouldn't consider what I did to be praying but it was. I talked to God about my fears and frustrations; I wrote letters to God when I needed to take that extra therapeutic step. I learned as a pre-teen what it meant to worship God, and way back then, I developed a theory that I still hold today. The core of my personal spirituality was inspired by a sermon that was preached at my church by our late family friend and longtime neighbor. One of the most memorable and dynamic women I have come across. She talked about the difference between praise and worship. She said we should think of praise the same way we would praise one another. In the same way, you would tell a co-worker or your child "good job" is the same way we should think of praise. It is merely us expressing to God how great and how wonderful this being is.

Most people think these things go hand in hand, but worship was something different. She taught that worship was something you did with your heart. The symbolism of the rituals we had like communion, baptism, attending service were all icing on the cake. They made things better in your life by reminding you of the principles you live by and serving an illustrative purpose, but they were not the cake. The substance is you. The work it took to be close to God was all about your heart. By keeping your heart as close to the heart of Jesus as you can, you were worshipping God. You worshipped when you gave to the poor and fed the hungry. You worship with your love, your patience, your kindness. Your worship was in being honest. You were worshipping God every time you forgave someone. You worship and honor the Life Giving Force with your own life.

Another principle that I have always held dear to me was illustrated in a story in the Bible where Jesus was addressing a crowd. One man asked him which of the commandments were the most important. Jesus basically answered that to love God and to love your neighbor as yourself was above all because in doing those things, all the other commandments will be obeyed by default. If you love other people as you love yourself, you won't want to steal from them or lie to them, or any other evil thing. I have always, throughout most of my transitions in life, tried to live by these things honoring God with my love for other people. There are those that would say that I need to do more, that there are confessions to be made, baptisms to endure, sacrifices, church services to attend, tithing, and the list goes on.

The size of that list will vary with each church, and each individual Christian you ask. Some (not all) of these people are so cold and callous toward other people, their prayers are nothing but empty recitation. The fact that these people make sure all the small rituals are done to perfection and make sure they are sitting in the pews every Sunday morning, doesn't put them any closer to Him than it puts me. Over time, I have learned and experienced things that have added to my spiritual richness in life, but these two sentiments have always been at my core. For many years since and to this day, I give all the effort I can to do these two things;

love God and other people. It's a labor sometimes to continue loving people but I consider it my duty. For me, it is all about love.

This way of thinking was still in the development stages then, but I returned to New York a more confident young woman. I was surer than ever that I didn't have to do things the way everyone else thought. I have always had this thing about being different and I was finally embracing that on so many levels. It was such a contrast to me, coming back after living in the mid-west, where people cared less about what you were wearing, back to fashion central. Indiana was a place where people valued relationships and made an art out of finding their own fun because there was not much to do outside on the street. As I got a job, and then another and I was making money, my parents kept hinting that maybe I should just stay since things seemed to be going well. I loved my friends and family, but I had this burning desire to leave New York. In my mind at the time, it was all because I was so in love with my boyfriend and wanted to marry him. That did have a lot to do with it, I would say that was mostly the reason, but there were other reasons that I didn't realize until it was all over. The most pressing being that, returning to my childhood bedroom as a woman after all that I had experienced and lived through, did not make my parents see me any different. Part of my happiness in Indiana was that I escaped the tremendous criticism that I faced all the time. No one out there treated me like an imbecile who could never make the right decision. Even if I made a mistake, no one held it over my head forever. It made me happy while I was there that there wasn't anyone around underestimating me (at least not out loud to my face) and shaking my confidence, so it had time to build itself back.

Of course, it didn't hurt to be able to come and go as I

pleased, which even as a woman in her early twenties I was still not allowed to do while living with my parents. My mom watched my every move and questioned me about everything. I was back to feeling stifled. I went to a bar one night with high school friends. I was over 21, I wasn't driving and I wasn't doing anything wrong. I came home really late and she was awake. She followed me down the hall to my room, all the way telling me how she smelled the alcohol on me, but I was unapologetic, much to her frustration. I wasn't even drunk, it was mostly the smell that stays on you when you spend hours at a bar that had her freaked out, but it just left me exasperated and missing my old life. That was the very night I set a deadline date to return to Indianapolis.

Chapter Twenty Five

Where We Left Off ...

One belongs to New York instantly, one belongs to it as much in five minutes as in five years.

- Tom Wolfe

In an effort to regain some autonomy, I decided that I would return to campus life at Stony Brook one last time. I was happy to just not be living at home. I did well there. I made a few friends who lived down the hall from me, was going home on the weekends when I chose and spending time with my friends when I felt like it. I got back in touch with my Indiana friend Favor, who was back in his hometown and miserable once again. We mended fences and decided that he should throw all caution to the wind and come to New York. He barely had money and nowhere to stay, but in that same spirit of spontaneity that we both shared, he bought a one way ticket, hopped on a plane and came to New York for the first time.

I asked a friend of mine to get him from the airport, and he was bursting with excitement when we first picked him up at LaGuardia. His excitement died down by the hour, as he first discovered that smoking cigarettes in New York was an expensive habit. We stopped by a store and he almost had a heart attack when he discovered cigarettes were twice the price they were in Indiana. His excitement went down another notch when he saw that the journey to the school I was going to was taking forever. We weren't as close to the city as he would have liked. When we got to my dorm room that was made for one person, he wasn't too excited about the super close living quarters. Despite it all though, he stayed with me for a few months in that tiny dorm room. He got a job as a waiter at a local restaurant, and we shared my meal plan to survive. It was frustrating at times but overall it was actually a really fun time for me, like an extended slumber party.

I was a little crowded in the room but I loved Favor so much, no sacrifice was too big. He became close with the other girls on my floor and we had some really good times. After a while, summer came, the slumber party ended as all fun things do, and it was time to move on. My time there was over and Favor also had business to attend to, he did ultimately come to New York to model after all. So he found him a room in an apartment in Washington Heights and decided he would cast his lot in the city of dreams. I took my mother's car without her permission because I knew in advance what she would have answered if I asked her. Favor and I moved his belongings from Long Island to the City on a gorgeous spring night in May, and so began a new chapter of life for him.

We kept in touch of course; I was the first person he knew here. But as he started to get settled and make a life for himself, and have new experiences, for better or worse, we drifted apart. I saw New York differently as an adult. I solidified my bond with childhood friends during this time of exploration and discovery for me. In a way, his joining me in New York spurred that need to be free and it stuck with me even when he didn't anymore. We were different people, headed down divergent paths in life. I was always happy for the connection I had with him and the role I played in helping him realize his lifelong dream of coming to New York and the role he played in my life, showing me what it was like to live and be unabashedly and unapologetically exactly who I am. He became an honorary New Yorker over the years. He has experienced life in that city in ways I never have, and in a reversal of roles, I have become the one with fantasies of visiting the place he now calls home.

Chapter Twenty Six

A New York Minute

I was mortified by the prospect of becoming hopelessly trapped in someone else's story.

- Lionel Shriver
We Need to Talk About Kevin

I begrudgingly moved back home after my chapter at Stony Brook was closed. I had a good paying job working for a local cable company. It was one of the more fun jobs I had. I really liked my co-workers. I made one really special friendship there that continues today. He has one of the greatest names I have ever encountered and I always just loved saying it. Something about the way it rolled off my tongue made me smile, so it's no wonder his name means *Brings Joy to the Home*. I want to call him the Homey. I met the Homey on the first day of training at work when he walked in super late. He looked a little mortified as he explained to the man standing at the front of the room that he had just moved here from Florida and it was his first time using public transportation in New York. He took an empty seat with all eyes on him and his face looking appropriately embarrassed. It was about a week later that he regaled me with his trademark wit one day outside during a fire drill that we started to really develop a friendship.

We had an undeniable chemistry. We shared a lot in

common and our differences were complimentary. We talked a lot, we started to carpool to work together, and then that turned into spending time together after work, and before I knew it, I had feelings for him. I always reminded him about my boyfriend in Indiana and that I would be going back. It's like I constantly talked about him to remind myself too. We shared so much with each other; it was an amazing experience getting to know him. He was new to New York so we did some exploring, and a lot of it was new to me too. We spent a lot of time together. We were both at turning points in our lives and had a lot going on. The time we spent together was therapeutic for us both. We had very similar musical tastes so a good amount of time was spent listening to and talking about music. We were very honest and open with each other, never judgmental. I think we were both using our pseudo-relationship as an oasis, a refuge from our complicated lives.

I had all these things I was figuring out when it came to who I was as a person, and the feelings I had about my family. I cried about my past and fantasized out loud about where I wanted to go. He had two children, one of whom he had full custody and one who was recently born. He was in a similar place, as you would find many people in their early twenties, looking to know yourself and where you belong. I told him all about mine and he told me about his. Every time I would feel like feelings for the Homey would get too strong, I would extinguish them with talk of my boyfriend and going back to Indiana.

I worked full time, 40 hours a week, at the cable company and then got a part-time job, about 25 hours a week, answering phones and making calls for a mortgage company. I saved almost every check that I received from the cable company and would use the checks from my other job as spending money. Even so, I was frugal with that money too and I often had money left over. I was determined to go back to Indianapolis with a lot of money so I could get a place right away and be a lot more stable from the start. Working these two jobs was stressful, but I was young and energetic and I had a goal in mind. I still found time to hang out with the Homey and my other friends. I was barely ever home.

I was not one of those kids who were in a rush to get a driver's license. I grew up in a place where getting around was fairly easy even if you didn't have a car. When I moved to the midwest I saw how different things were and I started to drive around town, although, legally I never made it past a learner's permit. When I first found myself back in New York, getting a little older and working two jobs I decided it was time to get my license. My parents had an older car sitting in the driveway that they always claimed I could drive but only after I got a license. My parents were adamant about not letting me drive any car that they owned. It was like they believed the minute I sat behind the wheel, it would spontaneously combust. I would be tremendously frustrated trying to convince them to let me practice driving in their car.

Since my then fourteen-year-old brother was given chances to get behind the wheel without even being old enough for a permit. I was told to find another way to get my license first and then we could talk about me driving. There I was twenty-two years old taking driving lessons. They were pretty expensive and I took a class once a week. I had the basics down because I drove around Indianapolis all the time. There, I hardly ever contended with traffic, I never got on the highway and I would drive these wide open roads over flat terrain as far as the eye could see. Not too much twisting or turning and no defensive driving necessary. I had a hard time with those concepts, three-point turns and parallel parking.

After the fourth class, the instructor was pretty frustrated with my lack of progress and he asked me if I practiced driving at all. I said no, I never drove, except for when I was taking the lessons. He said that if I didn't practice, I was wasting my money because no one passes the test only practicing once a week. I would never learn to parallel-park only doing it once a week for a few minutes. Sure enough, I failed the road test when it came around. After that, the instructor volunteered to talk to my mom and explain the importance of me practicing more than just with him. She nodded and smiled at the man and as soon as he left, she made sure she stated that she didn't really care what he said. She wouldn't be stupid enough to let me ruin her car when I didn't even know what I was doing. So, it continued that way for a few months, and I failed the road test two more times. Until one day after a frustrated and tearful plea for help, one of my friends from church agreed to help me and let me practice in her car. With about a week's worth of practice, driving every day, practicing my parallel parking over and over, I finally passed the driving test on my fourth try.

If I thought that it would make my parents happy at all, I was mistaken. My news was not met with joy at all, but with a new set of rules that apply when I am driving their car. They so graciously reminded me repeatedly of who actually owned the car and that I was a mere borrower. Even at 22 years old, I was being micro-managed about my whereabouts, especially when driving the car. I would be told sometimes I could not take the car and not given a valid reason, it often seemed like a power play. It was so frustrating for me. It felt like every time I tried to take an autonomous step forward, there would be deliberate actions to hinder my independence. It was solidifying the feeling that if I wanted to make my own decisions without interference, I could not do that living at home with my mother. I realized that I would always be a child to them, that I would always be that girl with book smarts and no common sense who cannot be trusted.

A year went by faster than it seemed at the time. I hung out with Homey a lot and was in constant contact with Wise in Indiana. There were a few visits back and forth. I told him about everything I was doing and he told me the same I assumed. He mentioned spending time with a girl and it was a little hard to hear but it didn't change my feelings for wanting to come back, although he was constantly throwing out hints to the contrary. I wanted things to work between us for a variety of reasons, none of them being the right one. I wanted to prove all the naysayers wrong. I wanted to see our relationship through because I always imagined myself married by 25 and it was rapidly approaching. I wanted out of New York, and away from my parents. So I ignored when he subtly let on that maybe it would be best for me to stay where I was. After a while, he moved in with his oldest brother in a town about 45 minutes away from Indianapolis to Bloomington. When he moved, he started calling less and less and was available even less than he was calling. One day he said, "Maybe we should take a break," and abruptly ended the phone call. I called him back over and over until (in my eyes) I convinced him we were meant to be.

Now that I look back at that time, I am almost ashamed of my willful ignorance when it came to that situation. I just wanted so badly out of my current life and I lacked the maturity and insight to know that moving back to Indiana to be with Wise was not the only way out.

Chapter Twenty Seven

Full Circle City

*The more we love the more we lose. The more we lose the
more we learn. The more we learn the more we love. It
comes full circle. Life is the school, love is the lesson.*
- *Kate McGahan*

I ended up back in the mid-west not long after summer
ended. My parents reluctantly accepted the move I made
when my determination was steadfast. They offered to
let me keep the car that I had been driving while I was
in New York. I shipped the old car to Indianapolis, and
I stayed with the Keeper again while I looked for a place. I
was so confident and optimistic about the future. This was
different than the other times I came to Indiana. This time, I
was armed with a decent amount of money, a car and a plan.

On my very first night there, I called my old friend Young,
one third of my old hard partying trio to see what was going on.
It was a Friday night so there was guaranteed to be some sort of
hang out situation happening. She nervously responded to my
inquiry which made me wonder out loud what was going on. She
reluctantly to told me that her cousin was hanging out with them
that night too. Her cousin was new in town, she moved there while
I was in New York, and she was the girl Wise told me he spent some
time with. I assumed maybe Young just thought I didn't know
about it, so I brushed her concerns aside and assured her I had no

issues with anyone. She informed me that her cousin might have issues with me. Young proceeded to tell me that things got a lot more serious between them than he let on. They were in a full-fledged, friends with benefits situation, and made no secret of it. While I was gone, they were very open about flaunting whatever semblance of a relationship they had. I was hurt that Wise actually had sex with someone else and also hurt that we had a plan in place to prevent this kind of hurt. I was so angry with him. Here I was the first night back, and I didn't do anything but cry myself to sleep.

I should have seen the giant red flag that was raised when I returned to Indianapolis and for that first whole week, Wise didn't even make his way to see me from Bloomington. A week after the devastating news, I drove with Young to Bloomington to a Halloween party and I finally confronted him face to face. He apologized and I forgave him easily because I was terrified at the prospect of the plan I had put so much time and effort into would not come to fruition. I comforted myself with the old notion that long distance relationships were hard and now I was back so we could work on things from here on out. I brushed all thoughts out of my head and wiped the slate clean.

I loved his family like they were my family. I had grown so close to all of them in different ways, at least that's how I felt. My boyfriend's younger sister was in High School by that time and did a lot of things that typical High School girls did. She had a best friend whose name means *One with Dark Hair.* I think it's quite appropriate to call her Dark Hair because she has had a natural talent for styling hair since she was little and has made a career out of it as an adult. Dark Hair had a rocky childhood, and her rough journey landed her on the doorstep of the Keeper's home when she was just fifteen years old. She moved into the house and even though she was so young, we formed a deep bond. We bonded over things that we quickly realized that the people around us did not understand. She lived there with us and the Keeper tried to be somewhat nurturing toward her. I think everyone around her failed to see the tremendous pain she was constantly enduring. I watched her work part time at Wendy's while going to school and always maintaining good grades. When she was a senior, she added cosmetology school to the load and she fought through it all so she could have a more stable life than the statistics said she should. She was an old soul living a young life. After we became close, she was more comfortable in the company of me and my older friends than people her own age. She had seen and gone through much more than not just her peers but some of us had. She remains a lifelong friend, and we have even lived together in short spurts at almost every stage of my life that came to follow.

I soon got a job at a clinic on the south side of town. I worked at the place where Wise's mother the Keeper had been working for twenty plus years. I worked in the office, filing charts, registering patients, answering phones, and all the usual drudgery that goes on in a doctor's office. The job, which paid fairly well, was a 9-5 Monday through Friday gig with benefits. I loved having my weekends off. Indianapolis didn't have the best job market, so I considered myself lucky to have such a stable job. I envisioned that I would work there for a long time as did most of the people who worked there. I would go to work all week, and then on Fridays, I would have a bag packed before I headed to work. After work, I would battle rush hour all the way to Bloomington to spend every second of my weekend with Wise. The apartment he shared with his brother had such a cozy feeling and I loved being there. I would cook sometimes, although my food wasn't all that great, I was still learning. We would order food sometimes and we would binge watch whole entire series' like the Sopranos and Arrested Development. He worked part-time at Subway and after that a liquor store, but he wasn't exactly hustling at that time in life. My car went through a lot, the windshield wipers weren't working at one point and neither was the heat. That didn't stop me from soldiering it in the cold and snow to get to Wise.

After a couple of months being back in town, I found my own apartment. I moved into the exact same building that I almost got evicted from when I left, which I considered very symbolic at the time. Its symbolism was further noted when I got an apartment on a much higher floor with a much nicer view of downtown. The view from my window could have been on a postcard, it was so perfect. I was overlooking the stadium where the Colt's played football and every inch of downtown, and on a really clear day, I could even see the flat landscape that lay beyond. I loved it. A co-worker who got all new furniture gave me her old furniture and I was content as can be in my new home. I really loved my place.

Chapter Twenty Eight

Things Fall Apart

*"Yes, she would love Logan after they were married. She
could see no way for it to come about, but
Nanny and the old folks had said it, so it must be so.
Husbands and wives always loved each other, and
that was what marriage meant. It was just so.
Janie felt glad of the thought, for then it wouldn't
seem so destructive and moldy. She wouldn't be lonely
anymore. But anyhow Janie went on inside to wait for
love to begin. The new moon had been up and down
three times before she got worried in mind..."*

- Zora Neale Hurston
Their Eyes Were Watching God

I hadn't been there long when I suggested to Wise that he move in with me when he complained about being tired of life in Bloomington. He took me up on the offer and I was more than excited to have him with me every day, which was a situation we had not had in years. He had a car that was so horrible that it was literally being held together by a string. He barely made it to Indianapolis with that horrible car and it didn't last long. Mine was also old and constantly having issues so I decided I would get myself a newer car because I had the income now to make payments. I got a small red ford focus and it felt like Wise drove it more than I did. His friend who was going through a rough breakup also needed a place and he took the second bedroom in the apartment temporarily. I had company over quite often and I had fallen into a nice routine with my life. I was in such a good space, despite the problems that I considered small at the time.

I loved Wise, but I was growing annoyed with his increasing insensitivity towards me. I started to realize that he was always this way, but now I woke up to the insensitivity every day. He always had this thing where he would brag about being an asshole. He and most of the people in his family are vicious with their words, always sprinkled with chuckles that gave the guise of humor. Sometimes it was humorous, but sometimes it was just plain mean. If you are at all thin-skinned and sensitive, then they are not people who would be advisable company. They are the last people you want to expose your weaknesses or shortcomings to, because they will mock you without mercy.

The most embarrassing and sensitive of subjects would never deter them from laughing at you. Wise was witty and had great one liners and quick comebacks, so this made for a gregarious person who everyone pretty much liked. Even as people laughed at his jokes that were often obnoxious, they would shake their heads and tell him how he is crazy or how much of an ass he is, which he seemed to consider a badge of honor. In the beginning, he wasn't like that toward me as much. Maybe he was but I might have been too infatuated to see it. Three years later, rose colored glasses broken, I frequently nursed my bruised feelings and started to realize that I wanted to be with someone who was nicer and more attentive. I was always realistic though when dealing with most people I was close with. I accepted his imperfections and told myself hey you can't have it all.

I was fairly content for months in the apartment. I was so

happy that he was living with me that I was blind to the fact that he was taking his sweet time looking for a job. He was enjoying the space he was in, which should have disturbed me more than it did. He would drive me to work every day in my new car and drop me off because he didn't want to be stuck in the apartment all day. About half the time he was late picking me up, and I would have to wait for him after having worked a long day. I supported our whole lifestyle. It was my job, my apartment and my car that kept us surviving. He found this job at a summer camp at a church that also had a school. They wanted to keep him on to do music with the kids, even after the summer. I was excited that he found a job but it was still winter and the job was months away. He was content with lounging around while I paid the rent for months with him jobless. At the time, it bothered me, but I didn't know how to say it so I never did. I just did my part as the dutiful girlfriend because I didn't want to ruin our path to marriage.

Ever since we had moved in together, my mother, who acted as though it was the end of the world and she went wrong in raising me (direct quote), was laying on the pressure really thick. Every time I talked to her on the phone she would talk about not liking that we lived together and pressuring us to get married. I obviously was all for that notion so I would pass the pressure on to him. Under all of that duress, he finally surrendered and reluctantly agreed to a wedding next year sometime, probably just to get me and my mom to stop. I was kind of sad about that at the time. Like every little girl, I wanted him to get down on one knee with a diamond and be happy and excited about marrying me, not reluctant like he was. In public, though I was more than glowing and excited to tell my friends we were engaged, and I wore a ring my mom gave me, when I told her, I didn't have a ring from him. I feel so silly now for doing this, but I just really wanted the fantasy so badly. I was ignoring reality and doing everything in my power to create it.

Chapter Twenty Nine
Holder Of The Heel

Now my belly is as noble as my heart.
- Gabriela Mistral

I started to feel sick in May of that year. At first, I thought it was severe PMS, but my period never came. It happened that way with me sometimes though so this didn't alarm me too much as I had a lot of issues and never got my period regularly anyway. I would often experience PMS without my period. I was driving in the car with a friend and was describing how I was feeling out loud. As I did, it felt like a boulder dropped in my stomach because the thought crossed my mind almost at the exact same time the words came out of her mouth "you might be pregnant". In the car that day, I explained to her about my medical issues and that it was highly unlikely that I was pregnant. I spoke confidently about knowing that it had to be something else. I went home and told Wise and the next day I took a pregnancy test.

I was in the apartment alone when I saw the two pink lines appear immediately. I didn't even have to wait the recommended two minutes. I looked at it in silent disbelief for the first few seconds and when it sunk in I screamed out loud "I'm gonna have a baby!" and started laughing uncontrollably. I sincerely believed that I would live a childless existence. I had come to accept and even embrace never having any children. I told myself and other people that I didn't want children. Wise and I even discussed adopting in the future. I didn't know that it was a defense mechanism I was using. Deep down, that fact really hurt me until that moment sitting on the edge of my bathtub crying tears of joy. I cried so very hard and was unbelievably happy.

Happier than I ever thought I would be. I sat on the couch in silence for what seemed like hours waiting for Wise to walk through the door. I remember hearing the key in the lock and bursting with anticipation. He barely had one foot in the door when I screamed, "I'm pregnant!" He was like "for real?" with a puzzled look of shock on his face. He fell on his knees in front of me on the couch and put his head in my lap. His eyes welled with tears but they never fell. He wrapped his arms around me as the tears rolled down my face. No other words. We shared such a sweet and intimate silence between us in that moment and I just knew everything was going to be okay.

My pregnancy was rocky from the very beginning; lots of cramping and spotting and morning sickness. I was actually diagnosed with an extreme version of morning sickness they called hyper emesis. I would throw up all day every day, no matter what. I could drink water or eat candy and I would throw up. Anything that passed my throat came back up. I shed weight quickly and was pale and sluggish and so miserable every day. I called my mom one day when I was in the office alone because everyone else went to lunch. I told her I was pregnant. She cried as if I told her someone she loved died. She was vicious in her expression of her disappointment, very harsh. I knew she would feel a certain way about me not being married, but I was so shocked and so hurt by her response. I couldn't stop crying for most of the rest of day in between fits of throwing up. She told me how she knew this would happen with us living together and how all the raising she did was in vain because I turned out to be a statistic.

She asked me if I took fertility drugs. When I said no she acted as if she did not believe me because she knew about my medical issues and that there was a slim chance of me getting pregnant. She made it clear to me about how much I hurt her, how much I disappointed her. I expected some of that sentiment from her, I really did. Her response was so much more vitriolic than I expected. Her words to me that day knocked the wind out of me. After having to step outside to gather myself, I went home early and spent the rest of the day in bed. As I laid there in silence, I remember being so angry with her. Why? How could she be like this to me? I saw this as the miracle it was from moment one. Instead of seeing the fact that I got pregnant despite the odds being against it as the wonder that it was. She thought it was a reason for her to assume I did something sneaky and reckless, not that I was the recipient of a real life miracle.

It bothered me that I had to always be made to feel bad about who I was and the things I did. I was living on my own, managing my own life just fine. I had a great job with maternity leave, a home, a reliable car, a boyfriend who was so great with his nieces and nephews that I had no reason to believe he wouldn't be a good dad. I felt good about the place I was in. When I got up the next day, I vowed that no one could make me ashamed of being pregnant. I was not a teen mom, I was twenty-three years old. I wasn't on welfare or asking anyone for anything. I was so honored and felt so lucky to experience something I never thought I would and no one would take that from me. Having this kid changed me in so many ways, almost from the second I was aware of his presence. He toughened my spine a little bit in the beginning when I needed it.

I had a little scare very early on when I started to have symptoms which usually happen when you are about to give birth. I was only about four months at the time so the doctor placed me on bed rest for the remaining duration of the pregnancy. I was diagnosed with yet another pregnancy condition not long after that, it was called preeclampsia. This meant that I was dealing with an abnormally high blood pressure which was dangerous for both me and the baby. I was told to stop working but I didn't. I hadn't been at my job long enough to get paid maternity leave so I was trying to save as much as I could.

Wise started working by then but he was not making a lot of money and it wasn't as if he was that keen on sharing it with me. He landed something better that wasn't supposed to start until the first week of August. Throughout that summer, He was growing increasingly distant, but I was so sick all the time, I barely had time to deal with myself much less him, so I didn't argue when he wasn't as nice as I felt he could be to his pregnant, sick-and-on-bed rest girlfriend. I just cried silently. I complained to my friends but never to him about his callous treatment. I was surprised because he was very happy when I first got pregnant.

I know I wasn't perfect. I was always prone to melodrama all my life, so I think this fact while annoying before, became a real issue. I think he wanted me to tough it out and I cried and was worried and neurotic every step of the way. He didn't give me any of that tender loving care that I expected. There were no offers to carry my bags or get me something to eat. If I asked, it was often met with annoyance. I went to work long after I was placed on bed rest with no protests from him. I would be so sick on the drive there, sometimes having him pull over so I could throw up. In the afternoon, I stood outside hot and dizzy and weak waiting for him to pick me up late in my car. I just kept telling myself that once I had this baby, everything would be better. Wise and I were just going through a rough patch in our relationship and it just happened to coincide with the pregnancy. I mean, we had been together for years, it happens, I told myself. We were still together, still planning to get married and raise our baby in the future. I kept holding on to these things, although they were slipping through my fingers.

I worked at a doctor's office and my medical insurance was through the same company but I used a different facility. It wasn't unusual that my personal doctor and my boss crossed paths often and had known each other for a long time. Apparently my name was brought up when they saw each other at a work conference. My boss said she was talking about the fact that we never go too long without an office baby, how we were always having someone pregnant in the office. She then mentioned me. I told them I was going to that doctor, the whole office knew. My doctor was shocked to hear that I was still at work. The doctor informed my boss that she placed me on bed rest a while ago and that I shouldn't be working.

When we were at work the next time, she called me into her office and asked me if the doctor placed me on bed rest. When I told her yes, she told me I had to take my maternity leave effective immediately. She expressed concern for my health but also for the office having liability if anything happened to me while I was working for them. I went home that day, a little upset because I needed the money but a little relieved too because it truly was becoming too much for me. I discussed it with Wise, and although he wasn't pleased with the loss of income, he assured me we would be okay when he started his new position soon.

Chapter Thirty
Eight Six

He walks away
The sun goes down
He takes the day
But I'm grown
And in your way
In this blue shade
My tears dry on their own
               - Amy Winehouse

About a week after being home on bed rest, on a Sunday morning the first week of August when he started his new job, Wise gently nudged me and woke me from a fitful slumber. He asked me to go for a ride with him because he wanted to talk to me privately and we had an overnight guest on the couch along with his best friend in the other room. As we left the apartment gates, we got right into traffic because the streets were blocked off for a marathon. As we slowly crept up the street and around the corner, he came right out and told me he didn't want to be with me anymore. My first reaction was disbelief. What? I'm pregnant with your baby and you're leaving me? When he insisted that that was how he felt and nothing could change his mind, I easily flowed into anger. I was livid. I threw a tantrum like a toddler and I truly don't even remember the rest of the car ride. I do remember getting back inside the apartment and calling my mother because it was her birthday. I tried to muster up the speck of joy I had left to sound happy when I said happy birthday but she immediately asked me what was wrong. I burst out crying and told her Wise was leaving me. She didn't say too much.

I felt so crazy like there was hot lava flowing through my veins and it made me want to rip my skin off. I was murderous with rage for days. I really felt lost, like I didn't know what to do, like I was walking around in a catatonic state, not doing normal things. Just staring off for hours sometimes, other times after hours of crying, I would get possessed by rage all over again and break things and throw things. I tried many times to reason with him and compromise, but he insisted that this relationship was not what he wanted, baby be damned. He talked about girls he met right in front of me, only days after we broke up. He flirted on the phone openly with girls, spoke disrespectfully about me within my earshot, and was trying his best it seemed to make me miserable. He would laugh when I got mad. It was torture for me. I was still sick and on bedrest and throwing up all the time when this was going on.

We still lived in the apartment together for about a week when one day he approached me and asked me what I planned on doing. I told him I didn't have plans yet. Well, he basically said, it's not like you can afford to stay here if I leave because you don't have any money coming in. The lease is in your name and you are going to have issues with that. Why not just let us stay here and pay the rent till the lease is over and *you* leave. The rejection I felt was the twist of the knife that he already drove through my heart.

I didn't hesitate to go because seeing him every day was making me want to kill him, and in retrospect, I think that was the plan. To make me miserable so I would leave the apartment. I look back at that moment as a crucial turning point for me, I wish I would have stayed and kicked him out of *my* place. I wish I would have toughed it out because now I look back and I had so many options. I had this heavy cloak of sadness on and as they say, I couldn't see the forest for the trees. I wasn't thinking straight, I was so devastated and physically drained from the nature of my pregnancy. I needed help in so many ways but I was utterly helpless. I often wish I had someone there to talk sense into me, but at the time, I had no one on my side and I was left wandering. For a while when I told the story to my friends, I would say I got put out of my own place. I had to come out of the haze of hate that I had for him to realize, he actually just manipulated me into leaving which is still nefarious, but not the same as putting me out. I wish I would have seen that I didn't have to leave at the time, but something in me was telling me I had to. I felt so alone and the depth of my despair and depression were indescribable. I couldn't see past it enough to make even common sense decisions. I think how I felt then was the definition of trauma.

Chapter Thirty One

Everywhere And Nowhere

There are wounds that never show on the body that are deeper and more hurtful than anything that bleeds.

- Laurell K. Hamilton

I stayed with his sister-in-law for a while who had two children. The deal was that I would stay there and in exchange, take her kids to daycare in the mornings. I ended up doing a lot more than that. She would come home in the afternoons and get sloppy drunk and pass out. Then she would ask me to get the kids in the afternoon also, who have been at the daycare from the minute it opened at 6 am till the minute they closed at 6 pm. The daycare wasn't all that close to her house and she never gave me gas money.

I was living off of my last check from my job and was penny pinching a lot and the majority of my money went to gas to drive her kids around. I had to witness a lot of her dysfunction which I didn't want to deal with on top of how I feeling physically and emotionally. To top it off, she talked badly about me to Wise, complaining about the fact that all I did was lay around (uh, I was on bed rest) and do nothing. I left there and stayed with my good friend Young for a while but her life was also in transition, she was breaking up with a long time boyfriend and had just been taken advantage of more than once. She was in a vulnerable space and I think feeling used at the time. It wasn't a great time to stay with her but I literally had nowhere else to go that was a remotely friendly environment. I felt so trapped.

I was still in touch with the Homey, who I had met at work in New York when I was there. When I went back to visit my family, we would see each other and catch up. He felt bad for me with everything going on; he was someone I talked to every day. He let me cry on the phone and complain as much as I want after which he would do his best to make me laugh. I was grateful for him. One day, he offered me a one-way ticket to New York with the promise of a return ticket after a couple of weeks. I jumped at the chance to get out of there. I flew to New York when I was about five months pregnant and I stayed there for about a month. When I told my mom I would be coming there, she was hesitant. I told her about everything I was dealing with and while I knew I needed to get certain things together, I was so overwhelmed and needed the break. She wasn't really moved by it. She felt it was not a smart idea to come to New York. She said that the church people are going to be using me as an example, like a cautionary tale for all the young girls and she didn't want me subjected to that. It hurt me that I was having complications and had been abandoned and she was not at all eager to see me. We had barely spoken since I told her what was happening and I was disappointed by the seeming lack of concern for me and my well being. As always, I felt that my shortcomings overshadowed everything in her eyes. I told her that people already knew I was pregnant and I was not ashamed, let them talk. I was met with silence before she muttered the words "Just don't go to church while you're here." That let me know that while I wasn't ashamed, she was.

I got on the waiting list for an income based apartment, that is to say, an apartment in the projects. I was just happy to get approved; it made me feel better about my future. The rent was cheap of course, I still had my job waiting for me to return six weeks after giving birth, I still had my car although I was dodging the repo man. I figured I would dodge payments until I started working again and hoped I could keep the car; as a backup though I chose a place close to the bus line so I could always get to work. I was starting to come out of the haze a little bit. It might sound strange to say, but it helped that he was being very mean to me. He would ask me why I was calling him with such disdain in his voice, it would pierce my soul every time so I stopped calling.

When I called to tell him things the doctor said or to say I needed something, he basically told me it was not his concern and to call him when the baby was born. He lashed out at me so harshly every time we interacted that I had no choice but to get it through my head. It took me about a month before I shook off the devastation enough to start picking up the pieces. I pretty much had my ducks in a row; I just needed a place to stay for about two months while I waited for my name to come up on the list. They told me a place would be available in January and I was due to give birth in February, so it seemed like it was working out somewhat.

I spent one glorious month in New York, faced the inevitable judgement (but not as much as I thought I would), saw my friends and felt rejuvenated. The Homey was just so nice to me. He would come get me every day after work because he knew about the tension between me and my family. My mom was ashamed and barely talking to me and my dad wasn't talking to me at all. I slept there but spent every second I could somewhere else. Other than that, the visit was awesome. Like salve on a third-degree burn.

The Homey took me to eat all my favorite things, was patient with me, offered me those back and foot rubs that I missed out on with Wise. As a matter of fact, the Homey gave me all the TLC I was missing and wanted so badly, carrying my bags and being considerate and just, in general, treating me like someone in a delicate condition. It highlighted to me how much I was not being treated like that by anyone else. My family was pissed and not talking to me so they couldn't really care less about how I was feeling. My child's father was treating me so badly, being rude, callous and not understanding at all. I never understood that either. I wasn't cheating on him, I wasn't cursing him out every day, I only ever had good intentions towards him. If I did do things to hurt or upset him, it was never with that intention. I know I wasn't perfect because no one on earth is, but I was lost as to why he was so angry and hateful toward me. I hated his guts for the way he treated me, I felt I didn't deserve to be treated as if I did something wrong when he himself said that the decision was about him.

Returning to Indianapolis after a month in New York was bittersweet. My pregnancy was advancing and I was ready to go home and get things straight but I was enjoying my time with my friends and the Homey in particular. When I got back, the reality hit me that I was homeless for the next few months until my name came up on the waiting list for the apartment. I had a hard time settling in anywhere so I was bouncing around and sleeping where I could. I even asked the Keeper of the Keys if I could stay with her until I got my place and she said no. Her reason was that Wise was her son and he was clearly upset with me and she didn't want to get in the middle. She wanted him to feel comfortable coming to her house and he wouldn't if I was there. She said "he's my family. If you need help you should go home to *your* family." That one statement devastated me. I didn't know that my status with them was officially demoted despite the fact that I was carrying her grandchild.

I thought her response rather cold and contrary to the way she treated me before, and it changed how I felt about her. I felt a little stupid and naive because I actually thought the love for me was about me. I clearly knew they initially accepted me because I was Wise's girlfriend but as the years went on I really thought that my bond with some members of the family, especially her, transcended that title and that we had a true connection between us as individuals. It hurt so much to know I was wrong. It was like a second heartbreak I had to endure from the situation. I cried and mourned the relationship between myself and the Keeper of the Keys and I had to come to terms with how it had changed.

Chapter Thirty Two

Southern Comfort

She took the moon over Georgia.
She'd rather have a million stars in the sky
than a gold mine.

She took the moon over Georgia.
When it came down to his world or mine,
she chose the moon over Georgia.
                                              - Shenandoah

One day after having a particularly salty argument with Wise, I was lying on Young's couch about a week after I got back to town from New York. I received a phone call on Young's house phone from my uncle. My mother's older brother was the elder in the family now that my grandmother was gone, and we all hold a respect for him that denotes that. When he called me at her house all the way from Florida and gave me a dose of tough love, I listened. Most of my mom's side of the family was living in Georgia and they had been talking to me since they became aware of the situation I was facing. Even my immediate family had purchased a home close to everyone else. They planned on moving there as soon as their home sold in New York. They found an amazing deal on a foreclosed house so they jumped on it. The house was sitting there empty waiting for them. Everyone, including my mom, was trying to convince me to move there since

I had nowhere to stay, but Georgia wasn't even on my radar.

Whenever I visited I always thought of the suburb about 45 minutes outside of Atlanta was so country. Even in Indianapolis, I stayed in an urban area. I just really hated the suburbs and loathed the country. I had no desire to move there at all, but my uncle reminded me that (even though it was hard to hear the same thing from the Keeper), they were my family and they were offering me help. He reassured me that there was no judgment waiting for me in Georgia, just people who love me and want to help. I made my decision to leave for Georgia before we even hung up. My uncle drove 8 hours from Florida four days later to pick me up at the Atlanta airport. I couldn't carry too much because of the condition I was in so I gave away 80 percent of my belongings and took only what could fit in the two duffel bags I could manage. He insisted that he wanted to personally pick me up because if I didn't get off the plane, he would immediately hit the road to Indiana to get me. I was so grateful for the display of love, the absence of judgment, because I needed it badly.

After all the initial fanfare of my arrival, and the requisite bad mouthing of Wise for leaving me when I was having his baby, my uncle went back to Florida and I settled in. I found myself alone in a six bedroom house at the end of a dark cul-de-sac, more depressed than I had ever been in my life so far. I felt so useless and unloved, so utterly low down. I was still throwing up multiple times a day. By that time, it had become routine, but the unpleasantness of it never decreased. I was losing weight and I was physically and emotionally drained beyond capacity. My thoughts of suicide were thwarted when I thought about the life growing inside me. I was in such a low place at the time, I am absolutely sure I would have done something drastic if I wasn't pregnant.

The thoughts going through my head were a threat to my life. My mom had come around, but only a little, they both still were very cold toward me and still ashamed about my out of wedlock pregnancy. It made me feel even worse that the person whose baby it was didn't even think me worthy of respect. Not even the small level of respect it took to have a phone conversation where he wasn't saying something hurtful or hanging up on me. I felt overlooked by the rest of the world. I felt no one cared about my physical plight. They all cared more about my shortcomings as a person. I felt I had no worth and I sincerely wanted to die. Sometimes it made me angry that I couldn't do anything to myself because I desperately wanted to hurt myself some days. My baby would kick in such an extreme way, it seemed as if he was flipping and doing somersaults. It was almost as if he was reminding me that it wasn't just my body at the moment. I was sharing it with someone else. I couldn't keep on thinking thoughts of suicide with life inside me. Before he was even fully formed, my baby saved my life.

Chapter Thirty Three

The Real McKoy

I note the obvious differences
in the human family.
Some of us are serious,
some thrive on comedy.
Some declare their lives are lived
as true profundity,
and others claim they really live
the real reality.

- Maya Angelou

My family that lived in Georgia is a unique bunch. After my grandmother died, they all seemed to want to live close to each other. For many years, none of my mother's sisters that were in America lived more than a 7-minute drive from one another, with two houses directly next door to one another. Their unique past has no doubt affected their way of life today. They are loud, animated, outspoken, jovial and they love their offspring so fiercely, that the intensity threatens to choke the life out of them. They will never say the words though. They won't hug or kiss or be especially affectionate at all but they will give anything and help family however they can. They are always ready to fight for the ones they love. When I first arrived in Georgia, I realized that I never really lived close to them as far as I could remember. When I was a child in Jamaica, I did, but not since I was a toddler.

I was always visiting them wherever they lived, so they always seemed like the cool side of the family. I saw my dad's side all the time when we lived in New York, and we spent most of our holidays with them. They were reserved people who didn't speak too loudly, who had impeccable manners, socially acceptable, politically correct topics of conversation and moderate laughter. They had dinners on nice plates and seemed so refined to me as a child. My mom raised us that way too. We lived in a quiet home where we were not allowed to raise our voices, slam doors or even speak harshly to each other.

My mother is a black sheep of sorts in her family because there is no one else like that among them. They are loud in speech, laughter, and life. Topics of a more tawdry nature are never avoided but discussed with reckless abandon. They are all extremely quick-witted which made following conversations among the adults one of my favorite things as a kid. Whenever they get together and reminisce or just talk in general, the laughter is constant and intense. I was really looking forward to being around them more often.

While I love my father's side of the family they were relatively close, the closeness among this side of my family was exponentially deeper. They were often at each other's homes and shared dinners spontaneously. They would take care of each other's children and share whatever someone else needed with them. If one went to the grocery store and saw something everyone could use on sale like say toothpaste, they would buy it in bulk and share them or at least call around and inform everyone else about the sale. Nothing was too sacred, they would share cars if need be. They would never ever deny you a plate of food if you rang their doorbell at dinner time. Despite their rambunctious nature, they were for the most part deeply religious. Everyone attended the same church religiously every Sunday. In keeping with my lifelong habit, I started attending their church too when I moved to Georgia. If only because I did nothing else during the week and it was a chance to go somewhere.

I officially lived at the house my parents bought by myself, but I spent most of the time at one aunt's house or another. I hated being alone. One of my aunts ran a daycare. Her name means High Tower. She remains one of my favorite people. Her generosity and compassion are unmatched. She is able to pull off this sense of warmth and welcoming about her without being affectionate. She is so easy to be around, that even in the few years that followed, sitting at her house watching her cook was all the remedy I needed for the trouble in my soul. I would sit at her house all day long back then while she watched a few children. We would watch hours upon hours of judge shows and talk shows all day long. I was eating so well and looking better than I had the whole pregnancy. I was drawing closer to my due date and finally got to a doctor after not having seen one for a couple of months due to the instability of my life at the time. My other uncle that lives in Florida was nice enough to let me have an old car of his that he no longer drove. It was old and had a lot of issues, but I was so grateful to have a car after my car was repossessed in Indiana while I was on the month long trip to New York.

My older cousin who has always been more like an aunt to me lived next door to her mom, the High Tower. My cousin's name means Palm Tree, and she is as firmly rooted as her name implies. She is one of the strongest people I have ever met, and I have always admired her ability to speak her mind sometimes ever so harshly and all the while remaining likable. She lived next door to her mom, the High Tower, with her husband and three children. Another aunt of mine lived not too far away, with the house my mom purchased being about five minutes down the street. During the last part of my pregnancy, I spent every day with them and drove home to my house some nights and other nights I stayed in the guest room at my cousin's house.

One of the times I spent the night there, very early in the morning my cousin knocked on the door before she left for work. She informed me that her husband's cousin was asleep on their couch so I should not be alarmed if I woke up and was alone in the house with this stranger. He had hung out with his cousin the night before and didn't want to take the long ride home after it had gotten too late. I thought nothing of it all. He woke up and left and I didn't lay eyes on him. A week later, I spent the night again and was awakened by a knock on the door and it was the same guy. He spoke through the door because my natural paranoia did not allow me to open it. He let me know that we were in the house alone together once again and that his cousins asked him to fix something so don't be alarmed. I thanked him and laid back down, a little weirded out by this phantom cousin of Palm Tree's husband.

The next day, I finally met him face to face and he stared at me as if he were trying to take in every detail of my face. I was six months pregnant by then and still going through all my issues. I sat on a couch with my feet up feeling sick to my stomach and annoyed by the fact that my family observed his interest and were joking about us getting together. I don't think anyone took it seriously given my condition, but he asked me for my number before he left that day. I saw no harm, especially since

I didn't know anyone else in the area. We talked on the phone for a couple of weeks and we hit it off in a friendly way. Not one time during those phone conversations did I think that he had any romantic intention or otherwise ulterior motive. It was nice to have someone to talk to after I was so depressed for so long.

Chapter Thirty Four

Crystal Child

...Then Jacob was left alone; and a Man wrestled with him until the breaking of day. Now when He saw that He did not prevail against him, He touched the socket of his hip; and the socket of Jacob's hip was out of joint as He wrestled with him.

And He said, "Let Me go, for the day breaks."
But he said, "I will not let You go unless You bless me!"
So the Man said to him, "What is your name?"

He said, "Jacob."
And He said, "Your name shall no longer be called Jacob, but Israel; for you have struggled with God and with men, and have prevailed..."
- Genesis 32:24-28

I woke up one Saturday morning in December and my feet were swollen to about twice the size they normally were. I was annoyed but otherwise, I chalked it up to pregnant people problems. I got out of bed and walked to the bathroom and was taken aback by the appearance of my face. It too was swollen. I was a little more worried but I didn't say anything to anyone. That evening there was a banquet at the church my family attended and I decided to go. I was getting dressed and when my foot literally could not fit into my shoes and I had to borrow a pair from my cousin, I knew I had an issue.

I called my mother in New York and while I was getting ready, while I was dialing I took note of my hands and fingers being stiff and swollen also. I told her what I dealing with and her response was, "it sounds like the preeclampsia is getting worse, get to the hospital immediately". I ignored her initially for a sort of complicated reason. I have always felt that my flair for melodrama came from my mother; she is the queen of it. She is the type of person who will warn you that a paper cut can get infected with gangrene, and your finger will have to get amputated if you don't put alcohol on it. Your aching left arm could be a stroke, "it happens to young people too, you know?" I could hear her say. She is quick to suggest a trip to the emergency room for the slightest of ailments because she is a firm believer in the better safe than sorry philosophy.

Sometimes (as I did this night) I brushed off her admonitions as pure histrionics. I went to the banquet. I woke up on Sunday morning still feeling a little bit off but not particularly sick. My mom so happened to call my cousin's house that night and she heard me in the background and was thoroughly upset about the fact that I didn't go the hospital. So early Monday morning I drove myself to the hospital very exasperated and annoyed because I kept insisting I felt fine. It was only a little swelling. I'm pregnant. Pregnant people swell. I fully expected to go back home later that day. I was planning in my head as I drove there how I was going to clean my room later and wondering what the upcoming Christmas season was going to be like because it was my first in Georgia. I chatted with my aunt in the car, laughing about mundane things. I never expected to not see outside again for ten days. I just went to shut her up basically because I knew she would not quit until I went.

As soon as they checked me in, the nurse took one look at

my blood pressure and decided that I would have to be admitted. She looked at me wide-eyed and asked me how in the world I was still standing. She said that with blood pressure this high, I should be passed out in a coma somewhere. This alarmed me because I wasn't feeling sick at all. I asked the nurse to clarify, "so does this mean I am not going home today?" She looked at me sadly and shook her head no. I asked her how long she thought it might be and she said, "probably for the rest of your pregnancy." I was so shocked to hear this and I kept thinking about the fact that I had two months to go. By noon, I had been poked by needles and prodded and subjected to all kinds of tests. I was told that the preeclampsia contributed to Intrauterine Growth Restriction (IUGR). This basically means that my uterus was not expanding the way it was supposed to in proportion to the growth of the baby. Instead of expanding like a normal uterus, the high blood pressure was making my uterus contract around the developing baby. IUGR increases the risk that the baby will die inside the womb before birth. My blood pressure continued to skyrocket which was putting me at risk for a seizure and possible death.

I surprised myself with how calm I was as they delivered this news. At first, they told me they would do an emergency C-section right away, but that decision was delayed when they realized the baby I was carrying was literally weighing barely one pound and had underdeveloped lungs. I had several doctors around me debating the solution because it was a delicate decision. The standard full-term pregnancy is 40 weeks; I was only 29 weeks pregnant. My baby was still developing so they really did not want to deliver such a premature baby for fear he would not survive. But the longer he stayed in the womb being restricted by my uterus and sending my blood pressure through the roof, the more both of our lives were in danger. The decision was made that they would wait a couple more days while they injected me with steroids several times a day so that the baby's lungs would develop while also doing all they could to stabilize my blood pressure. In those couple of days, I would also cross over into the 30 week mark which made a slight difference. They would plan a c-section in two days on Wednesday morning.

That night after everything settled, I laid on my back in the quiet stillness of the hospital room with tears rolling down my temples and filling up my ears, scared beyond belief. They emphasized how important it was for me to lay as still as possible and to stress as little as possible. The next two days were a blur of needles and tests and tears and prayers. The night before, the nurse came in to do a routine check and told me everything looked fine and we were on track for a 10 am c-section. That night I did not sleep even one wink. I watched the sun come up. My mom flew in from New York the morning my c-section was scheduled. That was an important night for me.

For the past seven months, I dealt with so much. I was so affected by how everyone else felt about me and my pregnancy. Wise's actions, my parents' disapproval and the judgment I faced from all sides was so overwhelming. It barely left room for me to think about the actual soul I had inside me. I was nervous, but it was such a dire situation, I just wanted everything to go right. I was worried about the six weeks recovery time from a c-section since I was going to be by myself in the house with the baby. The more I thought about being alone and not being able to drive or lift heavy things, the more I prayed, sometimes out loud, "Lord, please do not let me have to have this c-section." I prayed this at least a hundred times that night.

In between the prayers, I finalized what I wanted his name to be. I was debating the whole time about it. I had always wanted to name my first son Mandela because I had a tremendous respect for the man. I loved his story, I loved everything he stood for. His name was synonymous with bravery, strength, and greatness to me. In my heart I always wanted to be like him in some way or another, I always wanted to give my whole self over to something bigger than myself, something that actually changed people's lives. I was always lost as to where to even begin to be as great as this man. I sat up in the hospital bed with machines all around me, remembering sitting in this same position in the raggedy old bed that Wise and I had in the apartment discussing the baby's name. I love unusual names so I was excited to choose something.

Wise was named after his father, who was named after his father and it was important to him to continue the tradition so we settled it by giving me total power over his middle name which is what we would call him. I agreed to that and Mandela was the only name I considered. Whenever I told people about it though, everyone looked at me like I was crazy when I said it. I didn't get one positive reaction to that name, but it didn't matter to me. My family asked me one day when I first got to Georgia if I would give the baby his last name and up until that point I hadn't even considered that there was any other way, but the more I thought about it that night as I was in the hospital alone, dealing with this crisis, I realized it was just us; me and my baby. We were beginning this thing in such a rocky way and there was no one else there. Everyone who was closest to me, everyone who was supposed to care about what was going on with me and this baby was mad at me for one reason or another.

Wise didn't even want to talk to me, and my mom, even though she had thawed out some overtime was never joyous. We went from cold to tepid and I knew that was the best I could hope for. She gave me practical advice and made sure she was there for the birth so I won't say I was 100% alone. However, I needed to have a tender interaction. There were no hugs or special considerations made, I didn't vent my frustrations face to face with someone who cared. I had friends who were there for me by phone but they were all far away; no one to spend the night with me in the hospital to hold my hand. I had a few visitors in one hour spurts but I spent hour after endless hour alone in that hospital feeling each second as it painfully passed. I needed flesh and blood support and I had to shoulder the hardest burden of my life alone. Being alone was why I settled on giving him my last name because we were our own little family. I settled on the name Mandela Israel. Israel was another name that I loved since I was a child.

Growing up in church, everyone has a favorite Bible story. Mine was the story of Jacob when he was renamed Israel. From the outset of his life, my son had similarities to Jacob. He was born under odd circumstances and those circumstances were supposed to relegate him to a certain position in life. But Jacob defied tradition, defied the odds against him, and literally fought with God to become Israel. Jacob's brother was after him and wanted to kill him so he sent his family away and fled into the wilderness. As he made his way, one night he encounters an angel (some translations say it was God himself) and he proceeds to wrestle with a divine being all night. As the sun was coming up, the Angel frustratingly told Jacob it was time to end the fight and Jacob says, "I won't let you go until you bless me." The Angel (or God) then gave Jacob a new name, Israel. It means "He who struggles with God" some people say it means "Prince with God" and I will take either one. I gave my baby two strong names because I knew how cruel the world was, and that he was entering it with disadvantages already waiting for him on the other side of the light.

By choosing the name Israel, my intention was to conjure and infuse the strength of the one who would dare wrestle with God and not ever let go, to declare him a man who can change a nation like both of his namesakes. By choosing Mandela, I wanted him to have the spirit of the one who was brave enough to do whatever it took in the fight for his people, for himself. Smart enough to change strategies when need be while always keeping your eye on the goal. I wanted him to have the tenacity to hold on even when it's dark for a long time, and the grace it takes to forgive even the worst things in people. I closed my eyes and I asked the Spirit to give the soul I was bringing into the world the most strength possible because maybe I would need to draw on it someday too. I wanted to refresh my memory of the story and I pulled out a bible that was among the things my family brought to me in the hospital. I had an idea of where the story was but the fact that I opened right to the page the story was on gave me chills and made me even more sure about the name I chose.

Chapter Thirty Five

Labor Day

"Later on Lady Maccon was to describe that particular day as the worst of her life. She had neither the soul nor the romanticism to consider childbirth magical or emotionally transporting. So far as she could gather it mostly involved pain indignity and mess. There was nothing engaging or appealing about the process. And as she told her husband firmly she intended never to go through it again."

- Gail Carriger
Heartless

The time came for my c-section early the next morning. The nurse came in to do my final check before they took me back to the operating room. In the middle of the routine, she looked at me a little wide-eyed and told me that I was five centimeters dilated. Women who are in labor need to be nine centimeters to start pushing. She said, "I think we can go on let you push this baby out". I got excited but tried not to show it. Upon further examination, they discovered that overnight; the baby dropped down into the birth canal and was in the perfect position to be delivered. Although this was technically bad news because I wasn't full term, for the circumstances, it was a positive note. No need for the c-section. I was elated. I was so happy to finally have one aspect of this thing work in my favor. They decided to wait a little to see if I started labor naturally but I ended up being induced at 12 noon on the dot.

Early on into the labor, the pains were extreme, and one of the only things in the world I don't think I can find is the words to sum it up. It was unlike anything I have ever experienced. Fifteen minutes in, I was asking for the epidural. The nurse told me that she would give me the epidural for the pain whenever I felt it was unbearable. She didn't want to administer it too early for fear it would wear off at the last part of the labor which is when I needed it the most. She told me to hold on but I told her that the pain was actually already unbearable. My mom was the only other person in the room with me besides the medical professionals and I think they all thought I was being dramatic because the labor had just started.

My blood pressure skyrocketed during the labor which was a huge issue. It was a delicate hour. We all wanted a healthy baby to come into the world but my life was literally hanging in the balance. It was a difficult few days before the labor, with the doctors telling me bad news daily. If I moved too much in the bed or laughed too hard while on the phone the nurses would rush in and tell me to stop whatever I was doing and lay still on my left side. I was being monitored by machines so any little rise in my blood pressure alerted them at the nurse's station. The doctors told me that I should realistically prepare for anything. When I pressed for a more direct interaction, I was told that I should consider the possibility of going home without a baby. He was already so frail in utero and I was so sick that they felt one of us wouldn't make it. I was informed that if things took the worst possible turn and the doctors had to make a choice, they would have to save my life over the life of my baby. It was hard to hear these types of things day after day. To go into the delivery room with the voices ringing in my head telling me that we both, meaning my child and I, were in danger of dying, and it was so nerve wrecking. My labor was very anxiety inducing.

Thirty minutes in, the nurse gives in to my pleas and decides to call the anesthesiologist. He was with another patient and I had to wait for a very long fifteen minutes for him to get there. When I sat up in bed and took both of my mother's hands and exposed my back so I could get the longest needle I had ever seen stuck in the base of my spine, I felt like a boulder was slowly bearing down on my lady bits. Everyone was concerned about my hysterics and was repeating over and over again how important it was for me to be perfectly still while he is administering the epidural. I told the nurse in the middle of getting the needle, "I think the baby is coming". She must have been tired of my drama that day because she patronizingly pats me on the back and said, "Yes ma'am you are going to have a baby today, just relax, be as still as possible and it will be fine."

I ignored her admonitions and kept on telling her that I felt the baby coming out and she brushed me off because I was only one hour into labor. She kept reminding me how long labor usually takes and telling me to calm down. Once the anesthesia was administered, I laid back and put my legs back into the position they were in before, the nurse took one look down there and I could tell she was surprised. Although she tried to remain calm under pressure, there was urgency as she rushed to call the doctor. The baby's head was crowning just like I told her I felt before I got the epidural.

Only one hour and twenty four minutes after I was induced my only son saw the light of the world for the first time. I was so shocked at how small he was. I was told he was only two pounds before I had him but the sight of a two pound baby is not one that I was prepared for. I cried and screamed "He's so small!" over and over again. They didn't let me touch or hold my baby. He was shown to me for a split second before he had to be rushed to neonatal ICU. I had settled on his name being Mandela Israel the night before but when I took one look at his face and heard the nurses giggling about how feisty he was even in his first few seconds of life, I was moved. One of them called him a fighter. They were trying to put tubes in his nose and he kept snatching them out which they found so funny. It started to sink in, all that we had been through, all the odds that were against him from the beginning. My progeny had to wrestle God at every turn to stay alive and so I named him Israel Mandela instead.

Chapter Thirty Six

Nightmare

*"It's decidedly bizarre, when the Worst Thing happens
and you find yourself still conscious, still breathing."*

- Elisa Albert
The Book of Dahlia

It would be three days before I would actually see him again. I was not in a good condition after the delivery and was worried about the baby and myself. I was being monitored the first night to make sure I was ok, and on the second night, I had a seizure while I was sleeping. I don't remember anything about it in detail. I just remember waking up to several people in the room, sticking needles into my IV tube and making a general fuss about me. I was soaking wet with sweat from head to toe. I had to be told that the machine at the nurse's station alerted them to my condition and they had to rush in. What was even more bewildering for me about that situation was the fact that earlier that day, the doctor debated sending me home with some medicine and it just so happened that my mom was visiting at the time he came to my room. She spoke up and told him that in her professional opinion I was not out of the danger zone and that I probably required some more observation.

I was a little salty because I had been in the hospital for

days and was ready to go home but she managed to convince both me and the doctor that I should stay another night. Had that seizure happened when I was at home in my bed without medical professionals running to my side seconds after it started, who knows what could have happened? My newborn son was in a much worse state than I was. The worst part was that there wasn't a minute of the day that I did not have to think about or deal with some aspect of what was going on. There was no escaping and the stress, the sadness, and the loneliness. It was all so overwhelming. The list of ailments he was born with literally could not fit on one page of his medical records. He dealt with underdeveloped lungs and a bad heart valve, and a few very serious things. There were scores of "minor" issues like the jaundice and the need for a feeding tube, but they were the least of it. The first day of his life was a rough one and they didn't believe he would see a day two. When he did, they told me to tamp down my excitement until the end of the week. I was given percentages and statistics that far favored my son not living past a few days. I was given the option of turning off the breathing machine. A nurse sat with me and spoke at length about the realistic possibility of losing him. Every time they came to my room a small part of me panicked that maybe my baby passed away.

I went home from the hospital hours before the official start of Christmas day with baby-less empty arms and it felt so wrong, so out of order. I had instructions to remain on bed rest, not to drive or do anything remotely strenuous. My blood pressure was still extremely high and I was on medication for it. I was only allowed to be on my feet for a total of 30 minutes a day. I had trouble even showering without feeling like I needed to rest afterward. My son was still in the hospital fighting for his life, proving the doctors wrong every day. The end of the week came and he was still holding on. They stopped telling me what to expect, or maybe I just tuned them out. I just watched and prayed. He was so incredibly strong and even the nurses who took care of him every day were amazed that he held on like he did, in an almost defiant way.

When I was in the hospital I was anxious to get home but all the difficulties I faced before I went in were still out there waiting for me. Things were still strained between me and Wise and the situation was further complicated by his feelings about the fact that I didn't give our son the name he and I agreed on. According to him, the most egregious part was my not even having the decency to give him his father's last name. All the same, he said he was coming to town to see the baby in the hospital and I went out of my way to make preparations to meet him there.

I couldn't drive and I didn't really have any enthusiastic volunteers around me to take me to meet Wise at the hospital. There were two hospital bracelets, one for mom and one for dad, that would allow you to see your child any time of day or night. In the loneliest most painfully symbolic gesture of this whole ordeal, I put both bracelets on my left arm. I know I only needed one but I felt so much like I was in it alone. All the people around me who I felt should care did not show it and this was my small way of acting out. Only I was allowed admittance to the Neonatal Intensive Care Unit (NICU) with both bracelets on me. I was allowed one person back to the room with me. He never came. I was hurt and disappointed, especially because I got into an argument with my mother who felt I needed to focus on myself and not make any special consideration for Wise. The entire time I visited him in the NICU, only once did my immediate family come with me. I went through this difficult time feeling on the edge of insanity. The time was so starkly solitary.

Things were somewhat better between my mom and I by that point, there was still an element of discord between us because she frequently disagreed with and criticized my decisions from the very big ones to the mundane. It was achingly familiar. The vulnerable position I was in at the time had both of us reverting back to when I was younger. I once again felt like the seriousness of my situation and the emotional effect it had on me was overlooked. I was expected to fall in line and meet her expectations at all times. What I wanted or what I was feeling didn't matter. I felt that there was no consideration made for how I got through the ordeal or how I was feeling. I was frequently compromising and being asked on every side to understand how stressful it all was for everyone else.

I don't remember feeling particularly supported or being treated the way one would treat someone who has been through a life threatening trauma. The pain I felt was so overwhelming, I felt like I was drowning. I was lonely, feeling rejected and guilty about the state my son was in. That is not to say no one loved me or my baby or that there wasn't any concern. Concern is different from empathy and support, and those two things were what I needed most. Casual questions were asked, but no one offered to take me out or sat to talk to me on a deep level. In a family full of church-goers, no one held my hand and prayed for me. I sat in their church Sunday after Sunday and watched them pray and lay hands on other people but never was I called upon. Never was my baby's name called before God at the altar.

People underestimate the power of human touch. No one was treating me badly and cussing me out or anything, but it had been months since I had an affectionate physical interaction and it contributed a lot to my depression. Not since the month I spent in New York had anyone hugged me in a comforting manner, or treated me with any special kindness. When my uncle picked me up at the airport when I first came to Georgia, later on in the day when we were alone, he hugged me and told me he loved me. He cradled my belly with joy in his eyes and made jokes about my son who had yet to arrive. As he did it, I watched his beautiful smile and dancing eyes closely, soaking up the scarcely felt sensation of having someone express happiness about my condition.

My pregnancy was marred by discord with my mom, with Wise, with myself. It felt like my pregnancy ruined everyone's lives. I spent the majority of it in misery, as I did the months immediately following. One bright spot was that I was slowly getting better physically. My body stabilized and returned to relative normalcy. I found myself lonely and depressed and increasingly overwhelmed with my life. Human touch is often overlooked and it seems so insignificant at times, but at this point in my life, it was a need that went unfulfilled for so long. I didn't want or need anything romantic or sexual; it was quite contrary to that. I needed warmth and comfort and to feel at ease, I needed to physically feel loved. I needed so badly to be hugged and cradled and rocked back and forth and spoken softly to.

When I got a call from the young man I met at my cousin's house a while back when I was still pregnant, I jumped at the chance to go somewhere with him. My uncle had given me an old car so I had transportation but I rarely had gas money. All of my gas was used driving to the hospital which I did twice a day most days. I had been stuck either at home or in the hospital the last few weeks. I didn't interact with anyone who wasn't a doctor, a nurse or someone in my family. Dealing with heavy serious things, trying to keep sane and make the right decisions for my child.

I got a call from the hospital in the middle of the night one night saying that they needed to give my baby an emergency blood transfusion and I would have to come to the hospital immediately to sign off on it. It was such a difficult time. There were infections, he continuously pulled out feeding tubes and IVs, having them go to extreme measures to secure them. They had to put the IV in his head at one point because they had exhausted all his poor little veins. Every day there were tears and prayers. Every time I sat before the doctor to review his condition, I left in tears because no matter how much progress he made, they were always careful to put a cap on my optimism. I was told that if he made it home, I would most likely be dealing with a child with major lifetime health and developmental issues.

Even though I was going through all these things, and spending most of my time outside the house in the hospital, I still felt guilty as I sat across from this guy at the Olive Garden one cold January night making first-date small talk. That night I remember the strange mix of guilt and relief I felt. It felt good to relax, to have someone pay attention to me and want to please me. It was good to have a moment where I was around someone who I could talk openly with, to not have everything in the world revolving around my shortcomings and mistakes. I could still hear my mother's disapproving voice telling me that I shouldn't be going out.

I started to hang out with him more and more because being with him started to become a little bit of a reprieve for me. Life felt like it was choking me and he became a place where I could breathe. He drove me all around Atlanta and took me to places I had never been. It felt great to be with him. He was a unique person who showed me a side of life I had never seen, and as the meaning of my name implies, I am a sucker for all things new.

Chapter Thirty Seven

Follow The Leader

"She was as one who, in madness, was resolute to throw herself from a precipice, but to whom some remnant of sanity remained which forced her to seek those who would save her from herself."

- Anthony Trollope
Can You Forgive Her?

He was so different than anyone I had ever met. Even his name was one I had never heard before. It was a rare biblical name meaning to carry, bring along or to Lead. The meaning of his name is so relevant to my life because, I think more than anyone I had met before him; he did lead me in to a completely different place that changed my life forever. I was never the same after meeting him. We were seeing each other regularly for about a month when my mother really started to ramp up the criticism of the relationship. She first approached the subject with caution. She told me that she didn't think it was a good idea for me to get serious about someone. To her, I had just gotten out of a relationship and I just had a baby. I felt the need to remind her that I actually had been single for most of my pregnancy and it felt like forever. In my own eyes, I wasn't jumping into anything.

I had been so lonely for months, it started to make my ears

ring. Loneliness was just one item on the list of things that had been plaguing me the past year. I was hoping that she would understand that I had been through a lot and I wasn't doing anything that crazy. It was just a few dates. I tried to talk to her hoping she would understand where I was coming from. I explained how much hurt I had to deal with, how it felt good for someone to actually give me affection and seek me out, wanting to be around me. It meant so much to me but it was a point of contention between my mom and I. She went from quiet concern to righteous indignation. She started to tell me how I never listen to her, and every time I don't listen to her, things turn out badly for me and then I look to her to pick up the pieces.

Although it hurt, even back then, I had to admit that there was some truth to that statement. Every time things went south, my mom was always my go-to person. I never believed that things fell apart because I didn't do what she wanted. They fell apart partially because I went out into the world blindly and I wasn't always being wise with my decision making all the time. I was figuring the world out through trial and error. My parents were so focused on me not doing what they wanted and believing that their way was the only way to do things. They never gave me any advice about what I actually was doing at the time. I didn't know what to do. I didn't want to choose that path they illuminated for me so I walked blindly down the other side. If it wasn't their way, I was left to figure it out alone.

Whenever anyone steps into uncharted territory, there are missteps before one finds their footing. I couldn't ask for advice about say, Wise and I living together. The focus would be that we are living in sin and shouldn't live together before marriage, that's it. My mother would never accept it enough for me to feel comfortable to ask her if I was doing the right thing by paying all the bills and being ok with him not working "for now." I was torn about that even in the midst of doing it and when I posed the question to my friends, they could only offer me advice from their limited views.

It wasn't open for me to ask if it was ok to accept certain things when I wasn't sure if I should accept them or not, because I knew for them, the discussion would never get any further than what they saw. I stepped out blindly with only my inexperienced peers to look to for advice. I was also feeling that every time she would say what she thought I should do, it always was the path that had me doing the maximum sacrificing of my happiness. That's the lens I saw her disapproval of me dating Lead through. Why do I always have to be unhappy to do the right thing in her eyes? I thought to myself, after everything that just happened to me, I am being made to feel bad for going on a few dates and having leisure time. I knew from my recent experiences that I could not look to my family to fill that loneliness. They didn't want to hang out with me or go driving anywhere; they wouldn't hug me and let me cry on their shoulders no matter how many times I needed to. I couldn't count on them to help me fill this uber painful void.

I was facing so much criticism for being around someone who was willing. When she saw that I wasn't being moved by her admonitions, things between us grew as tense as ever. I continued to date Lead. For me at first, it wasn't so serious but the tension it was causing raised the stakes on the intensity of what we were doing. My parents were having a hard time selling their house in New York so they came back and forth often. I basically lived in their house in Georgia by myself for almost a year. After some time, my brother moved down to Georgia to live with me in the house. My brother was sixteen and my parents wanted to make sure that he started school as soon as he could down south. The plan was to move down to Georgia sooner rather than later but their plans were always being altered by life and circumstance.

My baby was released from the hospital on the same day he was actually due to enter the world. Ten weeks he spent there. When he was released, he still was only four pounds and very sickly. He still had his laundry list of issues and I had doctor's appointments multiple times a week for the first six to eight months after he came home. Most times, it was depressing and almost all the news that came through a doctor's office was bad news. That first time period was so hectic and full of worry and tears. I got used to it, but never was ok with it.

When we were approaching a year, the appointments slowed down to maybe once a week or so. They were always different places, different specialists, some of them over an hour away from where we lived. That old car my uncle gave me already had a lot of miles on it, but I was doing my part to add some of my own. Everything was a little extra hard with my son. I couldn't even buy his formula in the store; I had a prescription for special formula with medication, extra fat and steroids in it to help with him being sick and underweight. I had to order them and have them delivered to the house.

My parents finally sold their New York house and my mom and sister joined me and my brother in the house. My dad stayed behind because of his job, but he came down very very often to be with the family. I'm sure it was hard for them to be separated from each other. Over all the years that have passed, they still have one of the strongest marriages around. I can't remember any blow out fights or yelling or name calling over the years. Their disagreements were quiet and brief. They got along so well and were each other's partners in life so I have to imagine that being separated was not the desired circumstance.

On a daily basis I was miserable. I got a job at a factory and the work was grueling with long hours and not a lot of pay. I was having severe back pains that I still get to this day that I attribute to the epidural I got while giving birth; being on my feet for all those hours wreaked havoc on my lower back. I worked the night shift and the deal was that my mom would watch the baby at night while I worked from 3 in the afternoon until 11 at night. I needed my days to take my son to his many doctor appointments. It felt like I never slept for the short time I worked there. I spent my days awake with my baby, going to appointments all over metro Atlanta most days. My nights were spent slaving away in front of a conveyor belt. Grueling work aside, this plan would have worked out just fine if not for two factors, One was mandatory overtime and the other was still unknown to me then. My son was displaying the early signs of Autism.

When I would leave him with my mom, he would not sleep at all. Night after night, he would keep her awake, long after we passed that newborn stage where he woke up for feedings and whatnot. This was different, alarming. My mother would struggle with him at night and then have to wake up early to go to work herself in the morning. Also, most nights I was at work, they would tell us halfway into the night that we would have to stay until whatever time they have assessed that the work would get done. Sometimes it would be one thirty in the morning, even three a.m. My mom would expect me home at

11 pm and as she struggled to stay awake past that time, she would be calling me over and over asking when I was coming home. I tried to explain to her the concept of mandatory overtime which was something we were not familiar with coming from New York. It doesn't even feel like it should be legal that someone should have to work over the time they were contracted to work under the threat of losing their job. Here in Georgia, mandatory overtime is an option employers can exercise. They are allowed to mandate that you work beyond your designated hours and would be within their rights to fire you if you didn't.

My mom has never done well with taking things I say seriously, so I think a part of her didn't really believe that was the case. After I had been working there for about a month, a time came when I spoke to the supervisor several days in a row and told him I have no choice but to go home because of child care issues. My mom was insisting that I come home and she was fed up with being up all night and then having to wake up early in the morning for work, which I completely understood. Neither one of us were getting any sleep. Every time I went into that office and told them I had to go, I was met with shaking heads and disapproving looks from my superiors. They would remind me of the policy and that I was in danger of losing my job and I would tell them I had no choice. Every time I had this conversation with them it was after 11, which was when my job was supposed to end.

It was beyond frustrating to me that someone could demand that I work 12 or 15 hours at their whim, often not finding out what time I would be going home until a couple of hours before. It killed me that if f I went to work at 3pm and left at 11pm like I signed up for, I could lose my job. I hated being in this position, getting pressure from all sides of a situation while the people on either side of me refuse to understand. My final straw with that job came just six weeks after I started working there. My baby had been sick for a few days and after midnight passed and I fielded several miserable calls from my mother, I made the dreaded march to the office to tell them I had to leave. This time I was told that I only had one more opportunity to do this before I would be fired. I went home to my sick baby. His condition worsened; his fever spiked and we ended up in the hospital that night.

When the doctor told me he would have to be admitted because he had to be treated for a severe viral infection, I broke down crying. He was put back into the same Neonatal Intensive Care Unit he was in for the first ten weeks of his life. I remember thinking he's Back again to the battleground to fight for his life. I went to the job with a letter from the hospital and while they expressed their sympathy, they told me the show had to go on and they had to find someone to replace me. I walked out with tears in my eyes. I hated that job by every measure, but I needed the money, and I couldn't believe I just got fired because my kid was sick. Driving away, I remember thinking about how it threw a wrench into my plan to move out of my mother's house which was my main motivation.

My son recovered from the viral infection with aggressive treatment at the hospital. He stayed there for four days before he was cleared to go home. I looked for another job while taking care of my son. Appointments for the cardiologist, the ophthalmologist, pulmonologist, weekly pediatrician visits and all kinds of testing at the hospital were a full time job in itself. My son's sleeping habits were erratic. Certain things about his development worried the doctors. We were always going in to test for this or that. I endured a lot of questioning from my family about my working situation. Most people did not take the time to understand what my everyday life was like but they definitely offered their judgments and opinions about what they saw. I went a while without working because every time I went to the doctor, I was being given grim news about my child and his development and I had to deal with more appointments and other issues than I ever had in my life. Not that I wasn't applying for jobs every time I got an opportunity. I was met with roadblocks at every turn it felt like.

I was getting turned down for jobs for reasons like my low credit score or my lack of experience. It was disappointing that it was so difficult to find something worthwhile. If I ever got really close to working somewhere, the doctor visits were always an issue. I had so many appointments and things popped up suddenly and often. Sometimes I would be on lengthy waiting lists and would get called for something important with short notice. People had a hard time understanding I was never consistently available.

I know that my family loved us both but I don't think anyone understood or even tried to understand what I was going through. My extended family who lived here in Georgia gossiped about different aspects of my life including why I wasn't working and opinions were thrown around freely. No one bothered with being emotionally supportive and that hurt me a lot because I didn't need that with what I was going through. I had no one offering support or even a kind word. I was feeling so overwhelmed. Pressured by my mother about my job situation, worried about my son with no one to vent to about my emotions and worried about what I would do for money in the near future.

Conflict between my mom and I continued to abound for a few reasons; the chief of them being the fact that I was still dating Lead. She felt it was not the right time in my life for a relationship. There was some element of bias toward him personally, but the reason she always vocalized was that she felt I wasn't ready and had too much going on. She was completely correct in her assessment although I didn't think so back then. It was hard for me to see that because of an issue that we have always had through the years, it was her approach. It almost got to the point of insult that she kept dealing with me in a way that has never worked with me. She refused to look at me as an individual and tailor her approach to fit the type of person I was. I saw her do it with other people but never with me.

It felt after years of this like she thought I didn't deserve that, and wasn't worth that much thought. She was always aggressive with her opinions and so overbearing and would react so over the top when things didn't go the way she planned. I would get caught up in her reaction and not what she was saying. She never talked openly with me or showed me that she cared about how I was feeling. If she felt sympathy for me and what I was going through with my son (and I do think she was somewhat sympathetic), she never directly expressed it to me in those early days. What she would express to me was exasperation, impatience, judgment of my every move big or small. She would give me a hard time if I would be at Lead's house until late with the baby in tow. She gave me a hard time about driving around too much with the baby. She gave me a hard time about my habits at home, and was critical of how I was taking care of the baby. There were no hugs, no questions about how I was holding up, no tenderness. It was all so much. I was so frustrated with everything else going on that my mother and I's dynamic at home was making it worse.

I felt like I had no comfort with anyone else but Lead. It felt as if no one else cared about me on an emotional level. I was overwhelmed and needed support, and Lead was the only shoulder I had. Because of everything I was going through with my son's condition and his hectic work schedule, we had to really make time to see each other. I think that added a special element to the time we spent together. I literally had no peace anywhere else. We kept seeing each other despite my mother's vehement disapproval.

During those first months of chaos after my son came home, Lead was the only oasis in the desert of pain and frustration that was my life. I can attest to the power of feeling loved and wanted and accepted. People looked at my life on the surface back then and drew their own opinion. Here I was living in a nice house in the suburbs. I had a car (old as ever, but it did the job). I wasn't starving or needing clothes, my baby and I had all of our needs met and I didn't work. I heard countless times from friends and people in my extended family how lucky and blessed I was for those things. I was grateful for that, I truly was. Much like I felt during my adolescence, I had no nurturing. I was once again feeling the pain of the complicated space I was in when I first came to this country from Jamaica.

It was once again the aftermath of something traumatic for me in which my mom rescued me and gave me what I needed in the physical sense. The tenderness I needed wasn't offered. My physical and survival needs were once again being met while I was feeling desperately on edge emotionally. Subsequently, when I try to address the emotional part, it's brushed off because people feel like if you live in a nice house or have certain material things you should not have anything to complain about. I felt like I was dying inside. Even though I was an adult, I was still searching for that lap to curl up on metaphorically.

It was a truly epic struggle with myself. I wish I would have been able to see that through the fog of depression that clouded me. No one knew the struggle and almost no one asked. I woke up every day crying and I had never felt so hopeless before. No one showed concern for my mental and emotional well being, even when I cried out for help. Which I did so many times and in so many ways before I was forced to accept that no one cared. The black hole that existed inside me that needed affection and understanding and nurturing was still left void. Lead filled it with hugs and forehead kisses, and sympathetic, kind words. He filled it with his attention and gentle treatment of me. I fell hard and fast for the only person who acknowledged my pain and tried to make it better.

We started dating officially in January after my son was born. We spent as much time as we possibly could as the year progressed. By November of that year, he was faced with having to leave the house he lived in with his sister and her sons. He planned on renting an apartment by the time the New Year started. We talked so much about how frustrated we both were about our living situations. By that time, I had applied for and was receiving disability because my son had been diagnosed with a Developmental Delay. That just basically meant he was not developing normally and I was told that this diagnosis almost always got replaced with a more specific one as he got older. Right now, they determined he was not developing in part but they were still in the process of figuring out what it was that was causing it exactly. So I was receiving a little assistance at the time which made me feel a little more independent.

Early one Saturday morning while talking on the phone, we had a very practical discussion in which we came to the conclusion that it would be beneficial for us to get a place together. While I did love the idea of moving out of my mother's house, I told him that I was scared from the last time I lived with a boyfriend. I told him I didn't want to move in with someone I wasn't married to. Without missing a beat he said, "Let's get married then." I was shocked to hear him suggest that. I asked, "Are you sure?" He answered my question with a question, "Would you marry me?" I was confused as to whether or not he was asking if I would possibly do it one day or if he was actually proposing marriage. I asked flat out, are you saying you want to get married right now? He said, "Yeah why not do it? Let's do it." I felt a surge of excitement as we discussed that we could go to the justice of the peace in a week and get it done.

When I hung up the phone with him, I immediately left my bedroom and walked out into the living room where my mother was sweeping the floor. I sat in a chair a few feet away from her and I blurted out that Lead and I were planning on getting married. After her initial silent look of shock, her first question to me was "are you pregnant?" I said "No." She looked at me confused and asked why he wanted to marry me if that wasn't the case. She continued to press about it and when I insisted that we just wanted to get married because we were in love, she went back to her usual stony silence. I told her that we planned on doing it soon, like within the coming week. We were just going to go to the justice of the peace and do it and then start looking for an apartment. My mother was totally against the idea of getting married. She felt like it was too soon. We had been seeing each other for less than a year at that point. At the time that she said these things, I knew that they were valid concerns. I didn't feel surprised about her reaction and the warnings she gave me and even though I gave no indication to her, I considered everything she said, I really did.

My life was so stressful and anxiety ridden. I truly felt like I was on the edge of a breakdown and it was hurting me to realize how much no one cared. Like I said before, I tried to reach out and talk to people in my family and was disappointed by the responses and sometimes the lack thereof. What I really needed was counseling, or just a really good friend. I needed emotional support, I needed to be free of the situation I was in, I needed a change. My mistake was thinking that marrying Lead was the quickest way to escape some of what was ailing me. Not that I did not consider myself totally and completely in love with this man. I chose to turn a blind eye to certain things. This was not a subconscious thing, I literally chose to ignore red flags, both about his personality and the vulnerable situation I was entering with a man I did not know well enough. I was willing to brush so much aside for the fact that he was filling a very dark and painful void in my life. Giving me what I felt like I waited my whole life for. I told myself that this was a whirlwind romance, not a relationship that was moving too soon. Here I was blinded by the chance to once again be free. I couldn't see past that.

When it was clear to my mother that we had every intention of getting married, she stopped protesting the actual marriage and insisted that we skip the courthouse wedding and do it at the church so that our union would be blessed by God; neither one of us was particularly planning on a wedding, for one we couldn't afford one and secondly, both of our focus was more on getting out of our respective living situations. The money I was getting every month in disability and his paychecks were being pooled to cover our moving expenses. It all was happening quickly. I offered a compromise. We could still do it within the week, we will go to the pastor's office and he can perform the wedding with a few witnesses. My mom insisted that since we were doing that anyway, why not wait and have a little bit of a bigger event since the family was so close by and all. I gave in because it eased some of the weight of the disappointment she was heaping on me for my decision.

When we finally sat down and had the official conversation with both my mom and my dad, I was taken aback by how grim the mood was. I knew they weren't particularly happy but I was hurt that they didn't express one positive notion during the conversation and sat there with stony looks on their faces as if we were planning the funeral of a loved one. My dad lets me know that this was it, I was his problem now. This home is no revolving door, so this time you are gone for good. As far as the rest of the family went, I don't recall any of them being happy for us either.

My mom put together a very small event that took place three weeks from the day we decided to get married. There were less than twenty people there, all family, and one of my best childhood friends flew in last minute. I wasn't particularly enthusiastic about it because it really was not what I wanted. I wanted to just go to the courthouse. This wedding became a new source of conflict between my mother and I that came to a head the night before the event. She felt I was being ungrateful for everything she was doing. I thought I was putting on a good face out of respect. I wasn't fooling anyone. I walked down the aisle that day and was just counting the minutes till it was all over.

I left the wedding to spend the first night in the new apartment (he had moved in a few days before me). We stopped and got a cheap bottle of wine and went to our new home. It just so happened to be that time of the month so we drank and went to sleep. He went to work the next day. I was so ambivalent about it all that it bordered on sad. I loved him and I had resolved to do my best to make this marriage work, but I would be lying if I said that this was some great love story for the ages. Our union began with a small spark and little fanfare but it absolutely went out with a bang. Everything in between was so crazy that even when I was living it, I sometimes felt like I was outside my body watching a display thinking how the hell did I end up here.

Chapter Thirty Eight

Here's To You Mrs. Robinson

She knew now that marriage did not make love. Janie's first dream was dead, so she became a woman."

> - Zora Neale Hurston
> *Their Eyes Were Watching God*

L ike most relationships, things started out awesome. Some of the very same things that made me fall in love in the beginning, ended up being the things that ended our marriage after only four years. For example, in the beginning, I loved the fact that he wanted to talk to me all day long. He always wanted to know where I was and what I was doing and I thought it was sweet. I thought it was him being overprotective because he cared so much. After I got to know him better I realized it was about controlling me, not caring about me. When the day came that I didn't feel like talking or thought his line of questioning was too intrusive, it would elicit such a crazy angry response that was always intimidating. I started to realize I had little choice in the matter. Comply or suffer consequences. Consequences could affect me emotionally or physically but they will be faced. When I finally realized he wanted to control everything from what I wore, to how I lived in every way big and small, I was already in too deep. I came to find out that Lead was not necessarily evil, but he was a disturbed man with a lot of issues.

I often think about the first argument he and I had before we got married. It was the worst argument I had ever had with anyone before that day (although over the years we topped that one by far) and I remember feeling taken aback when it was all over, but I was really eager to forget it. I wish I had seen it for the red flag it was and ran the other way. He was at my mother's house where I was living at the time with my brother. I don't even think my son was out of the hospital yet. I was checking my email and he showed up to pick me up so we could go somewhere.

While I was on the computer the house phone rang and I got up from my seat to answer it. I came back to him staring with furrowed brows at the computer screen. It struck me as odd so I walked around to see what he was looking at and I realized he was reading one of my emails. It was the email I was reading before I got up. Even though I had went to a different website, he sat down and pressed the back arrow button that would go to every page you just visited in reverse order. It was an email from my old friend the Homey. I had recently discovered through the grapevine that he had a girlfriend the whole time we were hanging out in New York. We never had a relationship or any kind of commitment to each other but it still bothered me that he didn't tell me.

I wrote him an email about the subject and he wrote me back apologizing and explaining himself. He had moved back to Florida where he grew up and I was living in Georgia. We hadn't seen each other in forever and the mood of the email conversation was not exactly friendly. There were no declarations of undying love. Lead immediately jumped when I came up behind him and touched his shoulder. Not because he was surprised, he saw me. He said he was disgusted by me and didn't want me to touch him. He called me a liar and declared that he knew it was too good to be true and he knew he shouldn't trust me. I tried to explain the situation. He acted irrationally and started to storm out. Often when I think about that day I wish I wouldn't have stopped him. I forced him to hear me out. And even though I thought we had gotten over it that day, it turned out he never did. For years following that day, he would hearken back to those events as the first disagreement and therefore the root cause of all of our problems. Even when things were his fault, even when bringing up other past events didn't work, he would pull this first argument card. It was my fault; he said that he would rough me up when he got angry. Because on that day early into the relationship, he learned I couldn't be trusted.

This was a motif in his life; women are not to be trusted. He was born in Washington DC to a Trinidadian mom and a Jamaican dad. They were never married, and his father moved to Atlanta very early on in his life. His dad was a devout Rastafarian. He was serious about every aspect of the practice of his religion and raised Lead and his siblings (in the loosest form one could possibly use the term "raise") in that way. He told me that his mother started dating a man who was in the armed forces when he was about 8 years old. The relationship grew serious and his mother's boyfriend was being sent to a base in Germany. She was pregnant with his child. They got married and went to Germany where she gave birth to Lead's younger sister. The only problem is Lead and his two brothers were left behind; literally dropped off without warning on the doorstep of their paternal grandmother who still lived in DC. His father's side of the family didn't have the means to take care of them long term.

He told me about the pain caused by listening to his grandmother and aunts on the phone with his father in Atlanta complaining about their presence and demanding he come get his children, and his father's reluctance to do so. After these children were broken and felt thoroughly unwanted by anyone, and after a threat to give them up to the state if he didn't come, Lead's father finally made his way to get his children. He would live with his dad the rest of his childhood and wouldn't even see his mother again until he was nineteen years old. After that visit, he didn't see her again until he was in his 30s and married to me. They maintained a contentious relationship. Even after her abandonment, she was unapologetic and abrasive. She spoke badly of her children more often than not; she remained forever brazenly impenitent, brash, unfiltered, and arrogant.

When she came to visit us, she came into town like a whirlwind and left so much destruction in her path. Her first words to me were (as we were still hugging) "I brought some of my clothes to give you because Lead said you had lost some weight lately, but you didn't lose *that* much weight. I only buy designer clothes so I don't wanna waste it, I would rather give it to someone who they will fit". And so began our short visit. She came to town via car with her daughter from Colorado and two toddler-aged granddaughters. She was sponsoring the trip. They traveled to an army base in Columbus Georgia because her daughter's husband had some kind of ceremony and then would be leaving for a long time.

We met them at the base and after it was all said and done, they followed us home and planned to stay for about four or five days. On the second day she was here, Lead's mother, after being rude countless times, felt as if she was being disrespected when we chose to handle a sticky situation our own way. We walked out of the Atlanta Underground to see a boot on the wheel of the car. If she had her way, she wanted us to tell some story and try to finagle our way out of paying to get the boot off. Both her daughter and I felt like just paying and going home instead of causing any more issues because it had been a long day. Angry with both of us, and wounded by the perceived disrespect, on a whim she was gone. She booked herself a flight and called a cab to the airport. Lead's sister and two nieces were basically stranded because she was supposed to buy the gas and food on their way home. She had about three more weeks until the armed services would deposit her husband's pay, and they had no choice but to stay with us until then. For almost a month, his sister couldn't go home and we had three extra people in a small two bedroom apartment. He didn't speak to her again the rest of the time we were married.

Lead's father was no less dysfunctional. His Rastafarian beliefs dictate that people have as many children as possible and that was one edict he took seriously. The number of children he has had varies based on who I have asked, and truthfully I don't think he even knows. It's a number in the high teens. Lead knew and spoke to maybe 10 of them. With so many children and the chauvinism and misogyny that come with Rastafarian practices, Lead's father did what he wanted and often that was not in the best interest of his children or their mothers. I heard tales from Lead and his siblings about having to fend for themselves at a young age. My experiences with him were always brief and he could never remember me or my son's names. He was very aloof. Each time it was like telling him my name for the first time. He is a callous and selfish person by all accounts, although my experiences with him were quite limited.

This is the stock from which Lead sprung so it was no

surprise that he had a lot of issues. When we started living together, it took me a while to realize just how miserable he really was as a person. It felt like he woke up every day searching for a reason to be mad or frustrated or sad or anything negative. Whenever he told me the stories of his past relationships and breakups, they always seemed to end with the woman being a cheater and a liar and if it went especially bad, they were crazy for good measure. It struck me how similar the breakup stories were and it was yet another red flag I ignored completely.

He accused every last woman of cheating on him, even when he admitted he didn't have any proof, he still talked as if he was convinced it was true. All of his relationships ended with a physical altercation of some kind. In his stories though, he was always justified for his physical action. I sat and listened to these stories without feeling any sense of panic because I thought I was totally different from those women. Not only am I different, but so is he. He was younger then, I told myself. He was immature. I think back now with such disbelief that I ignored such glaring issues.

Lead felt he was always a victim of something. He said he didn't like to talk about his past and his childhood but somehow we ended up on those topics pretty often. It took me a little while to realize that he was using his sad past to manipulate me and keep me around. Later when our marriage was over and I looked back on things. I realized our whole marriage was a struggle for control. I was fighting for control over my own life in a weird way. I felt I had wrestled for control from my mother for so long and I only had it for a few years only to lose it again. The few years I was in control of my life, though not always good, did leave me with the undeniable feeling that I could not have it any other way. I hated every minute of having to depend on my mom again while I was pregnant.

In my mind, marriage was not about control, it was about sharing my life with someone. In the beginning, I was excited to move away and start my own family. I wanted to feel like a real woman in every sense. I relished in cooking dinner, doing his laundry, all the typical housewife stuff. It made me feel for the first time like someone needed me; at the same time though I was happy to feel like an adult. Finally free of the intimidation of authority over my life, which I have never done well with. Finally back in my own place where I could leave the lights on or not wash the dishes tonight if I felt like it.

We were equal partners in my eyes, meaning we were individuals in our own right who were sharing our lives together and walking down the same path. When I told him those exact words one day, he promptly let me know that in a relationship one person is always the leader and the other one more submissive. He also did not believe we were equal partners because he had a full-time job and I did not. In his eyes I did nothing while he did everything. What's funny is that he made it that way and worked hard to keep it that way. He started by just saying he was ok with me not working and that he didn't mind paying for everything. Whenever I would apply for jobs, he wouldn't protest outwardly but he was never happy. He would talk bad about each job and why I shouldn't take it. I ended up not taking a bunch of jobs for various reasons, often centering around the lack of childcare, but he always seemed relieved and almost happy when I would be disappointed about not being able to work somewhere. He paid the bills (which was basically a small electrical bill that never went over $50, and our phone bills which were on the same plan), and I paid the rent.

I used the disability money that I received monthly for my son. I never kept a dime for myself and Lead never helped out with that aspect. I paid all of the rent the entire time we were together. I did it because I felt terrible all the time because he would constantly remind me that I didn't have a job and to him, that meant I contributed nothing financially to our life. Truthfully, he was not the only one that felt that way. I know that members of my family didn't look favorably on public assistance, and I think everyone would have had more respect for me if I went out every day and worked. So from the first time we moved (my SSI paid our moving expenses), I felt obligated to put every cent I had into our family.

I thought I was doing the right thing. Having him always telling me how I didn't contribute to the household because I didn't go out and work did a number on me psychologically because I really started to believe it. I never kept one cent of that money while we were married; thinking about it now, I can't believe it got to the point that I sat there and believed him when he told me I contributed nothing even though all the while when we were married, this man did not pay rent once. The check covered all the rent, not a cent for him to pay, but also not a cent for me to hold on to. Not physically having any money all the time, always having to get permission and detail all my purchases to him became the norm. Even mundane things like a fruit smoothie or humiliating things like feminine products and personal items were all fodder for his scrutiny. If he didn't think it was worth it, we just didn't do it. I didn't have much say, after all, he constantly reminded me that it was him who got out of the house every day to work for that money.

I started to really believe I was worthless. Even though I took out several student loans during the course of my marriage to him and made large purchases like a down payment on a car, and furniture. I am always amazed at how easily he controlled me psychologically, where even though I paid the rent every month, and even though without me, he wouldn't be driving the nicest car he ever owned, he still convinced me that I did nothing, and he was the only one responsible for keeping us afloat. It was easy to believe him because the sense of worthlessness didn't start there, it started way before we even met.

All my life I felt this feeling that my presence was burdensome for my loved ones. I did not feel like I added any value to anyone's life and all I brought was pain, even when I didn't mean to, or had no control. All he did was reinforce a feeling of worthlessness that was already deeply rooted.

Things were only good for a few months after we got married. It was evident early on that he needed to have control over everything or else we would have major issues. It was also evident that this relationship would be high maintenance. I had to work hard to keep things good between us. I was back in school and he was supportive of that on the surface but always assured me that he was just fine with me not working. At first, I didn't see this as part of his whole control thing; I thought he was just overprotective.

Learning to live with him was not easy for me. It started to dawn on me about six months in that I had no idea who this man was when I married him. He was very paranoid about me being with someone else. He constantly and irrationally accused me of cheating on him. Our neighbor at our apartment complex unknowingly was the cause of many arguments. I never said anything but hello and I didn't even know his name but for some reason, Lead had it in his mind that while he was working at night, I was letting the guy into our apartment. I was constantly being accused of cheating in such an irrational way. I never cheated or even did anything that looked suspicious. I didn't really have friends that lived in Georgia so I rarely went anywhere without him, someone connected to him, or a member of my family. He never found me in any uncompromising situations, although he would pop up at unexpected times and do other things in an attempt to catch me. He never found any texts or suspicious behavior, although he would berate me for regular actions and make them into something suspicious.

For example, if I told him I was going to the store, he would determine how long that should take and raise hell if I came back any later. He justified his actions with that first argument and the email to a guy I used to talk to. We had blown out fights because some man would be looking at me and he would swear that I was giving him the "eye" and disrespectfully flirting with someone right in front of him. Sometimes he would see things that didn't happen. He would point out a man looking at me that I didn't notice. Even if I wasn't looking at him, he would swear that I must know the guy by the way he is looking at me. It happened so often that I started to make a conscious effort not to even look at any man around me so he wouldn't think I was giving him the "eye". He would get angry over the most minor things. Things that were at best mildly annoying to most people would illicit erratic behavior in him. Sometimes the very same words or actions that were ok the day before would cause a blow up the next day and it left me totally confused. I started to walk on eggshells. I woke up every morning calculating how the day would go so as to not upset him. I failed more often than not.

Chapter Thirty Nine

One Thousand Two Hundred Ninety-Eight Days

"Perhaps this is what the stories meant when they called somebody heartsick. Your heart and your stomach and your whole insides felt empty and hollow and aching."

- Gabriel García Márquez

A lot of those mornings I woke up tired, drained and depressed and it wasn't only because of my crumbling marriage. My son's health was a huge issue that loomed over everything. We got married a few weeks before my son's first birthday, but even before that, it was clear that there were issues with his development. For the first year of his life, the doctors assured me that he would have major health and development problems for the rest of his life. It was about waiting it out and monitoring him closely to see what specifically arises. I had appointments several days a week at different specialists and a check in with the pediatrician once a week.

It was difficult navigating this new city, which I learned a lot about through all these appointments in different areas. It was also difficult navigating life as a new mom, much less a mom to a child with Special Needs. I can't reiterate enough how lonely it all was and how doing it alone was probably harder than any other aspect of it all; dealing with the anger, fear, and uncertainty with only my own tears as comfort. After Lead and I were married, in my son's second year of life, it was determined that my son had a significant developmental delay. That was the actual diagnosis, SDD. He still wasn't walking or talking at two years old and he remained underweight and generally smaller than he should have been. He barely wanted to eat anything, so feeding him was always a challenge. He also only slept for a few hours at night.

Most people, myself included, would be tired after a full day and only four hours or so of sleep. He would pop up with the energy of the Tasmanian devil and hit the ground running, or should I say, crawling at lightning speed at first. He started to receive occupational and physical therapy. Those therapy sessions helped him to communicate with gestures and sounds and after a while, he was standing on his own. While I was dealing with my issues with Lead, I spent many days inside doctor's offices feeling a myriad of emotions. Confused, taking notes on things to look up later. Scared, because I had no idea and was getting no assurance from the doctors about what the future looked like for my son. Angry that even though my son had a father, I had a husband and a score of family members less than 10 miles away, I did everything alone. Not only was I left to shoulder everything alone, but when I told the people around me about what was going on, I was often met with casual responses like, "Oh what do they know anyway, the kid will be just fine." Sometimes, it was "just pray" or people would tell me about some miracle child of a friend of a friend who overcame everything and is in medical school. My personal favorite, they would tell me they saw a special on CNN or something about autism so now they know all there is to know.

I wasn't always sure what exactly I needed to hear but those things were not it. One thing that has always amazed me about this Autism journey has always been, even though my child and I are the ones who needed the understanding from everyone else, I often found that we were the ones forced to be understanding to everyone else. At family dinners on holidays, I couldn't eat because I would be following him around so he wouldn't touch or break things. Everyone would watch me have a difficult time, unable to touch my plate and pass their remarks. I had to remind myself in those times that they don't get it. If we are in a grocery store and something causes him to be anxious, neither he nor I can control his reaction. I have to dig deep to ignore the pointing and the stares. I have to remind myself that they don't get it. I have to constantly explain and apologize, stay out of the way, or ignore rude comments. It could really make you hate people if you aren't understanding of their ignorance. It has been a rare few times in a rare few places that we feel comfortable and welcomed.

My days were filled with so much stress and negativity. I had nowhere to run, and I could honestly call this time in my life the most difficult. I was being berated and belittled by Lead daily and being kicked while I was down by my son's Autism. I still felt a sense of strain in my relationship with my mom. She still at this point had never ever been proud of me and the shame she felt toward me was palpable. It felt like when I told her about the abuse I was experiencing, instead of feeling like she was sympathetic, it felt as if she was disappointed that I had made another bad choice and was living like a lowlife. I felt stuck with him.

After a while, his emotional abuse turned physical. This one was also hard for me to reconcile within myself while we were married because, in full disclosure, I threw the first hit. It was during an especially ugly argument that ended with the neighbors calling the police. He was angry about some minor infraction that day and I was on edge and feeling stressed. I don't remember what it was about particularly but I remember wanting to be left alone so badly. We yelled and argued for hours. At one point, he put his face so close to mine that we were almost touching noses and he spits in my face. When I incredulously exclaimed that I couldn't believe he just did that, he immediately denied that he did it on purpose. He claimed he was just speaking passionately and it came out, but there was no apology. He told me I didn't deserve an apology and that even though it was an accident. He said I deserved it and I slapped him in the face. He proceeded to manhandle me almost with a sense of joy. He told me that day that I opened the floodgates, so now it's on. He had free reign to do anything to me anytime he wants because I started it.

I never put my hands on him after that day, but he started to resort to that whenever he felt like it. Even two years after the fact, when I would be sitting in a chair across the room and he would get up to knock me off the chair and drag me by the hair across the room all because I woke him up early, he would blame me for hitting him that day two years ago. It felt achingly familiar to have all my shortcomings layered on, to never be forgiven. By the way, that day I came home from a doctor's appointment and woke him up about an hour before he usually got up to tell him that I would have to have surgery in a few days. He felt I should have respected his sleep and that it could have waited. He paid no attention to my emotional reaction from the doctor's news. They saw fibroids that needed to be removed from my uterus, and they would take a biopsy to send to a lab to determine whether or not there was cancer present. He admitted that it was a serious issue but he was thoroughly irritated about not getting that last hour of sleep. I proceeded to tell him that the doctor wanted me to do the surgery the next day, but I postponed it for when he was off of work in about three days because I had no one to drive me there and back. He flew into a rage because he felt as if I should not have confirmed anything without talking to him first. We had an ongoing disagreement about his days off. I stayed in the house a lot, dealing with issues with my son, with very little contact with the world outside.

Whenever he was off, I liked to make plans for us to do things, and sometimes it would conflict with how he was thinking about spending his day off. I tried to make him understand that this was my only reprieve from the stress I faced, that he was my only friend. But he felt like after having worked a long week, it should be up to him how he spends his leisure time; a point which I reluctantly conceded. I stopped making plans for his days off. But I felt that this was different because it was surgery. Surely medical issues did not fall under the same category as a trip to the mall. We fell into a huge argument when I tried to make that point to him.

I cried at how callous he was regarding the news from the doctor and called him a selfish bastard. I was sitting in a computer chair about 15 feet away from the bed he was laying in. He got up and came across the room and knocked me out of the chair, screaming the whole time. Then he dragged me by my hair across the room and into the living room. I ran out of the house crying. I decided to go to the store and then get my son off the bus from school like I had originally intended. He called my phone while I was out at the store and the bus stop to berate me for crying in public. He was always really sensitive about the way people saw him and he would get really upset when it was obvious to other people that he was treating me badly.

Whenever I would complain about the way he treated me, he never let me forget that one day, the original argument about the email. He drilled into my head that all of his behavior toward me was reactionary, and therefore my fault. He would hit me, drag me by the hair (one of his favorite moves), choke me, and manhandle me in all kinds of ways and more often than not in the end; I was the one in tears apologizing. I was often convinced it was my fault. I was thoroughly disturbed at the time and I couldn't see how crazy my life was. I honestly felt I had nowhere to go. My parents' disapproval of my marriage and their words that "this is no revolving door" made me feel like my one option for escape from this had disappeared.

My son was officially diagnosed with Autism when he was three years old. I don't know if I was as upset about the diagnosis as I was the uncertainty of it all. There was no way to really tell what end of the spectrum he would be on. Would he be an adult with a child's mind that needed supervision for everything? Would he be semi-functional and be able to go to school and work but maybe need to live with me for the rest of his life? Would he be a mostly functioning adult with a special talent and some quirks and a little social awkwardness? No one could provide answers. We just had to wait and see; my heart breaks just as much writing this right now as it did the first day it was told to me.

I spent two more years in a low down swamp of abuse, depression, anxiety, delusion and sleep deprivation. In the middle of all of this, I had two miscarriages, months apart. I felt so alone and I was hurting so much that I kept this away from my family and friends. I didn't want opinions and judgment about it. It helped isolate me. I lost a lot of weight. Here I was in Georgia, around scores of family members, and living with two other people and I was more alone than I had ever been. I had no refuge. Out in public, people would often stare and shake their heads at my son's behavior when he would have a meltdown. It would hurt me because I knew he could not control it. I was forever being apologetic and explaining for him. I still have to do that now sometimes, but I do it a lot less. I learned to deal with the staring and accept the judgment. At first, the harsh judgmental way people looked at me and my child was hard to deal with. A few people were even bold enough to walk up to me and rudely state their opinions. What was harder was that members of my family and even my husband were not always fully understanding of my son's condition or the stressful toll it was taking on me.

People in my family made attempts to watch him once or twice but it never went past that. He was with me all the time. When my son was a baby and a toddler, he didn't speak or walk. He was the kind of kid you could take anywhere. It wasn't hard to get one of my younger cousins to sit in my house at night while he slept so Lead and I could go out, which we did pretty often. They were teenagers who would have done whatever it took to be out of the house. We did a lot. We took him to the movies and on many excursions, all the while reveling in what a "good baby I had" only to, later on, be told that that behavior was the early signs of autism. Once he grew up a little and started to be more hyperactive and his symptoms changed, it became almost impossible to find anyone to watch him. I started to have to stay home with him all the time, even planning out my trips to the store. Lead did not slow down with me though. he continued to have the active social life that he and I both enjoyed, by himself. Every time he had the day off, he would be gone from morning until night, and sometimes the next morning.

I stayed in this relationship because I truly felt I had no other options. Several people in my life mentioned to me how lucky I was that a man would still want to marry me even though I had someone else's child; a child with a disability at that. When I first heard it from more than one person I was offended. At that point, I truly never felt that I was "lucky" because he accepted my baggage. He had just as much, maybe more than I did. I was surprised at this outdated sexist way of thinking was still around. I honestly felt like he was just as lucky to have me. We had some really good times peppered in with all the bad. That was another reason I held on to this relationship for years.

He was a charismatic person, he made me laugh and we liked to have fun. He loved to dress up and showered me with gifts. He always bought me clothes and shoes that were more expensive than I would have gotten for myself. He was very interested in presenting a nice glossy picture to the public. We both loved to go out and had a few other things in common. There were definitely some good times. Like the typical arch in a relationship, the good times decreased while the years progressed. At first, it was all good, that's the point where I and everyone else fall in love.

When the bad times started they were outweighed by the good times so it was still worth holding on to. Even when the scales started to even out and there was just as much bad as there was good, I still muddled my way through the best I could, never thinking about leaving. The more I put up with and the more I forgave, the worse things seemed to be the next time. I had to conform to a strict set of standards with him, and there was no room for deviation. I never was given the benefit of the doubt for anything. I started to be expected to forgive things like him going out and not coming home at all until the next day, while I would be yelled at and degraded and insulted (and a few times assaulted) for minor infractions like spending a few dollars extra at the store.

We fought incessantly and one day I looked around and thought, "I live in hell." Between the issues with my son and issues with my husband, I was perpetually depressed. While I was married, I had more medical problems than I have ever had before or after. I always had the flu. I wasn't taking care of myself. And while the vain world we live in had my family and friends complimenting my weight loss, it came from stress, from trauma. At one point after I begged for months and jumped through all kinds of hoops, we went to see a marriage counselor.

We only lasted three sessions, but it was an attempt. When we sat in front of the counselor, he told us that this would be a process that we shouldn't expect to be "fixed" after one, two or even ten sessions. The process is different for everyone but it takes time. He also informed us that he would be doing a psychological evaluation on the both of us individually and then we would discuss the results because, he said, sometimes issues between couples can stem from one person's issues in general. We completed the evaluation on the first visit, then the second visit he decided he would discuss mine first because he felt I was suffering from depression and anxiety. He felt like I should get a prescription for medication to treat my problems. He went through in detail the things that troubled him. He recommended an herbal treatment for depression and I began to take it after that visit.

On the third visit, we talked about whether or not I was feeling better after taking the herbal supplements. When we left that session, Lead declared he was done with counseling and we were never coming back. He felt like the doctor already found the root of our problem: me. So all that needed to happen was that I should continue working on me, no need to come back. When I mentioned that we hadn't yet talked about his evaluation, he agreed but said the fact that he was tired of every session so far being all about me was another reason he never wanted to come back. The counselor called and expressed his concern that I get treatment for myself even if we weren't doing the marriage counseling anymore. He felt I needed a combination of long- term treatment and medication. I never did either one.

Chapter Forty

Beginning Of The End

"Pain insists upon being attended to.
God whispers to us in our pleasures,
speaks in our consciences, but shouts in our pains.
It is his megaphone to rouse a deaf world."

— C.S Lewis

I know that the metaphor of the three strikes in baseball is so corny and overused, but I couldn't find a better fitting one for how my relationship ended. Three times I got that horrid feeling in my stomach and in my soul, right down to my bones. That feeling where you KNOW it's over. Not that I should not have felt that countless other times in the relationship, but there were three incidents after which I feel like a clear still small voice warned me to run for my life. We often ignore the feelings and try to deny it, fight it, and do whatever we can to make it go away. Each time the feeling was more intense than the last, like labor pains. The first time was the drive home from that last counseling session as I listened to him refusing to go back and saying that all of our problems stem from me. I felt the feeling sink deep and run through my veins. I chastised myself that day and replaced the bad feeling with the same stories I had been telling myself about anything being possible and I just had to work harder at this. The third time the feeling quite literally knocked me off my feet and I *had* to walk away, but that's getting ahead, let's talk about the second time.

I had my appendix removed about a year before we broke up. I developed appendicitis, which while it used to kill people a long time ago, is cured by a fairly routine surgery today. The fact that people in developed countries no longer die from it did not make it any less painful and dangerous. I honestly and truly felt I was going to die the day I went to the emergency room. The pain was intense and I was projectile vomiting until I had nothing left to throw up. It was added to the long list of horrible experiences I have had. I was in pain for a few days before things got bad, but I kept thinking it was other things. On the morning things got bad, I knew it was serious the minute I woke up. I went to school that day, performed all my daily rituals with my son, and all the while doubled over in pain. I literally had issues standing up straight.

By the time I had put my son to bed, I crawled on all fours to the bathroom and once I had thrown up for the umpteenth time that day, I could do nothing else but lay on the floor. Thank God my cell phone was in my pocket. I called Lead who was at work. I told him I felt like something really serious was going on with me and I might need to call an ambulance. He reminded me that an ambulance ride would cost about $300 with the insurance we had and we lived minutes away from a hospital. As a matter of fact, you could see the hospital from our apartment. He was at work with the car and I could never go to the hospital in my condition alone with my autistic son that would never work out well. Since he had issues with calling the ambulance, I begged him to please come home and drive me to the Emergency Room. He refused to come home and told me that I was being dramatic. Just try to go to sleep and if I didn't feel better in the morning I could drive myself there. I was getting so angry, even in the midst of my pain. I hung up the phone and laid there on the floor of my bathroom unable to move.

A light bulb went off in my head and I have to admit that I used Lead's fear of looking bad in front of other people against him. I called the office at his job. I told them I had been trying my husband on his cell and I couldn't get him. I told the woman who answered that she need not page him to the office or tell him to come home, I just wanted to him to know that I would be calling an ambulance to take me to the hospital. Sounding alarmed, she told me that it was no problem to get him to the office and she was sure he would like to talk to me. So she paged him. As he picked up the phone I could hear the lady who answered the phone expressing concern as he acted surprised as if I wasn't crying to him minutes earlier. He proceeded to tell me again that he couldn't leave work and an authoritative male voice in the background told him that it was more than a valid excuse to leave work if his wife was on her way to the hospital. He told Lead to go ahead and it would be fine. My plan worked. I knew that if other people knew I needed to go to the hospital and he was telling me to calm down, he would be embarrassed into helping me.

I called my cousin who took my son to my mom's house as Lead callously refused to help me get dressed or help me down the stairs. He was still annoyed with me and felt as if I was overreacting and being dramatic. Once my condition was confirmed at the hospital and they told me I would have to have an appendectomy early the next morning, he left me in the hospital and came to pick me up after surgery the next day. He was not apologetic about his treatment of me the night before; instead, he still seemed just as irritated. We went home that morning with instructions to be in bed for five to seven days and to not lift anything at all, not even my own body weight. I was to have someone help me up and down, someone to help me go to the bathroom and do things that might require stomach muscles.

I got no care from anyone during my time of need and it was so painful both physically and emotionally. Lead went back to work the next day and my mother, who had kept my son the night I went to the hospital and one more day after that, dropped him off saying he was too much to handle and she had to work the next day. I wasn't even supposed to be out of bed but on the second day I was home from the hospital, but I had to do all of my normal activities. I was alone with my son like I normally would be but this time I had three incisions in my stomach. I cried so much. I was in so much pain. My son inadvertently hits and kicked me in my surgery scars a few times. Sometimes I would have no choice but to stop what I was doing right in the middle of it and sit or lay on the floor right where I was. I was so angry with everyone around me. I was really angry with my mom for not keeping my son longer. I wasn't ready to have him back but I had no choice. It made me angry that when she told me she had to drop him off, she expected me to be understanding of what she went through having him for two days. She complained about the sleepless nights and the behavior we were still struggling to understand. She couldn't do it and that was that.

No amount of pain I was in mattered. The same could be said for Lead who not only left me home by myself, taking zero days off of work, but he left me alone in the house on his scheduled days off, claiming the same thing my mother did, it was all too much. I cooked, cleaned, took care of my son like I would normally, only I would periodically look down to blood stains on my shirt after I lifted something. I would feel the sharp pain of scars that were supposed to be healing. I suffered a lot in that third floor apartment in the days following my surgery. My heart was bleeding right along with the incisions in my stomach. I felt so abandoned and alone, which I had felt so many times before in my life. I felt angry that no one thought of me as important enough to them to help me in such a horrible time. I wasn't even worth taking a day off of work for. I was just as angry with my mom as I was with Lead. I remember the sinking feeling I had one day as I lay crying on my bedroom floor. I felt so low. Mentally, emotionally and physically, I was spent. A voice from somewhere warned me that if he couldn't love me at this point, our marriage was doomed.

All the same, as I started to heal, I had a new resolve to make my life better. See, I remember all these horrible moments with Lead, but I have memories of happy times too. That's what kept me in the relationship, the rollercoaster of it all. We had such phenomenal highs and incredible lows. If it would have been bad all the time, I would have left much sooner. There were rays of sunshine through the muck and mire and it kept giving me hope. Now that I look back, I was grasping at straws. A fun date night could never have balanced out or erased the pain of him physically assaulting me while showing me (and sometimes telling me) that I was worth nothing to him, but it was all I had. I held on to those sweet kisses, nice words and fun nights, even as they slipped through my fingers. The good times came less and less, until one day there were none.

The final year of my marriage was pure hell. Daily arguments and weekly fights made for a miserable existence. Every time we made up, it was from me apologizing and wanting things to be better and every argument was blamed on me. I took the blame because I wanted peace. When he told me that it was my whining and nagging that made him never want to be home with me, I accepted it and tried to be silent about his actions. Nothing changed, he still left home on his days off and would be gone until the wee hours of the morning. It didn't matter if I didn't say anything for months, the one time I would mention that it bothered me, I would be nagging again and have to take the blame for however, he chose to lash out at me for what I was saying. He blamed me when we were broke. He would spend money freely when we had it. When there was no money, he would proceed to micro-manage my spending and list all my purchases and declare it all my fault and mine alone that we were broke. Even when I paid our rent with my son's disability money, took out loans to buy furniture, or took out a loan to put a down payment on a new car, he still liked to tell me I did nothing to contribute to our family because I didn't have a job. I realized he was in a much better mood when we had a lot of money so I took out loans as often as I could to try and make things easier for him. I truly let this man convince me that the act of going out to work every day could never be matched by anything I did. He loved to make me feel bad, to make me cry. He brought up and spoke about hurtful things from my past. He used the things I told him, things that were personal and embarrassing, things about my family, to hurt me. I constantly was allowing him to say that every bad thing that happened was my fault. For about the last year and a half of our marriage, he treated me as if he hated me.

He interacted very minimally with my son. He showed his annoyance when he was woken up in the middle of the night or some other inconvenience. He made no bones about expressing his impatience with my son's condition, even going so far as to suggest the diagnosis was wrong and he was the way he was because I "treated him like a baby" and spoiled him. He wasn't very caring or nurturing and my son in turn never warmed up to him. He didn't smile or play as much when Lead was around.

My son started kindergarten in the special needs program. We had settled into a routine, frazzled and erratic though it was at times. It was a struggle over the years. He did not walk until he was almost three years old. At the time, the doctors and therapists were just beginning to say that he probably would never be mobile, and then one day he crawled across the room so fast it made me laugh with joy and amazement. it was a miracle. He gave no indication that he was gearing up for it. It caught us all, doctors and everyone by surprise. He reminded me of the baby in the animated movie The Incredibles. His speed seemed unreal. Less than a month later, my boy literally hit the ground running. He learned to stand on his own and wasted no time learning how to get from point A to B as fast as he could. When he started walking, there was only a small amount of time to celebrate the victory. We had to see an orthopedist and he had to be fitted with leg braces because of the awkward position of his feet and ankles. He wore the braces for about a year and his problem was corrected for the most part. He quickly adapted to life as a mobile person, but getting him to learn how to communicate was (and still is) one of our greatest challenges. I could see evidence that he understood certain basic things, and he had a handful of words, but he remained mostly nonverbal. I knew at the time, my son saw and heard all of the conflict at home, but I think I convinced myself that he didn't understand what was going on. Boy was I wrong, I would find out later. One of my greatest regrets in my life has been exposing my son to that life for four years.

I spoke earlier about the three huge incidents after which I knew that I would not be with him. These are the three incidents that led to the breakup process. I talked about the trip home from counseling where he expressed that he was convinced that all our problems stemmed from me, and the aftermath of my appendix surgery. The third was the most bittersweet of them all.

Chapter Forty One

Third Time's The Charm

Wednesday morning at five o'clock as the day begins
Silently closing her bedroom door
Leaving the note that she hoped would say more
She goes downstairs to the kitchen
clutching her handkerchief
Quietly turning the backdoor key
Stepping outside she is free

-The Beatles
She's Leaving Home

It started out innocently. At Lead's job, he got less hours in the summertime, and usually, there would be no loan money either. It was hard, but I learned to expect that the budget would get tight in the summer, but Lead never dealt with it well. His financial security was always directly related to his level of happiness. He found it hard to be satisfied with anything unless it was exactly how he wanted. When it came to money, if he was dissatisfied, he would be miserable in every aspect of his life until his situation changes. Until then, nothing I did or said would make him feel better. Part of being broke in the summer meant that his birthday celebration was always a little scaled back because it's in July. Meanwhile, when my November birthday came around, there was usually extra money. I must note that there was usually extra money because I anticipate it early every year. I would start saving money and also make my own plans. I have a thing about birthdays; they always seemed to suck when I was younger. I never had my own birthday party where everyone was excited to be there with me and watch me blow out my candles.

When I got older, it seemed like something always happened on that day to have me in tears. Plans would fall through or not turn out the way I hoped almost every year. My aunt ruined a surprise party that Lead planned for me one year. After my family found out I knew, I was pressured into changing my birthday brunch and museum visit so they could move the party up to an earlier time. People had work the next day, they argued. Come early since you already found out and it's not a surprise anymore. Just come so we can get this over with. I was told I was being selfish for protesting and wanting to keep the plans I made before I found out about the party. That birthday ended with me going to the museum anyway, and walking into my "party" to everyone already eating food, with our plates set aside and covered in foil, and a cold reception. After my 24th birthday when I was pregnant and alone, I vowed to always treat myself special that day even if no one else was going to do it. So every year since then, I make my own plans and try to do something I like, something that makes me happy. I set money aside and start thinking about it way in advance. After a couple years of fabulous birthday celebrations for me and very low key ones for him, it started to be something he complained about. He felt like I was being selfish and that I didn't think his birthday was equally as important as mine. In our fourth year together, in February, I booked us a trip to Jamaica on an all inclusive resort. I booked the trip for his birthday in July and he didn't have to pay a dime for it. I sat at the computer, debit card in hand, asking him if he was sure this was what he wanted. I started throwing out other suggestions of things we could do with the money, and he started to think twice about going to Jamaica. I was admittedly a little crestfallen because I was looking forward to the resort in Jamaica that we talked about. I have been there many times, but always to visit family. It would have been my first time with the tourist experience, and his first time on the island in general. He noticed my disappointment and said forget the other options, let's just go to Jamaica. At first, all seemed well but it felt like after only a few weeks, he was not only no longer excited about the trip, but he held some level of resentment toward me. Because of that brief interaction before I paid for the trip once and for all, he said he no longer considered it a present for him.

He allowed me to book the trip and everything before telling me he felt influenced into choosing Jamaica and did not feel it was for him. It seemed the closer the trip got, the more he would say it. When we got there, he went into full ungrateful mode and started angrily calling me selfish and manipulative. He said I was just trying to make it seem like I was being nice and going on the trip on the week of his birthday was just a ploy. I really was just all about me.

He never let go of that sentiment and it made the whole trip bittersweet. I had an awesome time at the resort, but in between climbing waterfalls, waking up with the ocean right outside my balcony, and delicious food, there were arguments. I was so hurt and upset that he couldn't just relax and enjoy his time there. I felt hurt that even though he is having this awesome time, and visiting a place he always wanted to go but never did, he couldn't just be happy with me. The first fight happened on the ride from the airport to the resort. I don't remember what happened but we didn't talk for most of the two hour drive. Every time I would come to him with soft apologies and remind him that we are in paradise.

I didn't want to pay all this money and come all this way just to argue. Almost every day on the resort, something made him mad.

On the way home, he got mad that a guy was checking me out at the airport. He insisted that he saw me look at the guy too and proceeded to make an embarrassing scene. When we reached our layover stop in Miami, we had to wait three hours for the next plane. As I was rushing through customs I dropped my passport. A deep masculine voice got my attention with "hey, you dropped something". I look up and it's the same guy. I politely said thanks and took my passport from him. He jokingly said, "You weren't going anywhere without *this*" and I watched as Lead turned on his heels and angrily marched away to the customs agent. I tried to talk to him and he immediately started yelling. It was so bad the customs person told me to move to another line so I could get checked out by another agent. After I got all my gate information and had everything I needed to board my flight home, I went my own way. I sat by myself in the airport for three hours, crying. I was on the phone with a close friend for a lot of that time too. I remember through my almost hysterical tears that the real reason I am so distraught and can't stop bawling is because I know it's over. I know I can't stay married to him.

After this trip, I came to the realization that nothing I could do would ever make him happy. I made a lot of sacrifices booking this trip, and it hurt me that it didn't please him, not even a little bit. It was almost as if it made him even angrier that I tried to fix the problem, which always seemed like the pattern with him. He loved to have something to point the finger at me for, to blame me for. For a long time, I would scramble to change and do anything I could to address his grievance with me. Often when I did, he made it a point to question my intentions and sometimes went as far as to outright reject me, even in my humble state. I asked him many times, as I did several times while we were on the trip, if I am one of the worst people in the world, why be with me? Why won't you just leave me? He would respond that it was because he loved me, and no one else did. He would then go on a rant about how he doesn't treat me bad compared to the other people in my life.

Lead would highlight my feelings of loneliness, being far away from my close friends, and finding it hard to make new friends because all my time was spent at home with my son. He would play into my insecurities about my mom and re-iterate that she probably hates me and is ashamed of me. He would remind me of the day we told them we were getting married when they pretty much said I wasn't welcome back home. He would remind me of the many times I felt left out by my extended family, how much they didn't want me around them. He would remind me that even though we have our issues, he is the only person in the world who was there for me. Sometimes those types of responses would shut me up because the truth is; I was more depressed and alone than I had ever been. His words were just fertilizer for the weeds in my mind.

Our arguments in Jamaica took on a different quality. I saw him in a different light. I watched as he went on a long hard search for something to be mad about. At home, you could not avoid certain frustrations, but out there with people waiting on us hand and foot, unlimited food and drinks, the ocean, the beautiful scenery, parties at night, anything you can think of, he outright refused to be happy. I realized that week that it wasn't me at all, that he was a miserable person, and no amount of submitting, no amount of sweet talking or changing my actions, no bending over backwards, no putting a down payment on a new car, not even booking him a vacation for his birthday on a five star resort overlooking the ocean in a place Christopher Columbus called the most beautiful place he had ever seen could make him happy. I sat talking to my friend and I came to the conclusion right there in the Miami airport, my marriage was absolutely doomed because I was spent. I felt useless, unhappy, dry, depressed and I had no more to give. Two weeks later it was officially over.

Days after we returned home, we had a huge fight in which he choked me. I truly felt like a subhuman specimen as I lay on the floor with his fingers squeezing my windpipe, only to look slightly to my right to see my son's tiny feet in the doorway. Something about that sight lit a fire under me. I fought him with all my might that day and every other day following where he came after me. All that did was provoke him to more and more extreme actions. Now smaller infractions warranted a bigger reaction. When I would (try at least) go toe to toe with him, he turned it up a notch because he refused to be anything less than dominant. I have a permanent scar about an inch from my left eye on my temple from him throwing something at me.

On the final day, we lived together, which was about two weeks after we came back from Jamaica, his daughter was visiting with us. She was about eight at the time. We were still broke, it was still July. We had food to make dinner that night but it was literally all we had in the house. We had a little money in the bank so we both thought it was a good idea to get them some kids meals from McDonald's around the corner, which we calculated would take about $6 from our already small balance in the account. I took them with me and he stayed home. While I was there, I decided to get a fruit smoothie for myself and the total came close to about $8. When I got home, all hell broke loose over that smoothie. I was selfish according to him. We didn't have any money because I liked to do things like this, he said. How dare I not clear with him before spending *his* money that *he* worked hard for? When I tried to say that the amount was trivial, he claimed it was not the amount, it was the principle. I was disrespectful.

In keeping with my newfound will to stand up for myself, I told him I didn't think it was a big deal. While we were talking about it, I actually have done a lot, so if I spend a couple dollars on a smoothie I shouldn't have to be made to feel guilty about it. He refused to back down and neither would I. All of our make-ups and ending of arguments in the past were dependent upon my submission, but I was done with that. I told him exactly what I was feeling, everything. I told him about how unhappy I was and how hard he was to live with and to love. I told him he should see someone, that he needed psychological help from a professional. That comment set him off. He came after me and we began to fight, knocking things over, causing mayhem.

Our bedroom door opened and I saw his daughter and my son in the doorway. I stopped, thinking that them seeing us like this would cross some sort of line, and I tried to tell Lead that the kids were watching us. He took advantage of my split second of weakness and pushed me on the ground, flat on my back. He straddled me and looked me dead in the eye, and silently slipped his hands around my neck and a single drop of sweat dangled on the end of his nose as he began to squeeze. In all, that second (and final) time he choked me and it was much easier than the first. While it probably lasted between five to ten seconds, it seemed like an eternity. Although I had been in danger for the past four years, it was laying there, on the floor, with breath being harder and harder to grasp, looking into those black eyes that I thought for the first time, "He could kill me." Honestly, the immediate moments following the incident are a big blur. I don't know if I fought him off or if he stopped voluntarily but I do know that the minute I got up off the floor, I was calling my Mom and packing a bag at the same time.

When my mom arrived, I was frustrated with her because I had to beg and plead and convince her to come get me. I called her sobbing and telling her I was leaving Lead in no uncertain terms. She was afraid of getting involved in the volatile situation. She was understandably afraid of him bringing the drama to her house if he knew I was there. At the end of the day she did what any mother would when their child cries for help. Once again, she came to rescue me.

As always with my mom, it was a mixed bag of emotions. When she came up to the apartment, Lead tried everything he could to turn her against me, to tell her how horrible I was. When he made no headway, he decided he would reveal to her that I smoked weed regularly, which he knew was a closely guarded secret of mine, especially from my family. Although she didn't give him the satisfaction of a reaction, when we got into her car, she tried to scold and lecture me. In between my loud gut wrenching sobs, I told her that I refused to talk about it. I just left my husband, my marriage is over. PLEASE! I cried. I just couldn't deal with a guilt trip on top of everything that just happened. We rode the rest of the way in silence.

Chapter Forty Two
Up The River

"If everything happens for a reason that means you made the right choice even when it's the wrong choice"

- Treyco

I found myself in a guest room at my mom's house. I barely slept that first night. The same went for my son. We were both traumatized, bewildered and somewhere we didn't want to be. Lead and I barely spoke over the next few days. It seemed like he was expecting to engage in our usual dance that involved me groveling and apologizing. To be honest, after about a week and a half I was a lot more willing to at least talk and meet him halfway. We had a somewhat cordial conversation one night that gave me more hope than it should have. The morning after our first talk, I dropped my son off at his summer program. I was passing our apartment, so I called him. I told him that I wanted to talk to him in person. He sounded hesitant about it but I pushed for it. I told him I wanted to decide once and for all what the plan is for the future, one way or the other. Even if we weren't going to be together, I just wanted to know something definitive. I was tired of our relationship status being up in the air. He reluctantly agreed to meet with me. The minute he opened the door to the apartment, he was already rolling his eyes and walking away, declaring that he wants this conversation over with as quickly as possible, and gave me a time limit. We engaged in a testy back and forth. I tried to talk about our relationship, but he kept repeatedly stating that he didn't care about me, or about this relationship. Whatever happened, in the end, he would make sure he was ok.

I was angry. He was dismissive. When he had enough, he told me to get out in such a cold way. I physically felt the hurt spread across my gut. He had used that tone with me many times, and it was usually effective if you wanted me to go away. I would usually comply and go somewhere crying because I would feel humiliated and helpless and worthless. This day, I told him I wouldn't leave. That this was my apartment, that it was my name and mine alone on this lease. That was the truth. He didn't have the credit history and I didn't have a job, so we had a hard time finding places to rent to us. I rented the apartment we lived in as a single person with a co-signer (my mom). I later went and added him on as a "resident" of the apartment, along with my son, but he was not the leaseholder. I told him he cannot make me leave, and he promised he would. That's when he tried to physically remove me from the apartment.

We ended up tussling on the floor for a little but he gave up on that and just started pulling me by anything he could grab, my clothes, my hair, dragging me toward the front door. It wasn't a long distance, the apartment was tiny. I tried my hardest to fight him off. We were both yelling and screaming it was one big chaotic scene. We trashed the apartment, as we fought. I tried to grab onto everything I could to gain ground but he kept succeeding at pulling me closer and closer to the door. When we got there, he physically threw me out the door, onto the concrete. I landed on my butt. I banged on the door for him to let me in, but that was an obvious waste of time.

I sat down on the steps and pulled out my cell phone that was still in my pocket. I held it and I remember my tears splashing onto the screen and my hands shaking violently. It drew my attention to the fact that my whole entire body was shaking. I wanted to call the police, but I was hesitating. I thought about the fact that I was the one who came over there and started to blame myself as I had been trained to do for the past few years. Yes, I went there to talk to him but did I deserve to be treated this way? It was not a question I asked myself often. I knew that getting the authorities involved could lead to huge repercussions for him. Never having been arrested or to jail, had been a point of pride for Lead; not that he hasn't done his share of things that might have landed him there, he would admit. He felt lucky to have lived the way he did, doing reckless things when he wanted and always escaping the consequences. I dried my eyes and I called 911.

As I started to dial, I saw him open the door. We locked eyes for a moment; we stared at each other silently. I stood like a statue, knowing he expected me to come toward the door. I stood perfectly still and stared icily at him with the phone at my ear and from the look on his face, I know he knew right away, and then he slammed the door shut. As I sat crying silently waiting for the police to show up, a guy who lived in the apartment across the hall came out and sat on the steps next to me. These two best friends who were openly gay had moved across the hall from us just about a month before. They had active social lives and were always having people over. He told me I was always welcome to hang out when they had get togethers but I never took them up on it. We had barely spoken before that day, with the only other significant time also centering around an argument Lead and I had.

He found a pair of expensive sunglasses of Lead's that I threw in the bushes for my revenge. When he knocked on the door to return them, I told him to keep them. Although we barely knew each other, he sat next to me on the steps and put his arm around me and drew me in. He talked as if he could read my mind like somehow he knew that I was sitting there questioning myself, wondering if I had done the right thing. He said to me "you definitely did the right thing. My mom was in an abusive relationship for a long time. It messed her up, it messed me and my brother up. You are doing right by getting out now, and you should never look back". He kissed me on the forehead and then got into his car. I was taken aback by a few things during that interaction. First and foremost, I was startled at the term "abusive relationship". I never considered myself in an abusive relationship, that term felt uncomfortable and I didn't want it. Deep down I knew it was true. I remember thinking that if my neighbor across the hall who has only lived there for a month can make such a definitive statement about my relationship, it must have been pretty obvious to everyone else around me, except me.

When the police got there, they took a statement from me and took pictures of my cuts and bruises that I wasn't even aware I had until the officer pointed it out. I had on a shirt that was completely ripped down the middle. The shorts I had on no longer had a button and the zipper was hanging off to the side. I stood in the heat for what seemed like hours, but was probably closer to about 30 minutes, holding my clothes together and being guarded by a police officer. I watched as they marched him out of our apartment in handcuffs. They went down a different staircase and took the long way to altogether avoid passing by me. I wanted to cry but I didn't dare. I watched them put him in the car and stood out there till they all drove off. If I was ever not sure before, I could not have been mistaken any longer, there was no going back.

It was as if a veil was lifted after that day. SO much was revealed to me. I was being lied to on a major scale for years and I didn't know it, but some of the things I found out were a result of my own willful ignorance. I chose to ignore red flags often in that relationship. He was bailed out of jail by a girl he was seeing while he was married to me. When I went to pick up a copy of the police report at the station, they informed me that there were two police reports with his name on it for the same month. I requested both. The one that did not have to do with our incident was involving a domestic dispute between two female roommates. It actually happened during the time I was staying with my mother when I had left initially. It stated that the roommates had a fight that started over one roommate's boyfriend constantly being there and had been spending the night for days. Interestingly, Lead was present when the fight broke out and had to give a statement to the police. The police officer identified Lead as the "boyfriend" who started the altercation.

Also in the time following his arrest, Lead began to tell people that I was close to things about me that weren't true. When I met Lead it was because he was related to my cousin's husband. He still had connections to people who knew me. He told them how I cheated on him over and over, how I used to be a prostitute. My habitual weed smoking turned into crack smoking when he told the story. When I called him, asking him about these things, it was clear he just wanted to hurt me and my reputation as badly as I had hurt his. He was livid that people at his job found out about his arrest, researched his mug shot and was calling him a woman beater. He had to even the score I guess.

Chapter Forty Three

The Moonlight Chronicles

"It's come at last," she thought, "the time when you can no longer stand between your children and heartache."

-Betty Smith
A Tree Grows in Brooklyn

W hile I was at my mom's house one night, I had the scariest experience I had ever had until then. I woke up from my sleep at about 10 pm, just because. There was no loud noise, no special activity; it was like a jolt up my spine. I sat up and looked in the bed next to me, expecting to see my son, but he was not there. I got up in a panic. I ran through the house screaming, waking everyone up, and frantically searching. When I saw the electronic garage door that can be opened from the inside with the push of a button was wide open, my heart sank. All I can remember thinking staring out into the darkness was, "He ran away…"

A year before that night, almost to the day, my son disappeared for the first time. I was going to my mother's house to pick something up when no one was home. I opened the garage door and my son and I went inside. After I grabbed what I needed,

I went to use the bathroom as he stood right outside the open door. While I was in the bathroom, he went out of my sight and I frantically hurried to get to him. He went back outside, and by the time I was able to get out there, I couldn't find him. I searched everywhere from the backyard bushes to each and every closet, and about 30 minutes later, I called the police. Just as the car was approaching the house, my mother's neighbor from across the street who was out for a jog, came up behind the car and said that he saw my son around the corner playing in someone's front yard. He was missing for about an hour all together.

On this night at my mother's house though, I felt like there was a steel ball at the bottom of my stomach. It was about 10 pm and we had both been sleeping for hours. I had no idea how long he had been gone or where he went. I called the police once again and I can't tell you how long it took for them to get there because I was in a haze. I walked around like a zombie, at one point sitting in the middle of the driveway not knowing what else to do. My mother was outside too at that point, barefoot and in a panic. She jumped in her car and went driving around the immediate vicinity. She cried and screamed his name, and all I could do was sit there on the concrete. The police did a search of the immediate vicinity and he was nowhere to be found. About an hour and a half later, they were ready to call out the helicopters.

As the officer was on his way to his car, he received a call that said that some people called the police to report that a child was in their backyard who matched my son's description. We picked him up about two miles away from my mother's house. He had wandered into the backyard of some gracious people who could tell that he was developmentally delayed somehow and took great pains to secure him until we got there. When they called the police and the match was made, an officer showed up to their house to bring him home to me. The fiery nature in him wouldn't let him get in the car with the stranger. He fought so fiercely that I had to get the address and go there myself. He didn't feel safe until I got there.

I deduced that he had to have taken one of two routes to this house, both of which made my stomach turn thinking about my baby going that way. One was down a dark windy road which people who were familiar with the area often sped up and down, and the other path was through thick forest that for sure contained wildlife that we would catch a glimpse of every now and then, most often in the form of their carcasses in the road. There were deer, raccoons, possum, snakes, foxes, and who knows what else. I am anxious even now thinking about the danger he was in at the time. He came home safely, without a scratch, and barely even any dirt on his bare feet. My mom said that he had an angel with him that night and I would like to think so. I stayed with my mom for about the next six weeks or so. After that, Lead moved out of the apartment we shared and went his own way. There were only two months left on the lease at that point anyway, and I had some money left over from a past student loan. I breathed a sigh of relief on what seemed like my first night of freedom.

I was awakened that same first night back in my apartment by a loud knock on my front door. As I walked toward it to open it, I saw the door was slightly open and I could see a chair behind the door and what I realized was a police officer on the other side. He stood there with my neighbor. My son had woken up, climbed on the chair and escaped the apartment while I slept. People saw him wandering by himself near the pool and called the police. The officer told me that they were close to calling the Department of Family and Children Services to come pick him up because no one knew where he belonged. It just so happened that the apartment manager, who was called out when the small crowd gathered with several police cars on the scene, recognized him and knew exactly which apartment he belonged in. They couldn't get him to come with them so they came to knock on my door so I could go down there by the pool and retrieve him.

I was in the apartment manager's office earlier that day explaining to her that I had a restraining order against Lead and am removing him from my lease. He threw a tantrum the whole time and tore her office up so I'm guessing that's why he was easy to remember. She processed my paperwork just before closing the office for the day. I started to research and ended up finding out that it was common for children with autism to wander. He would do so a few more times in the years to follow. As time went on, I learned to adjust and take extraordinary measures to make sure our place is secure, especially at night.

He started to improve in so many ways right after my marriage dissolved. I didn't realize it at the time, but I was not the only one being traumatized by the fighting and the hostile environment. He would often join in on the screaming when things got out of control. Now that he had all of my attention, and I was in a more clear headed space, I focused all of my attention on improving life within my two person family. I took him to see a new child psychiatrist who put him on medication to manage his autism symptoms. My son's vocabulary grew exponentially. When he first started speaking he was three years old, going on four. He made sounds before that and he had his own way of communicating with me, but he did not form coherent words. I cannot remember the first word he said because the words came in a barrage. He went from not saying anything to suddenly speaking a couple dozen words clearly. He did not yet have the concept of expression down, but he was just making the sounds. The doctors described it as echolalia, a condition in which you compulsively repeat the things you hear. I was told not to expect that he understands the words he was saying. I was just happy to hear my son speak. Before this, the experts told me that if he wasn't verbal by three, he would most likely never be talking. Here we were looking at his fourth birthday. It was a miracle, and the smallest utterances from him would bring me the greatest joy.

To everyone's surprise, he began to show that he understood more than we thought. He started using words in their proper context with time. He had lots of intensive speech and occupational therapies and has been in programs with the public school system. He had some wonderful people work with him over the years. It takes up all my time. Guiding him through life is my full-time job.

When I left the relationship with my ex-husband, my son was still in diapers. He was always small for his age so he got by wearing the largest size baby diapers at even three and four years old. As he got older and bigger, I was on the brink of having to put him in adult diapers. I have to admit that the thought was a bummer. I talked to his occupational therapist about it years before that point. I made so many attempts to potty train and they fell flat. It was hard to do when he could not effectively communicate. I went back and talked to someone new who gave me a new method to try. I hated when she compared this new method to how one would train a puppy. Although it took almost a year, the new method eventually worked. He was potty trained at almost five.

Under the umbrella of autism comes a variety of other issues that make life difficult. My son has problems sleeping, which is also another common thing people with ASD endure. He is high energy and can go all day off of a two hour nap. If he is going all day, I am going all day. If he slept two hours, I slept two hours. Lack of sleep was a big issue and it drove me to the doctor's office in tears. More recently, we have developed a routine that includes medication to help the situation. It only works sometimes though. I went from a two to three hours a night, to about four to five on average. Every now and then on especially grueling days, it seems an angel from heaven blesses us with a full night's sleep. I feel blessed every time. He continues each day to amaze the people around him with his continued progress. He went from a kid who barely had a few words in his word bank to expressing himself in gradually clearer and clearer ways.

Chapter Forty Four

Sackcloth And Ashes

"If you desire healing, let yourself fall ill
let yourself fall ill."

- Jalalhudin Rumi

When Lead and I were together, he liked to make me feel as if I was worth nothing, that I did nothing and that he propped up our whole lives on his shoulders. He blamed me for everything negative and took all the credit for the positive. When he left the apartment for the final time, he declared that I would have nothing because he was taking everything he bought with *his* money with him. On the day I walked back into my apartment, I was prepared to see a bare bones place and was telling myself that it would be ok, and I would move on and be fine. It shocked me (although it shouldn't have) that when I swung the door open, my apartment pretty much looked the same. My living room furniture was there, along with the TV. As I thought back, I remembered I found my couches at a discount furniture store and paid for it with some leftover student loans. The same went for my bed. My kitchen table and chairs were a hand-me-down gift from my mom. My washer and dryer were the cheapest ones on the floor of the appliance store and they were also on sale.

I remember waiting forever until I could stop hauling my laundry up and down three flights of stairs. I also had some hand me down furniture that I had gotten from various places. When it was all said and done, he took a big screen that we had recently purchased for our bedroom, a Sony PlayStation and the computer. That was it. Well, I guess I should include the little things he took since he did. He took several glasses, plates, pots and pans that we bought right before we broke up. The majority of the things we had when were together, he left behind. Little by little as I walked around the apartment, I thought about the stories behind how we got some of that stuff and it all started to sink in. I thought about the fact that I paid the rent every month that we lived together. In the first few minutes of life in that apartment without Lead, I realized he was at the very least unappreciative of me and my contributions.

The more likely explanation was that he was manipulating and controlling me. It was an instant boost to my confidence, realizing that he intended to hurt me by "taking everything he paid for" with him, but he did me a huge favor. He showed me my contributions plain as day. I was not the useless leech that he convinced me I was. In the coming weeks and months, I began slowly to restore myself. Maybe restore is the wrong word; it was more like a rebirth. Restoration implies repairing the broken parts and a return to an old (albeit better) state. This wasn't that. I was altogether different. I became new.

Now, this newness did not materialize overnight. It took getting to my lowest point first. It was only then that I started to really survey my life and wonder what it all was for. I was incredibly depressed. I cannot remember a time when I felt so low. The need to take care of my son kept me from surrendering when my body didn't want to get out of bed. I had to. He needed me on so many levels that I knew if I allowed myself to waste away, so would he. As I scraped myself up off the floor I slept on those first few weeks and got him together for school, or fed him, or stayed up with him on one of the many sleepless nights, it slowly became easier. Sometimes I would be crying into his oatmeal as I stood at the stove. I would count the minutes until the bus came to pick him up for school some days.

As soon as he left, I might wallow in my feelings all day but every afternoon I had to get it together for him. I couldn't stay down too long. It's like I was forced to practice being functional when I wanted to shut down. I had doctor's appointments and IEP meetings at school. I had to be vigilant in watching him so he wouldn't wander off, cater to his sensory needs, his frail sickly nature and his picky eating. Taking care of him sped up the process of my slow healing. It got the wheels going, even though I was still broken. The practice paid off because eventually, I wanted to get up, I didn't have to force myself. I started to talk to people and come out of my shell more.

I picked up one of the pamphlets I received when I had to go to court because of Lead's arrest. When I went there, they let me know that the state would be handling the charges because too often women who are being abused come to the court and drop charges against the abuser. This often ends in a worse situation; they end up assaulted again down the line or worst yet, dead. They told me that the restraining order was also mandatory for a certain amount of time but I could extend it, which I chose to do. I was asked once again to give a statement about what happened that day and I was handed some pamphlets about Domestic Violence and ushered out, walking past the next poor soul who probably didn't want to be there either.

I remember feeling so uncomfortable with terms like Abuse and Domestic Violence. I did not consider myself in an abusive relationship; which seems so crazy now that I look back. How delusional was I? I threw the pamphlets down somewhere when I got home that day, only to pick them up spontaneously a few days later in a moment of jest. Almost mocking and rolling my eyes as I opened them up. The very first thing I read struck me and changed my mood instantly and it is still the thing I remember most from that reading. It started by declaring that being abused is not your fault. You should not feel responsible for someone else's actions, but you do however have an obligation to yourself. It read that often if someone is allowing themselves to be abused continuously, there is usually a really big underlying issue with the person being abused that was there before they even met the abuser. It cited examples like low self-esteem and various other emotional issues, but it urged the reader that the journey to getting over this starts with a self-evaluation.

Why did I stay? What issues did I have that contributed to my miserable situation? In that apartment, feeling alone, which I had been familiar with for a long time, I searched. I had nowhere else to look for the answers except within. The search for those answers brought me to my darkest place yet. Sometimes I found myself in a battle inside my head; talking to myself, asking and answering questions out loud. When I felt empty I tried talking to God out loud. I felt so crazy.

Chapter Forty Five

Ars Longa, Vita Brevis
(Art is Long, Life is Short)

"If your heart is broken, make art with the pieces."

- Shane Koyczan

One day while I was in one of my darkest moods, I felt the urge to paint something. Just like that. I had never thought about painting before a day in my life and the thought surprised me. I have always been artistically inclined but never in that way. I have long been a lover of books, and for years I have done writing of all different kinds. I attempted a couple of musical instruments as a kid, and for most of my life, I sang regularly with some sort of organized group. Sometimes multiple choirs and groups at once. Through my exploration of art, I have never even conceived of painting. I honestly don't know where it came from. I thought about it once and just decided to go to the arts and crafts store that was up the street. I got up and literally wiped tears from my face as I was wondering what came over me. The urge was surprising and sudden but unmistakably divine. I bought three canvases, one tube of black paint, one white and one green. Green has always been my favorite color. When I read once in middle school that the human eye sees more shades of green than any other color, I loved it even more. Even more yet when I read somewhere else later on that green was the color that symbolizes New Beginnings. That's the exact meaning of my name.

It only made sense that it came naturally for my first display of artistic expression through painting would be dominated by that color. I bought a pack of three canvasses and painted all three of them within hours. It's as if this art was always in me. I didn't have any real form or formula; I just painted what I felt. It felt amazing, like a therapy session. I went back the next day and got blue paint and did three more. I have been painting what I felt ever since that day. My art has certainly evolved from those first three green paintings, but they are among my favorite. One is an infinity symbol and the other two were totally free-styled but ended up also being two very different representations of the Cosmos, the Universe; like I needed to connect myself to the Divine.

Those first paintings remind me of the start of this new life. They were also a reminder that even at my darkest hour, when I feel like I am about to lose myself, that omnipresent Divine Presence that brought me this art has always and will always be around me, within me. It was through my art that my spiritual life improved vastly. I was spending so much time alone that it almost was unavoidable. I faced myself, I faced God. I came to a much deeper understanding of my Creator and I became so aware of my actual connection to the Spirit.

I was raised in a deeply religious manner. I have a very deep understanding of the Christian religion and I could probably quote the bible right along with the best preachers. I have been well schooled in religion. There was a time when I was a very young adult, that I made a decision to devote my life to what I thought was a spiritual purpose at the time. It turns out I was just deeply religious. I was baptized and I was living the life. I felt at the time that all I was doing was totally sincere, and it was. The understanding I had of what God meant at the time was sincerely expressed.

Despite all the years of indoctrination and the fact that my religious life was on point, I had no real spiritual connection. I heard countless people preach, teach talk about it and I thought I knew what they meant but I never had it. I had religion. Religion without spirituality can easily be something you can be persuaded into and out of. It relies on the external, it relies on reaching out for something to validate. When the external factors disappeared, so did my religion. During this, the lowest point of my life, I was reaching out for something but found emptiness in religion. My despair was unspeakable, and the rituals and recitations did nothing. I cried out to God because that's all I knew how to do, but I can't say that I actually expected an answer. I had to realize that I was crying in the right direction (outward), but I needed to look inward to hear the answer.

My many years in church taught me a lot for better or for worse. I learned more from the interaction and closeness with people than I did through the actual preaching. There were negative aspects of it, as there often is when institutions are run by men. It was the place I learned about human nature. Even when people try to be their best selves, they can still falter. From the lowest of lowlifes to greatest person on the highest pedestal, all are subject to the same temptation and all are imperfect. On the positive side though, I have never in my life felt more loved and like I belong to a community of people than when I went to my church in Westbury. I still miss that sense of family that I was never able to achieve even in my own extended family. It was the first place I was shown the real meaning of love. It laid the spiritual foundation for me without me knowing. While I decry "religion" I couldn't value my time growing up in church any more than I do now, because, without it, I don't know if I would have been able to recognize the Spirit at that time of my darkest place. It was years later, in retrospect that I realized that when I just suddenly "felt like" painting one day, that was the Spirit of God within me, coming to my rescue and setting me on a path of discovery, speaking a language that I would understand.

Through art, I learned to stop being lonely and I learned to how to look forward to and enjoy being alone, which I always hated. I found I had a harder time painting when other people were around, even on the phone. I needed solitude. Through the silence, the solitude, I found peace. I learned that a true connection with the Spirit is almost the opposite of religion, which is an outward show, it requires a turning inward. That's where I found my connection to the Divine. I spent time in meditation and prayer in a way that I had never done before. I reached conclusions about myself that I was way overdue for, and saw my life through a whole different lens. I even felt a deeper spiritual bond with my son. I think in the midst of my depression and my struggles in the previous years, I subconsciously thought of my son as just this entity that I was obligated to take care of. Believe me, as callous as that sounds, I loved him tremendously and that obligation saved my life a few times.

During this sacred time, I started to feel a more deeply rooted sense of connection. That he is an extension of me that I have to love and take care of me, just as much as I loved and took care of him. We were our own two-person family. Though I have always loved my son, I started to take care of him with an attentiveness I was not emotionally free enough to give when I was married. Too much space was taken up by Lead and our issues; as more days passed with no angry raised voices, no fights, no tension in the air; it felt like my son made progress by the minute. He did and said so many new things, that I wondered if they were in him for a long time. The stress and trauma of my turbulent marriage was too much for his sensitive nature. I started to look in his eyes and really see his personality. His reactions and behavior became more and more appropriate and typical. His smiles and laughs became so much more frequent and more genuine. That could probably be said for the both of us.

As my days in the apartment were coming to a close, I woke up one day and I realized that I love myself. I know because I had been searching for a few days for the right sentiment to describe this new feeling I was having. I had never felt it before. I spent most of my life feeling like the people who were closest to me would be unforgiving of my shortcomings. I was familiar with the feelings that came with having to answer for things that happened long ago. The most important piece for me was learning first to forgive myself. I had to acknowledge and accept where I went wrong, but it was just as important to learn to let it go.

The forgiveness I worked on and then the love snuck up on me. When I had a genuine love for myself, flaws and all, I started to forgive the flaws in others so much more easily. There were flaws in other people that caused serious issues for me in my life, just as much as my own flaws did. Other people's flaws hurt me, scarred and traumatized me. I couldn't love my own self, good and bad without realizing that other people in my life deserved that same grace. In this time, I learned to forgive myself, my father, my dad, and my mother. I came to terms with the several times I felt abandoned in life by friends. I dealt with my bad feelings toward Wise and Lead and actively worked to exorcise those angry demons. When it was all said and done, I had the burning desire to be better.

As I moved out of the apartment that Lead and I shared a few months later, I left it in shambles. I didn't even argue with the huge bill that the apartment complex left me with. I paid it, almost with joy. I was literally paying to get rid of a horribly stained carpet and to paint the walls but symbolically it was a purging. I was accepting the price, paying it, and I was leaving it all behind. There were stains on the wall from various things being thrown by one person at the other. Holes that Lead punched in the wall. My son's room was symbolic of the chaos that autism plagued us with while we were still trying to figure it all out; a broken window here, a dismantled closet there; things that were done out of frustration. Lead and I were acting out our individual suffering. My sweet angel acted out because he couldn't express himself. That apartment was a visual display of the pain we all had endured the past four years.

My baby and I were both leaving there bandaged up and healing. He was better and so was I. When we moved into our new place, it solidified my move forward in life. As the cloud of depression lifted, I was excited about what the future was going to bring.

Chapter Forty Six

Phoenix

"On the girl's brown legs there were many small white scars. I was thinking, do those scars cover the whole of you, like the stars and the moons on your dress? I thought that would be pretty too, and I ask you right here please to agree with me that a scar is never ugly. That is what the scar makers want us to think. But you and I, we must make an agreement to defy them. We must see all scars as beauty. Okay? This will be our secret. Because take it from me, a scar does not form on the dying. A scar means, I survived."

- Chris Cleave
Little Bee

I started to date casually. This was a first for me. Since I was 13 years old, I was someone's girlfriend. It was not that no one tried. I changed my status on Facebook from Married to "It's Complicated." My inbox was like fresh meat in a shark feeding frenzy. For the first time I looked at the attention I was receiving in a different way. For the first time in my life, I did not want to be in a relationship. I felt that what I had done before hadn't worked. For the first time since puberty, I put more energy and thought into myself and what

I wanted than I did into being with someone. Dating casually was an adventure, but I'm glad I did it when I was more mature.

My old friend the Homey, who I met at work in New York years ago, became someone special to me all over again. He came to visit me from Florida pretty often and we rebuilt a solid friendship. Both of us wanted more, but we both had reasons why we could not uproot our lives and we eventually gave up on the romantic pursuit. Although nothing came of it, in the end, I learned during the brief liaison with the Homey, how it felt to accept gifts and good deeds without feeling unworthy. I experienced the respect I deserved. I acted with confidence. Although I was initially disappointed that it didn't work between us, I walked away feeling great about it. It felt easy and free and lovely while it lasted, and we were meant to be for a season.

I found so much beauty in our mutual acceptance of that. I think the most important thing that came out of it was that I had a change of heart. Over a year after my separation, I was more ready to settle down that I was admitting to myself. There were aspects of being single that I enjoyed very much and I was so used to turning men away once they spoke of a relationship that the feeling of wanting more caught me by surprise but I couldn't deny it.

When I was married, I was slowly isolated from my family which often happens in abusive relationships. I barely spoke to anyone in my extended family. I spoke to my immediate family (mom, dad, siblings) fairly often and visited them a little, but I never let anyone in on my real life. I didn't open up completely about all that was going on with me until close to the very end. When I got out of the marriage, I had the full expectation of being closer to my extended family. I expected this because of their extreme closeness to one another. I saw them support each other and offer a helping hand to one another. I realized that I had been gone, but I expected a seamless return. I knew they all knew what was going on. I figured at times they didn't remember to include me because they were not used to my presence. I resolved to give it some time.

I came around a lot more, as time went on, and I started to notice that they would still often do things without me. I was slightly hurt by that in the beginning, but once again I blamed it on the fact that I was in a horrible place for a while and I didn't come around too much before. Maybe they needed time to get used to us. I said how I felt, made it clear that I was feeling a little left out, but nothing changed. As a year passed, and another year passed and I watched them take each other's kids on trips or to their houses for a day and never invite me or mine. I have to admit, it started to cut a little deeper.

Whole summers would go by with all the kids exclaiming how much fun they had at this pool or that mall; the adults often meeting for dinner, both in restaurants and at each other's homes. No invite. Each time I brought it up, I felt silly. The truth was, I had no other support system, no other sounding boards, no friends. I needed them, but for some reason, I will never know, my extended family often ignored me. I don't want to say that no one reached out to me ever, but more often than not, it was so I could do them a favor. I would jump to it, thinking if I help them out then they will remember me. Unless they needed me to do something for them, no one called, no one came by. My younger cousins did, but the people who could have offered me the support I needed seemingly didn't care.

Even when we had major things going on, like a runaway incident, like my son having surgery, like losing my car for about 9 months, not even a fire that gutted my whole kitchen and did damage to other parts of the house in which I was living warranted even a phone call from them. When I would see them and mention any catastrophe in my life they would all casually mention that they knew about it, most of the time hearing about it through my mom, and I guess they felt that was sufficient. I would sit back and watch them visit or cook dinner for each other when they had things they were going through, sometimes for much less serious hardships.

Although I had no kitchen for two months, no one bothered with me or my son. I try to be an understanding person. I know people have their lives and their own children to worry about. My family not being there for me in that way wouldn't bother me so much if I didn't see them do it for each other all the time. I shed many tears over it and wondered if it was me, if I just wanted too much and didn't deserve it. It was hard, but eventually, I learned to take a back seat and to not feel bad for not being wanted somewhere. To top it off, the little I hear of their opinions of me are mostly negative. I had even heard of a few rumors being spread by my ex-husband being discussed and believed among them.

They never once asked, but they certainly talked about it. I don't think any of them know the real me enough to make some of the assessments they have made about me, but they persist anyway. Although we are relatively close in distance from each other, my extended family remains relatively distant from me. They don't invite me or my son to too much outside of the requisite Thanksgiving dinner and those sort of things. They don't offer to have him tag along when one person is taking all the kids somewhere. It took a lot for me to really deal with that. I even ended up in an argument (shamefully) with one of my aunts. The subject matter was a petty one, but for me, the anger came from knowing what they were saying about me, and from feeling like an outcast. After that disagreement with my aunt who is everyone's favorite, it pretty much solidified my isolation from them. I still see them fairly often and I struggled to get to a place where I can still own my love for them as my blood, but to place my desire for belonging elsewhere because I obviously don't belong with them.

Following the end of my marriage, I stayed single by choice for over a year. When things had died down with the Homey, I became a lot more selective and I was turning every guy down for even the simplest of date requests. I got a lot of attention of all different kinds when I was single. Lead tried his very best to convince me that no one would want me for various reasons. It wasn't just Lead, I had been told by friends and other family members in the past about their fears that I "had nothing to bring to the table" and would not be able to stay in a steady relationship. I had also had it expressed to me that having a child with a disability would also turn men off. I experienced the opposite.

Here were men who had known me since we were children together who wanted to marry me. There were men wanting to get to know me, and of course, there were the good for nothings only after one thing. I sent them all packing, even though they served such a great purpose in my life. The time with the Homey added to it too, I was able to let the admonitions that I "would be lucky" to find a man roll off my back. I knew for a fact they were wrong. I remember writing a journal entry that was kind of like a prayer. In it, I listed the characteristics that

I wanted any man I would be with to have. When I was done with the list, I felt almost amused by the unrealistic specifics on the list. I halfway jokingly resolved that I would probably be alone for the rest of my life. That thought did not completely depress me or make me sad. I was truly alright with being alone.

There were a lot of specifics on the list, but I was open to negotiation on some things. Some of the highlights include a man who was strong, a wise man of few words like my dad. I love a man who works with his hands and knows how to fix things; someone spiritual who can appreciate my art; patient, a good listener, and so this list went for pages. One of the more unusual things on the list was that I wanted someone who would be a feminist. I once read that a feminist is merely someone who cares about the issues of women. In that same piece, it contained the caveat that any man who had a mother, sisters, daughters, a wife, should care about whether or not women were treated fairly. That was important to me.

I had spent so much time with myself, intensely working on myself and analyzing where I had been, the mistakes I made, where I wanted to be in the future. The casual dating, the intensifying of my spiritual life, the introspection and retrospection, the realization that the work on myself would be never ending. I was a different woman. One that would settle for nothing less than what I deserved, one who loved herself enough to find just as much joy in being alone. Even though I never cried out or took the things from that list and turned them into actual formal prayers, the result was as if I had. It felt as if on some level that was not conscious, I put that out there into the universe. It did not go unnoticed. When I finally found him, it wasn't long before I knew for a fact I called for him in the spirit and God responded.

Chapter Forty Seven

Kismet

*"I thought about one of my favorite Sufi poems,
which says that God long ago drew a circle in the sand
exactly around the spot where you are
standing right now. I was never not coming here.
This was never not going to happen."*

- Elizabeth Gilbert

The first few times I encountered him, my eyes were closed. Everything about the way he came into my life held so much symbolism. It felt like God was going overboard in showing me he was the One. I could have no doubts. I had glimpsed the frame of this tall ebony colored man with a bald head in two different dreams where I was walking along a road. In the third and final dream I had about him, I woke up feeling immense joy and I knew it meant something. In this dream, I was in the basement of the house I currently lived in. My entire extended family was crowded in my family room and they were all looking sad. Some looked angry. I was angry with them because I wanted them to be happy for me. It was my engagement party I cried. My betrothed in the dream was a familiar face, it was the Homey. I looked at him desperately and he shrugged. No one spoke a word to me and so I walked outside feeling angry.

I stepped into my backyard and there he was, a stranger wearing white pants and a sky blue shirt. He turned to me and asked me whose house this was. Although I had never seen his face before, talking to him in the dream flowed naturally. I told him it was my house and he began to tell me that I was unaware of the rare flowers and plants I had back there. The Homey walked out silently and stood next to me for a while and then he started to walk away, still wordless. I was so enchanted with the flora that this stranger was opening my eyes to that it was impossible for me to care as I watched the Homey disappear down my driveway. It felt like as he gestured toward places in my yard, these beautiful plants and flowers appeared. They didn't quite appear out of thin air though, it was as if they were always there and I didn't notice them until he showed them to me.

At one point, as we stood under a giant tree that hangs over my house. He pointed upward with awe and when I looked, there were some giant white flowers growing from the branches of the trees. I can picture the beautiful white flowers right now. A gust of wind came through and the white flower petals started to rain down on us. We laughed and he kissed my lips and swept me up in a big hug, all while flower petals rained all around us.

I had the first two dreams before I met him. Even after I met him, I never would have thought he was the man in my dreams. About a month after knowing him, I had the third dream that was so detailed and I knew it was him.

Chapter Forty Eight

Walking Dream

"The wound is the place where the Light enters you."
- Jalaluddin Rumi

Since my separation, Lead had no qualms about taking the car I made the down payment on. My dad had let me drive an old car that he only drove to work sometimes. The car was old and had a tremendous amount of miles on it but I was grateful to be able to get around. It started to have some issues and I was too broke to take it to a real auto repair shop so I was looking for someone to maybe just come to my house and take a look and tell me what was wrong with the car. My aunt knew a guy from her job who had looked at her son's car, so that is how we connected and exchanged numbers before we met face to face.

He came over one day in July, about a year and a half after I had moved into the house. He often says I was rude that day because it was a blistering hot day the middle of July and I didn't offer him any water or to come inside with the air conditioning. I didn't even stand out there with him while he worked. I went inside and closed the door. That was just an indication of where I was in life when it came to men; very closed off and standoffish. I didn't make the greatest impression that first day. But he had to come back another time to look at the car again about a week later. In between that time, my aunt sang his praises to me whenever she could. She let me in on what details she knew about his life, told me all about what a good guy he was, and all but encouraged me to give him a chance. Unknowingly she was doing the same thing with him. When we reconnected, we were both a tad bit annoyed with all the meddling, which became our first point of agreement.

We started to talk on the phone about things other than my car. We were fast and easy friends. We have so much in common. We both were coming out of tumultuous complicated relationships, so we were on the exact same page about taking it slow. Since our first conversation, he was saying things I never heard, but desperately need to hear. He was like a breath of fresh air and the longer I knew him, the more and more I would see my list/silent prayer manifest itself before my eyes. I saw the instant connection between him and my son. The patience he shows for my son and his condition is beyond what has been shown by anyone, even my family. It was like he was meant to be in his life too. Up until he came into our lives, my son never had a consistent male figure in his life. Heck, there was no other figure in any role, male or female, he has only had me. I have been the only person at the appointments, the only person dealing with scary proclamations from the doctor. I was by myself on the emergency room visits. I dealt with him and all his issues alone. Now there is someone else who cares just as much as I do. Someone else who has genuine questions for the doctor, someone else worried about what he ate today and how we are both holding up.

The love we had did not catch a fire. It didn't need some outside source to ignite it; the heat came from somewhere purely organic. Our love developed as its own entity, the blaze ignited from within. Just the same way a flame needs an outside source to spark it; it can also be easily killed by outside sources. I feel like what we have is made of the same stuff as the moon and the stars. It has always just been. God created it in all its glory. All the phases of the moon, the falling stars, black holes, all the chaos in the Universe was perfectly orchestrated so things would happen as they did. Things wouldn't happen without all of the chaos, and it had to happen in the time that it did for it to be perfect. This Love didn't need any person for its spark of creation and doesn't need any person or particular element "fan the flame" to support its continued existence. It was written, it was meant to be. It just is. We were written, we were meant to be. We just are.

Chapter Forty Nine

Art Is Life

"life beats down and crushes the soul and art reminds you that you have one"

- Stella Adler

Music was my illumination. It was the art form I fell in love with first and it will always have this organic place in my heart. I have also always loved to write. That has seemed at times like a natural effect for me, like breathing or blinking. I didn't start painting until more recently in life. After all the difficulty I have been through, my art, in whatever form I am inspired, has become so essential to me. I don't necessarily need to share it or have other people approve of it, it is purely mine. I feel like it is a gift God gave me to give myself. I put what is inside me on the canvas. When I am done and the paint is dry, it is like a catharsis every time.

I can't help but see art the same prism that I view almost everything, a historical one. The beginnings of art stretch back before written history. Of course, we know about the famous European painters. The Michaelangelo of the world have been widely celebrated, but what gets less attention is that there was a tremendous amount of art created on the continent on which life began. Africa has a rich art history that is often stifled. Thousands of years ago, the people occupying the third largest continent created art from wood, bronze, gold and whatever materials that they had available. When discovered by Europeans, they called these expressions primitive in public. In private, the likes of Van Gogh, Gauguin, Matisse, and Picasso would draw inspiration from them.

Looking back at ancient African art, one cannot help but notice that there is a focus on the human figure. Often they would be paintings, carvings, and castes of faces, bodies. Things were displayed in an abstract way, representing reality in a non-realistic distorted manner. This art reminds us of our ancient collective soul. That we did not hail from a "dark continent" void of civilization and culture as we would be led to believe. We were once a part of great civilizations whose images have been distorted and misrepresented in our modern world, just like the distorted faces of the abstract van Gogh paintings that Africa inspired him to create. We are still expected to believe that nothing great came out of Africa before the Europeans came in contact with it. When African people were sold into slavery, they were quite literally beaten down and crushed. Looking at this ancient African art reminds us of our soul, and that it existed before the slave ships of the 1600s arrived on Africa's shores to barter for people's lives.

Time moved on, as it is meant to do, and new ways of life were embarked upon by Africans in the Americas. Art created in the new world of the Americas and the Caribbean, was its own combination of the influence they were born into and the influence forced upon them. These cultures, while heavily influenced by African roots and their European oppressors, formed their own hybrid culture, unique to their experiences. We know the stories of the Negro Spirituals that the enslaved African Americans sang. They were often coded with messages, whether it was to report that one of their own had fled North or to alert those who were awaiting the right time to flee. These songs became the main form of artistic expression among an oppressed people. It gave them a connection to one another and to a higher power in a world where they were discouraged from connecting. They had minimal resources, so with their voices and makeshift instruments, they refused to let their spirits die. It reminds us, as it did for them back then, that they were not property, as people were trying to convince them, but human beings with souls.

Art has served up this reminder for Black people over and over again through time. The end of slavery gave way to an incremental increase in resources. With that came an increase in artistic expression. The Blues were born out of the pain of slavery that may have been too much to talk about while in the midst but could be channeled through guitar chords of the generation that followed. Jazz came about showing us the desire of Black people to think outside of the parameters that were set for them and play their own tune. No matter how chaotic it sounded to those who were used to more structure, these two art forms tapped into the collective consciousnesses of Black people and moved their souls. It reminded them once again of their existence.

Another reminder came in the 1920s as the explosion of black writers, musicians, and painters brought a voice that was uniquely Black and uniquely American simultaneously. Decades later, during the Civil Rights Movement of the 1960s, political and social action was taken to ensure the equal treatment of African Americans. Through all that action, musicians, writers and the like kept our soul-provoking art alive. Reggae music became a form of expression across the water in my personal homeland. In the 1970s, the Black Arts Movement saw a demand for art as a form of protest. It should always shed light on injustice and uplift the people. The creation of Hip Hop in the early 1980s was born from those movements. Despite what Hip Hop has become, it began as the voice of voiceless people. It was that new generation's turn to manifest the notion that Black people are, in fact, here, and our souls do, in fact, exist.

Art can mean different things to different people. Although the perception can vary, its purpose does not. The world seems to be falling apart, and there is so much injustice and hate going around, that sometimes it is hard for us, individually and collectively to have a bright outlook on the future. Just as we, as a human race are still here despite all the negative things, despite all the soul-crushing entities we have to endure, art remains. That propels and inspires my life. I love that it lives and that it still permeates the souls of some people to such a degree that they must bring it forth. That art, in turn, touches other people, reminding us that our Collective Soul is still here. I'm still here.

Chapter Fifty

Izzy

"There is more to a boy than what his mother sees.
There is more to a boy then what his father dreams.
Inside every boy lies a heart that beats. And sometimes
it screams, refusing to take defeat. And sometimes his
father's dreams aren't big enough, and sometimes his
mother's vision isn't long enough. And sometimes the
boy has to dream his own dreams and break through
the clouds with his own sunbeams."

- Ben Behunin
Remembering Isaac

I was having a conversation with a good friend one day when my son was about five years old. She was relaying a story about a child throwing a tantrum and knocking over a display while in the grocery store. She had just witnessed the scene moments before so she was still reeling. She talked about the mom and how she was not angrily chastising her child, but rather was attempting to talk the child down. My friend talked about what she would do if that were her child and of course there was a lot of judgment and criticism for the parent. I silently listened to her vent like a good friend should, but my mind wandered. I have had many scenes like the one she described and I wondered to myself how many people had this same conversation about me. There were some people who would not be shy about expressing their disapproval for my son's behavior and the way I would handle things. I wondered about those too shy to shoot me disapproving looks. Did they call their friend and talk about it, or use me as an example if the conversation arises?

My son's disability makes traditional forms of discipline and punishment very difficult. We have spent years in therapy and done countless hours of personal research to find the right balance, but this disability is unpredictable. It's a mixed bag. Therapy and research have been the biggest reasons for his relative progress. Without some of the wonderful people who have worked with us over the years, I don't know where we would be. Some methods take a while to work and you have to keep at it not knowing when or if this is a good fit for your child. Some days, all you have learned was for naught and you can do nothing but try to protect him. Try to make sure he doesn't hurt himself or other people. All this was too much to try to get my friend to understand during this random conversation as she left the store. My heart broke a little, but not because of her. I understood. I once held some of the same opinions. It was heartbreaking to be on the other side and know that understanding would not come easy.

At one time, I had all these ideas about what kind of parent I would be. I had such strict parents growing up and I was able to see the benefits and the drawbacks to being that type of parent. I planned to be different in some ways. I wanted to be realistic about the things they would face and give them real life advice, I wanted to listen to my children and respect their feelings, which was a big thing for me growing up. I hated that I felt insignificant. I vowed to be different than them, to be affectionate and tell them good things about themselves every day. On the other hand, I saw the value of being protective; of making sure you knew a lot about your child's life.

I saw the value of discipline and teaching manners and respect along with a strong moral structure. I wanted to strike the perfect balance. I didn't want to be one of those parents who were desperate to be their child's friend, nor did I want to be an authoritarian. I wanted to shower my child with love and impart wisdom and raise an extraordinary human being. I wanted to pass on to them my love for learning and books; I wanted to improve on the mistakes I made. I had so many hopes and dreams, but it was all shattered by Autism.

There are so many ways in which I have to parent differently. For example, he didn't learn to speak until he was almost four years old. That was just the point where he learned to say words. I was told by the professionals that it was a toss up as to whether or not he would get to the point of understanding what he was saying and using his words in the right way. For now, they said, he was basically just mimicking. Echolalia, they called it. Through therapy and lots of work, it was about a year until he started to correctly label things and understand some concepts. It was a huge milestone for us when he began to request things after two solid years of working on that specific thing with speech therapists. Once he started to request things appropriately, it was important to honor every request so he would learn that asking is how you get what you want.

Now if my child were typical, I would be spoiling him by going out of my way to give him everything he wants as soon as he asks. The person that I was would never approve of that kind of behavior from a parent. I adjusted because I had to. Now that he understands the concept of requesting, I have to carefully begin the next stage of that lesson; you don't always get what you want. These simple lessons are years in the making sometimes. I received criticism from family members and strangers alike, who did not understand the calculations I had to make with all my actions toward him. This is just one example. Take this and multiply it dozens of times over. The same amount of effort or more had to be put into the learning of a whole lot of things that most of us typically take for granted. Life with my only progeny always has been and continues to be a full-time job.

I am still determined to raise as extraordinary of a human being as I can but there have been a few detours on the road to get there. The plans I had went out of the window, and especially in the beginning, I had to parent by the day. It didn't all hit me at once just how different this experience would be, but slowly, and painfully, the revelation was made clear. It would hit me over and over again in all kinds of ways. It could be as gut-wrenching as watching him struggle to do the things most people put in minimal to no effort, like learning to walk or to say what he wants. Some of the milestones were delayed, some have yet to be reached, and some, I have to accept, may never be reached. Sometimes that two ton feeling in my chest that I cannot put into words would hit me by surprise at more ordinary moments. It could be as mundane as a passing joke between other mothers about grandchildren far in the future. I would laugh and then it would dawn on me that my Izzy may never have children, never get married or fall in love. The sadness that would creep up at moments of realization like this one is such a hard feeling to describe. Maybe I never tried because it's a darkness I cannot dwell in.

His father, Wise and I had a rough and rocky relationship

through the years, to say the least. He didn't visit him much or really reach out. When I initially had Izzy, I was devastated. I knew Wise was upset that I had moved so far away, but I honestly felt it was the best move for me at the time. I had no one to depend on at a time when I was desperately in need. Being far away naturally made it harder for him, and while there were a few attempts to do right, they never stayed consistent. He moved to Georgia for about a year once and we had a hard time coming to common ground on how things should work. I was married to Lead then, and he had his own issues, as he tried to be in control of the situation. The two bumped heads often. Wise left out of frustration with his job situation and he had only seen our son twice in the year he lived here. When he moved back, I went to Indianapolis every year, sometimes he helped pay for our trip, sometimes he didn't. When we were in town, sometimes he saw our son, sometimes he didn't. The tension was at its worst when he got married and his wife seemed like the female version of my husband. We both had two people who actively didn't want the two of us speaking so things were distant for a couple of years.

We both got separated from our spouses around the same time, and we had a Kumbaya moment and decided to leave the past behind us. We had both grown and admitted our faults and decided to move on as friends and co-parents. I had high hopes. They were quickly extinguished because we found it hard to agree on what was "fair." There was so much back and forth, during which time he got re-married and seemed to be progressing in life. He became a business owner and treated his wife's children as his own. It was good to see him grow, but hard for me because I felt my son was left out of his progression.

It felt as if my son was some burden that he only wanted

to do the bare minimum (sometimes not even that) to fulfill his obligation. I decided on my son's 9th birthday to take him to court for child support. I was tired of the negotiations between us getting nowhere. It seemed like I was constantly ending up with the short end, doing all the sacrificing and he just lived life as he pleased. The case dragged out for almost a year on account of us being in different states, and his name never having been signed to the birth certificate. During this time, the tension of the old days seemed to return. One day, after a particularly tense conversation that ended with me hanging up on him, he called me back. I answered the phone gearing up for another fight, but his voice was noticeably calmer and it forced me to turn it down a few notches. He said to me, "You are always angry at me. You know, we haven't been able to have a normal conversation in years. Even when you are not yelling, there is always so much anger behind every word you speak to me, but it's okay", he said. He told me, "I realize that your anger probably comes from the fact that I have never acknowledged or apologized to you for how I treated you when you were pregnant." I was in my car at a red light with my mouth slightly open in disbelief as he apologized to me for the past. I didn't want to let on that there were tears rolling down my cheeks. I mustered up my best tough guy voice and just said "Ok. I'll talk to you later."

I cried so hard when we hung up that phone call. It was a gut wrenching purge of a wail that came from my belly. When it was all over, I called a couple of my friends because I couldn't even believe this. I went to sleep that night so full of optimism and hope for what the future could hold for my son. He had visited Izzy a few months before with his new wife, who was anything but new to his life. They have been friends since childhood. She was so sweet and accepting of Izzy that I was surprised. I felt encouraged between that visit and his apology. The conversation we had was at about 3 in the afternoon and that very same night I got a phone call at 2 am from Young, my old friend from Indianapolis.

When I answered she told me that Wise had died in his sleep a few hours ago. I said his full name with a question behind it several times, and it took several times hearing "yes" before it sunk in. He died. It still doesn't feel real. We went to his funeral, we saw him go into the mausoleum, but it still feels like a dream. He was so young and so many people loved him, his loss has been difficult for so many, including my son. Before he died, Wise probably made his best decision when he married the gem of a woman that he did. Since his passing, she has been adamant in her support and love for Izzy. To add a mixed bag of joy and sadness, when he died, they had just found out she was pregnant a short while before. It was so early, they hadn't announced it yet. Later on, she gave birth to twin boys. Izzy's brothers look just like him. Her family treats us like family. I have had a hard time in the past few years because of the isolation from my family in Georgia. I prayed all the time that God give us some foundation. In His infinite mercy, He has not only facilitated closeness with my parents like never before, we also were blessed with a new Indiana family.

I hate that the newfound belonging we have is rooted in tragedy and despite my rollercoaster of a past involving Wise, I mourn for him in my own way. Despite it all, (and it has been a lot) he will forever have a place in my heart because he gave me my greatest gift.

My son hasn't been the only person developing and changing through this process. I have totally become a different person. I have learned so much from him and from the struggle. I have had to find so much perseverance and strength throughout this whole journey with him. When I had him, I was a little girl and I was forced to learn to grow, learn to be strong. I had to learn how to speak up, literally. He wouldn't listen to the thin wispy way in which I spoke, so I had to adjust and add some base to my voice. Adding some strength to the way I spoke served me well in general. Having to get over my shyness and ask endless questions to the doctors or therapists, or having to ask for special arrangements somewhere have helped me get over some of my social awkwardness. I have always hated being stared at, but it happens so much that I had to get over it. I had too much to worry or cry about to waste time worrying about people who don't even know my name.

When I felt isolated by my extended family, his sweet unsolicited kisses let me know that he will never leave me. Izzy is a huge part of the reason my parents and I actually do more than just get along, we are extremely close. He has been the reason for the most time I have ever spent in prayer and meditation, the reason I have felt the most profound joy of my life. I have yet to experience a joy as intense as watching my child defy expectations.

Chapter Fifty One

Ismail

"...So I love you because the whole universe conspired to help me find you."

- Paul Coelho
The Alchemist

He sat at my kitchen table one day after only knowing me a few months. He had never met my son before. A six-year-old Izzy came sauntering down the stairs with his thumb in his mouth. He always takes awhile to feel people out before he gets comfortable, but a few times in life, he has had an instant connection with people. This was the first time I was to witness it. Without removing his thumb from his mouth, he silently sat on his knee and slipped his other arm around his neck, as if this was the most natural thing. He seemed to be welcoming him home. One of the greatest parts of our whole relationship for me is the genuine love that exists between these two. They have a bond that has little to do with me. He is the only other person who has been as invested in Izzy as I have been, sacrificing time at work, sleep, convenience, and everything I have had to sacrifice over the years. Only now, having someone fighting with you in the trenches makes it a little easier. He makes every part of my life better. He makes me better.

The more I dealt with the man in my dreams, the more I

realized that I was dealing with a unique individual. So unique, it feels like he was tailor made to fit me. God made him with me in mind, I'm sure. Just like when a person is tailoring a garment, there was a process involved. The process entails lots of measurements that have to be taken that might prove uncomfortable or wrong at first. One has to try it on several times. There is nipping and tucking, sewing and constructing involved. It takes time. I like to think that the time we had growing up, living our lives not knowing each other, was our tailoring process to ensure that now we fit just right.

Before I fell in love with him, I remember a conversation in which I expressed my hesitation about a serious relationship. Without missing a beat, he told me that he was just as fine being friends with me. All he knew was that something was telling him he had to be in my life.

In a lot of ways, he is strong where I am weak and vice versa. In a lot of other ways, we are twin flames. We think alike; have a lot of the same interests and philosophies. Nothing is ever perfect, but after a lifetime of pain, I am blessed with the Nearly Perfect, which is more than I could have ever conjured up. I couldn't even write a better life. We both constantly learn from each other, and there is a mutual honoring that takes place daily. He is the treasure I wandered the earth looking for.

After a couple years together, he took me to visit Hilton Head Island, where his family is from; they have owned land there since right after the United States decided to stop holding people in bondage. His family, for generations, have returned to the this land where their roots are, and there has always been something so beautiful about that to me. The first day I put my bare feet on the soil his ancestors toiled, I felt welcomed. I felt a connection; I felt without a doubt that I was meant to see this place. One tree, in particular, caught my eye before we even parked the car. I couldn't stop staring at it, I felt drawn to it. I was so compelled, I took my shoes off and climbed up into a nook and sat. I was overcome with emotion from out of the blue. I cried because I needed to release. I felt so grateful for everything, good and bad that led to me being there at that very moment. As I walked away, I was overtaken by the feeling that I would marry him under that tree. Not that I wanted to, or maybe it might be nice, but I knew right then for sure that I would. Two years after that, in the most magical ceremony of my dreams, I did.

When we had been together for a while, I looked up the meaning of his name one day, as is my custom. When I read it, the feeling of confirmation swept over me and I knew everything was as it should be. The tingle on my skin brought a smile to my heart. Ismail means *God Has Heard You*.

If freckles were lovely, and day was night,
And measles were nice and a lie warn't a lie,
Life would be delight, - But things couldn't go right.
For in such a sad plight,
I wouldn't be I. If earth was heaven and now was hence,
And past was present, and false was true,
There might be some sense,
But I'd be in suspense,
For on such a pretense,
You wouldn't be you. If fear was plucky, and globes were square,
And dirt was cleanly and tears were glee,
Things would seem fair,—Yet they'd all despair,
For if here was there,
We wouldn't be we.

-"If" by E.E Cummings

Made in the USA
Columbia, SC
02 January 2018